SNOOKER

THE RECORDS

CLIVE EVERTON

GUINNESS BOOKS

B11

C000174662

Editor: Beatrice Frei
Design and layout: Jean Whitcombe

© Clive Everton
and Guinness Superlatives Ltd, 1985

Published in Great Britain by Guinness Superlatives Ltd,
2 Cecil Court, London Road, Enfield, Middlesex

Phototypeset in Times and Helvetica
by Input Typesetting Ltd., London, SW19
Printed and bound in Great Britain by
Hazell Watson and Viney Ltd, Member of the BPCC Group,
Aylesbury, Buckinghamshire

'Guinness' is a registered trade mark of
Guinness Superlatives Ltd

British Library Cataloguing in Publication Data
Everton, Clive
    Guinness snooker: the records.
    1. Snooker——History
    I. Title
    794.7'35'09   GV900.S6

    ISBN 0–85112–448–8 Pbk

CONTENTS

ACKNOWLEDGEMENTS

Picture Acknowledgements

All Sport/Adrian Murrell: 27, 29 (bottom), 43 (top left), 115

BBC Hulton Picture Library: 7

Central Press: 47, 95, 96, 98, 103, 104, 105, 109, 110, 135

J. Hawken: 23

Illustrated London News: 88/89

Marshall's Sports Service: 14 (bottom), 114

David Muscroft: 5, 10, 11, 14 (top), 19, 25, 29 (top), 31 (bottom), 33, 35 (top), 37 (bottom), 39, 41 (top and bottom left), 43 (bottom right), 45, 49, 52, 66, 70, 153

Peter Reed: 21 (bottom), 35 (bottom)

Snooker Scene: 124, 143, 147

Sport and General: 85 (bottom)

Tyne Tees Television: 119

Nigel Wigley: 102

Line Drawings and Table Diagrams: Bert Hackett

Colour Section: All Sport/Adrian Murrell
                 David Muscroft
                 Graham Trott

Right: Jimmy White, left, and Alex Higgins, winners of the Hofmeister World Doubles title in 1984.

SNOOKER

Snooker in the television age

Snooker is one of television's most popular sports and extensive coverage of the game's major events is now taken for granted. Since daily BBC coverage of the Embassy World Professional Championship was instituted in 1978, the British public has become as obsessed with snooker for a fortnight in spring as it has traditionally been with tennis for the Wimbledon fortnight in mid-summer.

Each year, new peaks have been reached in viewing figures. The midnight audience for the climax of the 1985 Embassy World Championship was 18.5 million, the highest figure for a sporting event on any British channel, the highest ever midnight audience on any channel and the highest audience BBC–2 have ever had.

But in television's early days, the structure of snooker counted against it when it was in competition for screen time with more obviously physical or more sharply condensed activities.

Snooker's World Championship, for instance, ran at various venues throughout the whole season. Matches, even in the early rounds, were rarely of fewer than the best of 37 frames, spread over three days, and 73 frames, spread over a week, was regarded as necessary to provide a true reflection of ability in the event's later stages. From 1946 to 1949 it was judged that there was sufficient public demand for the final to be extended to 145 frames spread over a fortnight.

Particularly in the days when there was little recording and editing, there could be no guarantee that the part of the match which television would be prepared to cover would be its climax or even a meaningful part of it.

A few attempts were made, in the days of black and white television, to cover other events, the first involving the use of balls which had their numerical value inscribed on them in the manner of American pool balls. Segments of matches, including some coverage of the contest for the World Professional Billiards Championship between Clark McConachy and John Barrie in 1951 which was highly praised by the *Daily Mail*'s distinguished television critic, Peter Black, gave way to makeshift versions of the game to fill limited time slots.

The latter invariably revolved round Joe Davis, as indeed the whole professional scene did. On one occasion, another professional was deputed to open the unbroken triangle of reds as vigorously as he could in order that Joe could then make three – in the event unsuccessful – attempts to make a century break.

Inserted into *Sportsview*, the Wednesday night forerunner of *Sportsnight*, was a feature in which, from a set position, Joe attempted each week to compile as large a break as he could in two minutes. One week, the luckless referee, as if to exemplify the adage 'more haste, less speed', sabotaged his effort by scattering the balls as he went to replace a colour on its spot.

As it was with Joe that the BBC conducted all its snooker negotiations, it was hardly surprising that such BBC coverage as there was should convey the impression that Joe was the only player of any real quality. Snooker on television settled into endlessly repetitive, totally lifeless 'challenge' matches between Joe and a series of opponents he himself selected.

When BBC's Saturday afternoon programme *Grandstand* was live, snooker was found to be a useful standby if racing or some other outdoor attraction fell foul of the weather. As is the way with live television, items did not always run to their predicted length so the snooker players would frequently be informed at the commencement of a frame that it had to be completed in say, fifteen, twelve or even ten minutes. For none of these matches was there even a pretence of competitive interest.

In its early days, ITV adopted a more enterprising policy. With a mere half-dozen active professionals at the time, the professional scene as such was clearly played out so ITV, in conjunction with the amateur governing body, formulated a tournament in 1961 in which four amateurs, receiving small, face-saving handicaps, wiped the floor with four professionals.

The matches were only of the best of five frames and, live as they were, television missed some of the finishes, but at least they were genuine contests. There was live coverage too in 1964 of the Northern final of the English Amateur Championship featuring a future world professional champion, John Spencer, an international amateur tournament featuring representatives of the four home countries and, at various times, much other interesting if not particularly well planned snooker. Two amateurs, Mark Wildman (1962) and Jonathan Barron (1963), made century breaks on television before any professional did.

Tragically, genuine competition was not deemed

Early days at *Pot Black*, mobile cameras, trailing cables and all.

exciting enough and the amateur governing body, desperate even for the modest television fees which at the time represented a financial lifeline, disgracefully connived to pre-arrange certain aspects of the matches, instructing the players to ensure that the result depended on the fifth and final frame. In the ensuing hullabaloo, snooker disappeared from ITV's screens altogether.

Since BBC's last flicker of interest in snooker had been extinguished soon after Joe Davis's retirement in 1964, there was for a while no snooker on either channel. In such travestied or corrupt forms as the game had come to be seen, this was the best thing that could have happened for when a new opportunity eventually presented itself a fresh start could be made.

With the advent of BBC–2 and colour television, the BBC were casting about for ideas which would stimulate the sale of sets which could receive colour transmissions and which would thus increase viewing figures on the infant channel. One BBC producer, Philip Lewis, who had been involved on the *Grandstand* coverage of snooker, was convinced that colour – which was after all intrinsic to the very rules of the game –

would make the game much more attractive on the screen than ever it had been in the days of black and white.

From this perception, *Pot Black* was born in 1969. With Joe Davis long since retired, there was no temptation to build the programme self-destructively round one player or a few tired old permutations. Indeed, various factors amounting to little more than chance had led to three leading amateurs, Gary Owen, John Spencer and Ray Reardon, becoming the first new professionals since 1951.

Eight professionals, initially split into two round robin groups of four, took part. All matches (except for the best of three frames finals of some series) were, and have remained, sudden death affairs of one frame, a format which the snooker world itself, brought up on 37 and 73 frame matches, would never have devised but which, with the game only just emerging from the worst depression it had ever known, it was prepared to accept.

The non-snooker public responded enthusiastically to this simple but carefully presented formula. Millions new to snooker were fascinated by the quiet delicacy and precision of the game and the cool, controlled demeanour of the players, such a contrast, as Philip Purser put it in the *Sunday Telegraph*, 'to the hysterical pooves of the football field'.

Players invariably found that appearances on *Pot Black* stimulated demand for the one-night club exhibition engagements which were then their staple income and which, even now, remain an important portion of it for most professionals. Slowly, very slowly, snooker began to attract sponsors.

John Player sponsored the World Professional Championships of 1969 and 1970 but as the event was still a season-long affair of week's matches, television understandably displayed no interest.

Gallahers, the second tobacco combine to enter snooker, employed a different strategy. Their agents, West Nally, the West End company who rapidly established themselves as the leaders in the expanding trade of servicing sports sponsorship campaigns, devised a tournament not only to capture the interest of the snooker world but to serve twin objectives: a relatively immediate merchandising return and indirect advertising by means of obtaining television time for an event carrying a company name.

Just as cricket's Gillette Cup had been introduced on the assumption that many spectators who would not watch a segment of a three day match might be attracted to a one day contest which they could witness, result and all, in its entirety, the Park Drive £2000 offered a complete snooker match of seven frames in one evening. The four best available professionals played a triple round robin – 18 matches in all – in prime club venues, a highly favourable situation in which to promote a particular brand of cigarettes.

None of the matches constituted an attraction strong enough for television but – so West Nally put it to the BBC – a seven frame final between the first two finishers in the league table did. BBC responded by covering all the four Park Drive £2000 finals for edited transmissions on *Grandstand*. Both Park Drive £600's, another West Nally brainchild, were recorded in their entirety by Yorkshire TV and screened as a seven week series.

The success of the Park Drive events persuaded Gallahers and West Nally that snooker had wider possibilities. Under Park Drive's sponsorship, the World Championship was telescoped into a fortnight with simultaneous play on eight tables and, for the first time, substantial television coverage of a semi-final on the first Saturday afternoon and the climax of the final, still a five day affair of 75 frames, on the following Saturday.

Eager as snooker was to encourage television, the medium's technical requirements often caused problems. In the second Park Drive £2000 final, the heat from the lights was so intense that it caused the formica on the cushion rails of the table – admittedly of new design – to curl up. So hot were the cushion rails that a player who had to rest his bridge hand on them completed his shot with a rare sense of urgency! Special television lights, unnecessary in the days of black and white but essential for colour, provided the players with problems of glare and dazzle which they coped

with as best they could until the eighth session of the 1973 world final, an occasion so important to the players that they had to put their own preferences well in front of television's, brought the matter to a head.

After only a few minutes under the blinding newly installed lighting it was obvious that Eddie Charlton could see but that Ray Reardon could not. Leading 27–25, Reardon lost two frames with ludicrous ease and a third after his protests had led to two of the largest floodlights, which were in any event needed only to illuminate the crowd, being switched off. Further discussions took place at the mid-session interval during which Reardon was able to compose himself and then emerge to win four of the remaining five frames of the day. With the hiatus which had threatened to change the course of the final having passed, Reardon went on to win 38–32.

ITV covered the 1973 and 1974 Norwich Union Open finals from the Piccadilly Hotel, London, recording the 15 frame matches in their entirety on the Friday night and transmitting the highlights on their Saturday afternoon *World of Sport* programme. The BBC adopted a similar procedure for the inaugural Benson and Hedges Masters in 1975, a tournament from which television has since gradually increased its coverage.

Both Norwich Union and Benson and Hedges were clients of West Nally, thus emphasising that snooker needed someone outside the sport to look at it dispassionately and create packages which, without belittling the game itself, were acceptable to sponsors and television companies. What chiefly transpired was that a huge number of frames was not required either for the public to take a match seriously or indeed for it to constitute a fair test of skill.

Television lighting continued to vary in acceptability. The 1976 World Championship, having been played up to the semi-finals under traditional lighting with a shade over the table, switched to television lights for the final but these were hung in such a way that there was an altogether unacceptable degree of glare and dazzle from the balls. Reardon erupted, the lights were re-hung and the incident was of value in that Nick Hunter, the BBC producer who from this daunting beginning came to assume executive responsibility for the BBC's entire snooker output, instituted research with BBC's lighting engineers and consultation with the players to produce a lighting system acceptable both to the competitors and television itself.

Substantial improvement, followed in due course by certain refinements, led to such a good system, now

Pot Black Winner			
1969	Ray Reardon (Wal)	1977	Perrie Mans (SA)
1970	John Spencer (Eng)	1978	Doug Mountjoy (Wal)
1971	John Spencer (Eng)	1979	Ray Reardon (Wal)
1972	Eddie Charlton (Aus)	1980	Eddie Charlton (Aus)
1973	Eddie Charlton (Aus)	1981	Cliff Thorburn (Can)
1974	Graham Miles (Eng)	1982	Steve Davis (Eng)
1975	Graham Miles (Eng)	1983	Steve Davis (Eng)
1976	John Spencer (Eng)	1984	Terry Griffiths (Wal)
		1985	Doug Mountjoy (Wal)

adopted as standard, that players no longer feel that television lighting is in any sense a handicap in producing their best form. They have also welcomed the practice of suspending a gauze-like filter beneath the lights, not only because it reduces the glare, but because any exploding lights cannot thereby rain down on their unsuspecting heads. One such explosion at the William Hill Welsh Professional Championship in 1977 had burnt a hole in the cloth, fortunately, not while a player was at the table!

The 1976 world final provided the BBC with another problem. It was planned to record the climax of the match on Friday to transmit highlights on Saturday but Reardon obtained such a commanding lead in the best of 53 frames final against Alex Higgins that a hasty decision had to be taken to record on Thursday in order to ensure live action.

Even then, it was not plain sailing. Higgins, falling hopelessly behind in some frames, conceded them with reds still on the table in order to deny Reardon the further boost to his confidence of potting the remaining balls. In turn, when Higgins was set for victory, Reardon lost no time in throwing in the towel. In this way, frame followed frame at what some felt was excessive speed.

A clause was inserted in the playing conditions for subsequent championships to the effect that frames could not be conceded until the brown had been potted, but the players, reluctant to abrogate their right, for tactical reasons, to concede a lost cause at a moment of their own choosing, rightly ignored it.

Undeterred by his trying baptism, Hunter appreciated as no one in television previously had snooker's potential as a television sport. While *Pot Black*, which had attracted between one and two million viewers from its inception, was now attracting a highly respectable three to four million viewers on BBC–2, Hunter believed that bigger audiences could be obtained if the BBC developed its coverage from a glimpse of the final to a portrait of the event. The public, initially prepared to accept snooker only on a short simple basis, was now becoming familiar enough with its leading players and the game itself to accept more substantial fare.

West Nally, unappreciated by the professional game, had save for retaining its connection with the Benson and Hedges Masters pulled out of snooker in 1975. Chaos was looming when a new promoter in Mike Watterson providentially emerged to stage the 1977 World Championship.

BBC coverage was extended to the last three days, less than Hunter wanted and less indeed than could have been accommodated in the schedules but for a change of dates for the event. The viewing figures were encouraging but, even more, the BBC, the sponsors, Embassy, and the snooker world were reassured by the overall quality and efficiency of the promotion.

Thus encouraged, BBC gave the 1978 World Championship daily coverage by means of a late night 50-minute compilation, sometimes with live inserts, in addition to Saturday afternoon exposure in *Grandstand* and, a final triumph, live coverage of the final on BBC–2 on the second Thursday and Friday of the 13 day championship and early on Saturday evening.

The very first late night compilation, edited from simultaneous recording of two matches, a total of 26 playing hours through the day, attracted a near midnight audience of four million which built to seven million by the end of the tournament. The nation stayed up late and went to work red-eyed as some 150 BBC personnel were involved in recording and editing some 300 miles of video-tape during the championship fortnight.

'Backstage at The Crucible', wrote Peter Fiddick, *The Guardian*'s television correspondent, 'there is a sense that the result scarcely matters, that something new is happening. The top professionals are very conscious of their new audience and its implications. For them, the game is at last being shown properly, at length, with all its tactics, and the fact that it could prove even more popular that way opens a whole new future even to men said to be potting £30 000 a year. "What the public are getting here", says Fred Davis, "is the feel of what it is like playing under pressure hour after hour for days on end".'

The 1979 and 1980 World Championships built on these foundations as coverage was extended – in 1980 to a staggering 70 hours – and television audiences increased.

This success bred other successes. The new United Kingdom Championship, another Mike Watterson promotion, attracted BBC's *Grandstand*'s cameras to its inaugural final in 1977 before coverage was stepped up to embrace the semi-final and final in 1978 and 1979 and to eight days, that is, from the quarter-finals onwards, in 1980. This coverage included the significant breakthrough that most transmissions were on BBC–1, still the corporation's senior channel. A third Watterson promotion, the State Express World Cup, a new world team championship, was covered by BBC in its entirety for eight days in 1979 and nine in 1980–3.

Pot Black not only continued as an annual series of fifteen 25-minute programmes but in 1981 and 1982 screened a *Junior Pot Black* with the same format featuring young unknowns; coverage of the Benson and Hedges Masters was extended by degrees until it was covered in full; and BBC Wales covered the Welsh Professional Championship. Snooker on BBC had reached what even its most enthusiastic supporters were prepared to concede was almost saturation point.

One by-product of all this tournament coverage was more public interest in the game's personalities, techniques and reminiscences.

Next page. The television set-up at the Embassy World Championship. Two cameras on the floor and either one or two above the scoreboard cover each match. The lighting rig has been specially designed for television. The commentary boxes for each table are immediately above the words 'World Snooker'.

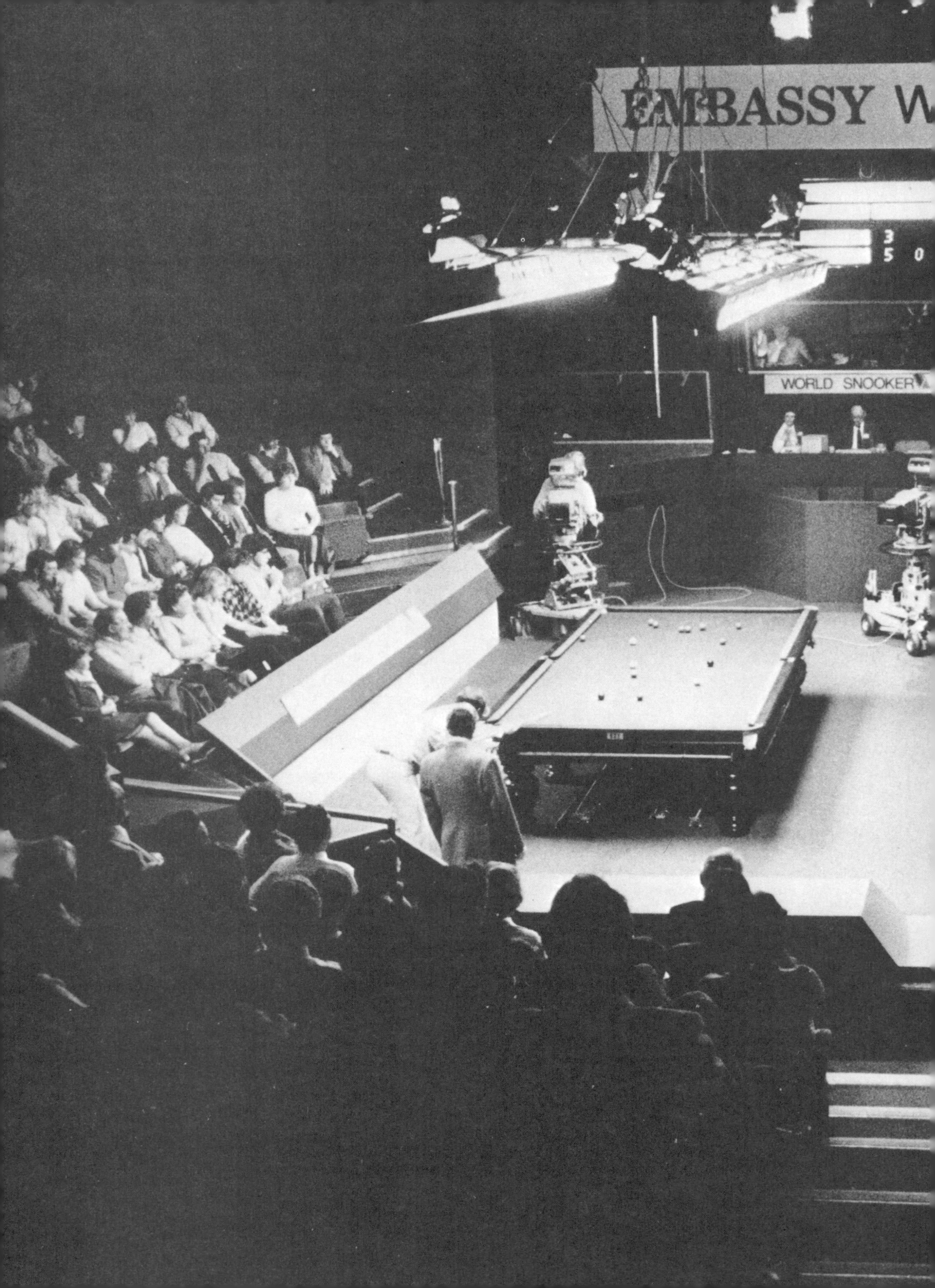
EMBASSY W
WORLD SNOOKER

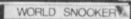

Snooker – Scheduled Network Television Coverage

By television channel in hours/minutes.

	BBC–1	BBC–2	ITV	Channel 4	Total
1980	16h 45 min	85h 50 min	17h 30 min	—	120h 5 min
1981	21h 20 min	129h 25 min	18h 10 min	—	168h 55 min
1982	24h 28 min	126h 58 min	67h 20 min	—	218h 46 min
1983	42h 5 min	152h 11 min	81h	2h 50 min	278h 6 min
1984	55h 49 min	174h 56 min	89h 18 min	15h 30 min	335h 33 min

By tournament in hours/minutes and prize money.

Tournament		1984		1983	
Embassy	BBC	105h 43 min	£ 200 000	95h 56 min	£135 000
State Express/ Rothmans	BBC	37h 6 min	225 000	36h 47 min	60 500
Corals	BBC	45h 35 min	100 000	33h 10 min	60 000
Lada/Mercantile Credit	ITV	24h 8 min	83 000	21h 50 min	65 000
Yamaha/Dulux	ITV	18h 55 min	65 000	21h 45 min	55 000
Jameson	ITV	27h	150 000	21h 45 min	85 000
Benson and Hedges	BBC	33h 36 min	150 000	15h 33 min	55 000
Hofmeister	ITV	29h 45 min	150 000	14h 20 min	75 000
		321h 48 min	£1 123 000	261h 6 min	£590 500

While snooker became a mainstream sport on BBC, its position on ITV was less satisfactory, largely because of the internecine strife which is inherent in its federal structure. Nationwide network television on ITV could only be guaranteed if an item was accepted for the Saturday afternoon *World of Sport* programme but sponsors became reluctant to support tournaments from which their total television exposure might be only some 40 minutes.

The Norwich Union Open finals of 1973 and 1974, the one-off Dry Blackthorn Cup of 1977 and the one-off *Daily Mirror* Champion of Champions in 1978, all recorded Friday night for Saturday showing, provided top class snooker on this programme and Thames committed themselves to three days of 'same day' coverage from the Holsten Lager tournament at Slough in January 1979.

This project misfired through difficulties peculiar to the television industry. The hours of play in a snooker tournament are long and arduous, too long for union regulations to permit a complete day's play to be covered by one crew. A television company thus has to choose between incurring more labour costs or covering only a proportion of a day's play.

Thames, having failed to secure the agreement of other ITV companies to show the tournament nation-wide, were screening it only in their own region, in itself an argument against extra expense. It opted not to cover the first three frames of the semi-final between John Spencer and Cliff Thorburn and thus missed an historic 147 break by Spencer, the first ever maximum in tournament play which would, of course, also have been the highest break ever made on television. The snooker shown was keenly competitive and of high quality but Thames's misfortune in missing the 147 led to the formation of a body of executive opinion, not confined to ITV, in favour of covering either the whole of an event or none of it. It was a possible compromise to cover the latter stages of a tournament but once coverage had started it was all or nothing.

Snooker on ITV settled back into a routine of recording events for much later showing and a few of these series saw the light of day in areas not covered by their originating companies. They were good pay days for the players but the tournaments could not and did not achieve any great status either within the game or with the general public.

Two of the smaller companies, HTV and Tyne Tees, ran annual amateur series. The HTV event, featuring the leading Welsh amateurs, provided such future professional luminaries as Terry Griffiths and Doug Mountjoy with their first television exposure, and in 1978 Tyne Tees secured a scoop when Joe Johnson, later a professional, made an official world amateur record break of 140 in their final.

ITV's coverage of snooker was fragmented and lacking in continuity. There was some agreement that snooker made good television but inter-company rivalry and lack of administrative backbone within the game left the situation untidy.

The professional governing body, as such, made no attempt to control televised snooker. Any promoter, not necessarily possessing any previous connection with the game, could approach a television company and/or a sponsor and concoct a deal to put to the players. Confusion and squabbling were common.

Ironically, the only snooker to be nationally if not simultaneously networked was Yorkshire's annual Pro-Celebrity tournament which the snooker world regarded as a travesty of the game but which achieved satisfactory audiences for the television companies.

The Wilson's Classic (Granada 1980, 1981), the Padmore Super Crystalate International (ATV 1980) and the Tolly Cobbold Classic (Anglia 1980, 1981) were well enough received in their regions but it was not until March 1981 that 'same day' network coverage of a major tournament was achieved with the Yamaha International Masters from Derby. Mike Watterson had established himself so clearly as the leader in his field that he was again the promoter.

It was not only in its federal structure that ITV continued at a disadvantage to the BBC. Its programme times could not be so flexible and the availability of only one channel restricted the time which could be devoted to one event. Nevertheless, snooker continued to attract such high viewing figures on ITV that the feeling grew within the network that it should adopt a more coherent policy for the sport, building up the continuity and status of the tournaments it covered so that its portfolio matched BBC's. Trevor

Televised sport			
1975	1200h	1983	2331h
1981	1830h	1984	2558h
1982	2102h		

East was given executive producer responsibility for the ITV network as the opposite number of Nick Hunter at BBC.

The Wilson's Classic, which became the Lada Classic in 1982, moved on to part- and then full-networking; both the Jameson International and the Hofmeister World Doubles were fully networked from their respective inceptions in 1981 and 1982.

The Yamaha International Masters was networked annually until 1984, whereupon the sponsors withdrew from the sport. In early 1985, the Lada Classic was replaced by the Mercantile Credit Classic and the Yamaha by the Dulux British Open. With the Jameson, Mercantile and Dulux events carrying world ranking points and the Hofmeister World Doubles established as an authentic world championship, ITV had the rights to four tournaments which were substantial by any standards. In addition, the Tolly Cobbold Classic, a small invitation event, yielded in 1985 its February slot on Anglia TV to the Tolly Cobbold English Professional Championship.

The Embassy World Championship remained by far the most significant event of the year and thus the jewel in BBC's snooker crown. Another world ranking tournament, the Rothmans Grand Prix, took in 1984 the nine day early season slot previously allocated to the State Express World Team Championships; the Coral UK, covered for nine days in November/ December, was awarded ranking status in 1984 when it was de-restricted from UK nationals and permanent residents; and the Benson and Hedges Masters, though not a ranking tournament because it was not open to all professionals, maintained its special status with a field comprising the top 16 players in the ranking list. The World Team Championship, newly sponsored by Guinness, was given four days network coverage in March; the Langs Scottish Masters, annually from 1980, gave BBC Scotland a major tournament in September; and BBC Wales continued to cover the Welsh Professional Championship.

Such a tidily co-ordinated picture would not have emerged without a belated but total change of heart by the WPBSA in its attitude to the control of television coverage. Early in the 1980s, it was perceived that the health and financial prosperity of the professional game depended directly and indirectly on television, not only through the contracts negotiated with BBC and ITV but with the tournament sponsorships which were conditional on television coverage. The WPBSA therefore resolved that, as the governing body, it would hold all television contracts for professional snooker. This effectively prevented promoters from gaining commercial control of the sport as they otherwise might have done.

Disillusion and acrimony, not least over money, set in between the WPBSA and Mike Watterson. The WPBSA set up its own promotions company and the number of Watterson events dwindled so that by 1985 only the World Team Championship remains from a clutch which had also included the Embassy World Championship, the Coral UK, the Jameson International and the Yamaha International Masters.

Having absorbed this lesson, the WPBSA adopted a similar attitude to television coverage of overseas tournaments since it was crystal clear that, with the domestic market virtually saturated, the establishment of an overseas circuit was the next major step in snooker's expansion.

It was and in some cases remains necessary to overcome problems which snooker took years to conquer in Britain before it achieved its high status as a television sport. Countries like Australia, New Zealand and Canada are well aware of snooker's British television success story but have themselves proceeded cautiously in attempting to repeat it. However, the Winfield Australian Masters, which began as an antipodean counterpart of *Pot Black*, changed to longer matches and an authentic tournament format in 1983 and there was also a Winfield New Zealand Masters the following year. A Canadian Masters is scheduled for 1985. Thailand, who buys miles of BBC snooker footage, themselves covered professional events in Bangkok and Hong Kong showed similar enthusiasm, Barry Hearn, manager of Steve Davis, who has invested considerable effort in building up an embryo circuit in the Far East, has with WPBSA approval negotiated the television elements of this operation. Nearer home, Radio Telefis Eireann have covered the Benson and Hedges Irish Masters annually since 1975.

The next few years seem certain to see a consolidation of television's relationship with snooker in Britain and a very wide development of it overseas. From this will flow benefits ranging from increased equipment sales and more profitable snooker clubs to more opportunities for more players just as has been the case in Britain.

Snooker has always been a great game but, held back by administrations variously weak, autocratic or out of touch, it has taken outside influences, of which television is the chief, to bring this home to the public at large.

Top 10 televised sports
Scheduled network coverage in hours/minutes

	1984	1983
1 Cricket	349h 46 min	281h 14 min
2 Snooker	335h 33 min	278h 31 min
3 Horse racing	285h 2 min	283h 21 min
4 Tennis	189h 50 min	190h 51 min
5 Soccer	187h 9 min	187h 55 min
6 Golf	137h 43 min	162h 6 min
7 Bowls	68h 9 min	48h 30 min
8 Athletics	57h 21min*	111h 29 min
9 Rugby Union	54h 20 min	63h 10 min
10 Darts	54h 9 min	53h 35 min

* Affected by Olympic Games coverage

The circuit

Rankings and Tournaments

World rankings used to be assessed solely on the basis of performances in the previous three world championships, and the Embassy World Championship is still the most important event in the ranking system.

A player scores ten ranking points for winning the world title with the runner-up taking eight, the losing semi-finalists six, the losing quarter-finalists four and losers in the last 16, two.

However, in order to reflect more fairly the season's form – and also to give certain sponsored tournaments added prestige – the WPBSA came to sanction other ranking events carrying a reduced scale of ranking points – five, four, three, two, one as opposed to ten, eight, six, four and two.

One 'merit' point is awarded for reaching the last 32 in the world championship and half a 'merit' point for the same stage of any other ranking event, provided that the player has not been exempted until that stage.

When ranking points are equal, placings are determined by merit points in cases where there has been equal opportunities to earn them.

Players without either ranking or merit points are ranked solely according to performances in the latest Embassy World Championship, even frames being

Doug Mountjoy

taken into account where other criteria are equal.

Apart from the Embassy World Championship, which traditionally concludes the season in late April/early May, the events currently designated as ranking tournaments are: Jameson International (September/October). Rothmans Grand Prix (October); Coral UK Open (November/December); Mercantile Credit Classic (January); Dulux British Open (February/March).

The Jameson International was due to be replaced for the 1985–6 season by the Goya Matchroom Trophy. The Rothmans Grand Prix was formerly the Professional Players Tournament, the Coral UK Open became a ranking tournament in 1985 after being previously restricted to players with UK qualifications. The Mercantile Credit Classic replaced the Lada Classic and the Dulux British Open replaced the non-ranking, but nevertheless televised, Yamaha International Masters.

Any ranking tournament must be open to all professionals but the circuit also contains several prestigious non-ranking tournmanets, in particular the Benson and Hedges Masters, which is restricted to the leading 16 players in the ranking list and which takes place in January. The Langs Scottish Masters (September) and the Benson and Hedges Irish Masters (March) have also earned regular places in the calendar, and other annual events include. The Guinness World Cup for national teams of three and the Hofmeister World Doubles.

John Virgo

The World High Rankers 1984/5

		Jameson International			PPT/Rothmans Grand Prix			UK Coral	Lada/ Mercantile Credit Classic		Dulux British Open	Embassy World Championships			Total (£)	Merit Points
		1982	1983	1984	1982	1983	1984	1984	1984	1985	1985	1983	1984	1985		
1	Steve Davis (Eng)	2	5	5	–	0	3	5	5	3	3	10	10	8	59	1½
2	Cliff Thorburn (Can)	1	4	0	1	2	4	3	0	4	1	6	0	6	32	2
3	Tony Knowles (Eng)	5	1	4	0	5	2	2	2	0	1	6	0	6	34	2
4	Dennis Taylor (NI)	2	1	2	1	0	5	1	0	0	2	2	6	10	32	1½
5	Kirk Stevens (Can)	3	0	0	0	2	2	3	2	1	4	4	6	2	29	2
6	Ray Reardon (Wal)	1	1	1	5	1	1	2	0	2	0	2	4	6	26	2
7	Jimmy White (Eng)	1	0	2	4	0	0	2	1	1	0	0	8	4	23	2
8	Terry Griffiths (Wal)	2	3	1	2	1	0	0	2	2	0	2	4	4	23	1½
9	Alex Higgins (NI)	1	0	2	0	0	0	4	1	1	3	6	0	2	20	1½
10	Tony Meo (Eng)	0	0	1	1	3	1	1	4	0	2	4	0	2	19	2
11	Willie Thorne (Eng)	0	2	2	0	3	1	2	0	5	0	2	2	0	19	3½
12	Eddie Charlton (Aus)	0	3	0	3	1	1	1	2	0	0	4	2	2	19	1½
13	Silvino Francisco (SA)	–	2	3	–	1	1	0	1	0	5	0	2	0	15	7
14	David Taylor (Eng)	4	0	1	0	0	1	1	0	0	0	2	2	2	13	1½
15	Doug Mountjoy (Wal)	0	2	0	0	0	2	1	0	0	0	2	4	2	13	½
16	Joe Johnson (Eng)	0	–	1	2	4	0	1	0	3	0	0	0	0	11	6
17	Bill Werbeniuk (Can)	1	0	0	2	0	0	0	0	0	0	4	2	2	11	1
18	John Parrott (Eng)	–	–	0	–	0	0	0	3	0	0	–	2	4	9	4½
19	John Virgo (Eng)	3	0	1	3	0	0	0	0	2	0	0	0	0	9	4½
20	John Spencer (Eng)	1	2	0	1	0	0	0	1	0	0	2	2	0	9	1½
21	Eugene Hughes (Ire)	0	0	3	0	2	0	0	0	1	2	0	0	0	8	6
22	Cliff Wilson (Wal)	2	0	0	1	1	0	1	–	1	0	–	0	0	6	4½
23	Neal Foulds (Eng)	–	–	0	–	0	3	0	0	0	0	–	2	0	5	3½
24	Dean Reynolds (Eng)	1	0	0	2	0	2	0	0	0	0	0	0	0	5	6
25	Mark Wildman (Eng)	0	0	0	1	1	0	0	3	0	0	0	0	0	5	4½
26	Murdo Macleod (Sco)	0	0	0	1	0	0	0	1	1	1	0	0	0	4	5
27	Rex Williams (Eng)	0	0	0	0	0	0	1	1	1	0	0	0	0	3	7
28	Mike Hallett (Eng)	0	0	0	0	1	1	0	1	0	0	0	0	0	3	6½
29	Dave Martin (Eng)	0	1	0	0	1	0	0	0	0	1	0	0	0	3	3½
30	Perrie Mans (SA)	1	0	0	0	–	0	–	–	–	–	2	0	–	3	½
31	John Campbell (Aus)	–	0	0	–	2	0	0	0	0	0	0	0	0	2	4½
32	Dene O'Kane (NZ)	–	–	0	–	–	0	0		0	2	–	–	0	2	2
33	Patsy Fagan (Ire)	0	0	0	0	0	0	0	0	0	0	0	0	2	2	2
34	Steve Newbury (Wal)	–	–	1	–	–	0	0		0	1	–	–	0	2	1
35	Warren King (Aus)	–	0	0	–	0	0	0	0	2	0	0	0	0	2	2
36	Graham Miles (Eng)	0	0	0	0	0	0	0	0	0	1	0	0	0	1	4
37	Steve Longworth (Eng)	–	–	0	–	–	–	0		1	0	–	–	0	1	1
38	Eddie Sinclair (Sco)	0	0	0	1	0	0	0	0	0	0	0	0	0	1	3½
39	Marcel Gauvreau (Can)	–	–	1	–	0	0	0	0	0	0	0	0	0	1	2½
40	Malcolm Bradley (Eng)	–	–	0	–	–	0	0	–	0	1	–	–	0	1	½
41	George Scott (Eng)	0	1	0	0	0	0	0	0	0	0	0	0	0	1	2
42	Mike Watterson (Eng)	0	1	0	0	0	0	0	0	0	0	0	0	0	1	2
43	Mario Morra (Can)	0	1	0	0	0	0	0	0	0	0	0	0	0	1	1½
44	Robert Chaperon (Can)	–	–	0	–	–	0	0	–	0	1	–	–	0	1	½
45	Colin Roscoe (Wal)	0	0	0	0	0	0	0	1	0	0	0	0	0	1	1
46	Jim Donnelly (Sco)	0	1	0	0	0	0	0	0	0	0	0	0	0	1	½
47	Ian Williamson (Eng)	0	0	0	0	0	1	0	0	0	0	0	0	0	1	½

Remaining rankings based on merit points and/or world championship performance:
48 Jim Meadowcroft (Eng)– 3; 49 Wayne Jones (Wal)– 2; 50 Tony Jones (Eng)– 2; 51 Ray Edmonds (Eng)– 2; 52 Jim Wych (Can)– 2; 53 Les Dodd (Eng)– 2; 54 Mick Fisher (Eng)–2; 55 Danny Fowler (Eng)– 1½; 56 Fred Davis (Eng)– 1; 57 Ian Black (Sco)– 1; 58 Tommy Murphy (NI)– 1; 59 Peter Francisco (SA)– ½; 60 Paul Medati (Eng);– ½; 61 Paddy Browne (Ire)– ½; 62 Robbie Foldvari (Aus)– ½; 63 Eddie McLaughlin (Sco)– ½; 64 John Dunning (Eng)– ½; 65 Vic Harris (Eng)– ½; 66 Bob Harris (Eng)– ½; 67 John Rea (Sco)– ½; 68 Tony Chappel (Wal)– ½; 69 Jack McLaughlin (NI)– ½; 70 Steve Duggan (Eng)– ½; 71 Billy Kelly (Eng)– ½; 72 Frank Jonik (Can)– ½; 73 Clive Everton (Wal)– ½; 74 Jack Fitzmaurice (Eng)– ½; 75 Paddy Morgan (Aus)– ½; 76 Jack Rea (NI)– ½; 77 Gino Rigitano (Can); 78 Geoff Foulds (Eng); 79 David Chalmers (Eng); 80 Jim Van Rensburg (SA); 81 Matt Gibson (SA); 82 Bernie Mikkelsen (Can); 83 Mike Hines (SA); 84 Ian Anderson (Aus); 85 Bill Oliver (Eng); 86 Pascal Burke (Ire); 87 Joe Caggianello (Can); 88 Dennis Hughes (Eng); 89 Graham Cripsey (Eng); 90 Anthony Kearney (Ire); 91 Maurice Parkin (Eng); 92 Bert Demarco (Sco); 93 Paul Watchorn (Ire); 94 Bernard Bennett (Eng); 95 Derek Mienie (SA); 96 David Greaves (Eng); 97 Mike Darrington (Eng); 98 Leon Heywood (Aus); 99 Dessie Sheehan (Ire); 100 Roger Bales (Eng); 101 James Giannaros (Aus); 102 John Hargreaves (Eng).

The Big Earners 1984/5

	Langs Scottish Masters	Jameson International	Rothmans Grand Prix	UK Coral	Hofmeister World Doubles
1 Steve Davis	10 000	30 000	15 000	20 000	5625
2 Dennis Taylor	–	4300	45 000	2000	1500
3 Cliff Thorburn	1500	1350	27 000	6750	9375
4 Alex Higgins	3000	4300	2000	12 000	17 250
5 Tony Knowles	3000	18 0000	6500	3000	5625
6 Jimmy White	6000	4300	2000	3000	17 250
7 Willie Thorne	–	4300	3500	3000	9375
8 Silvino Francisco	–	10 125	3500	1000	1500
9 Kirk Stevens	1500	1350	6500	6750	2812
10 Ray Reardon	–	3000	3500	3000	2812
11 Tony Meo	–	3000	3500	2000	5625
12 Terry Griffiths	1500	3000	1000	1000	2812
13 Doug Mountjoy	–	1350	6500	2000	1500
14 Eugene Hughes	–	10 125	1000	1000	750
15 John Spencer	–	1350	1000	1000	5625
16 Eddie Charlton	–	1350	3500	2000	1500
17 David Taylor	–	3000	3500	2000	2812
18 Joe Johnson	–	3000	2000	2000	750
19 Neal Foulds	–	1350	15 000	500	750
20 Murdo Macleod	1500	1350	2000	1000	–
21 John Virgo	–	3000	2000	500	2812
22 John Parrot	–	675	2000	1000	2812
23 Bill Werbeniuk	–	1350	1000	1000	1500
24 Dene O'Kane	–	1350	1000	150	1500
25 Dean Reynolds	–	1350	6500	500	1500
26 Mike Hallett	–	675	3500	1000	2812
27 Rex Williams	–	1350	2000	2000	1500
28 Cliff Wilson	–	675	2000	2000	750
29 Warren King	–	–	1000	1000	750
30 Graham Miles	–	675	2000	500	1500
31 Dave Martin	–	675	2000	500	750
32 Steve Newbury	–	3000	1000	150	750
33 John Campbell	–	1350	2000	1000	750
34 Steve Longworth	–	–	–	150	–
35 Marcel Gauvreau	–	3000	1000	1000	750
36 Mark Wildman	–	675	2000	500	1500
37 Eddie Sinclair	–	1350	–	500	–
38 Tony Jones	–	150	2000	1000	1500
39 Danny Fowler	–	1350	1000	1000	750
40 Patsy Fagan	–	–	–	–	
41 Malcolm Bradley	–	150	1000	500	750
42 Wayne Jones	–	1350	1000	–	1500
43 Jim Donnelly	–	–	1000	500	750
44 Paul Medati	–	–	1000	–	750
45 Robert Chaperon	–	–	1000	–	–
46 Tommy Murphy	–	–	1000	1000	2812
47 Peter Francisco	–	–	2000	150	1500
48 Roger Bales	–	675	1000	150	1500
49 Ray Edmonds	–	–	–	–	750
50 Dave Chalmers	–	150	1000	–	750

Mercantile Credit Classic	Benson and Hedges Masters	National Championship	Dulux British Open	Guinness World Cup	Benson and Hedges Irish Masters	Embassy World Championship	Total (£)
12 800	3843	17 500	17 500	6900	6900	35 000	182 501
2000	3843	7500	9000	13 333	2400	60 000	150 876
24 000	37 500	–	4625	2500	4100	10 000	128 700
3750	8250	4500	17 500	13 333	10 000	5250	101 133
2000	3843	9375	4625	8333	6900	20 000	91 201
3750	12 000	2750	2000	4166	17 250	10 000	84 466
40 000	3843	1500	2000	4166	–	2500	74 184
2000	–	–	50 000	2500	–	2500	73 125
3750	3843	–	30 000	2500	4100	5250	68 356
6000	8250	1500	2000	4166	2400	20 000	56 628
2000	8250	5625	9000	8333	2400	5250	54 983
6000	12 000	6000	2000	4166	2400	10 000	51 878
2000	21 000	3750	750	4166	–	5250	48 266
3750	–	2000	9000	13 333	4100	2500	47 558
2000	8250	750	2000	4166	–	2500	28 641
2000	3843	–	750	2500	4100	5250	26 793
2000	3843	2750	750	–	–	5250	25 906
12 800	–	1500	750	–	–	2500	25 300
1000	–	1500	2000	–	–	2500	24 600
3750	–	3000	4625	2500	–	2500	22 225
6000	–	2750	2000	–	–	2500	21 562
1000	–	1500	2000	–	–	10 000	20 987
2000	3843	–	750	2500	–	5250	19 193
–	–	–	9000	2500	–	2500	18 500
1000	–	2750	2000	–	–	2500	18 100
2000	–	1500	2000	–	–	2500	15 987
3750	–	1500	750	–	–	2500	15 350
3750	–	1500	750	–	–	1500	12 925
6000	–	–	750	2500	–	750	12 750
1000	–	750	4625	–	–	1500	12 550
1000	–	1500	4625	–	–	1500	12 550
1000	–	375	4625	–	–	1500	12 400
1000	–	–	750	2500	–	2500	11 850
3750	–	5625	2000	–	–	150	11 675
2000	–	–	750	–	–	1500	10 000
1000	–	750	2000	–	–	1500	9925
1000	–	2000	750	2500	–	1500	9600
1000	–	750	750	–	–	2500	9650
1000	–	750	2000	–	–	1500	9350
2000	–	2000	–	–	–	5250	9250
–	–	750	4625	–	–	750	8525
150	–	–	2000	–	–	2500	8500
1000	–	750	–	2500	–	750	7250
2000	–	1500	–	–	–	1500	6750
–	–	–	4625	–	–	750	6375
–	–	750	750	–	–	–	6312
–	–	–	750	–	–	1500	5900
1000	–	–	750	–	–	–	5075
1000	–	–	750	–	–	2500	5000
–	–	750	750	–	–	1500	4900

The top players

Steve Davis

ENGLAND   1957 –

World Ranking: 1
Turned professional: 1978

	World	Ranking tournaments	Other tournaments
First prize	3	5	19
Second prize	1	1	2
Semi-finalist	–	3	2

Helped by his father, Steve Davis taught himself to play in accordance with Joe Davis's instruction books, and with his textbook principles of style and control he has dominated the professional scene since his first major success, the 1980 Coral UK Championship.

When he has harnessed his emotional drives – particularly those of aggression – to his intimidating technique, he has been well nigh unbeatable. In contrast, he has displayed vulnerability when it has been least expected, notably in losing by the odd frame to Alex Higgins in the 1983 Coral UK final, after leading 7–0, and on the final black to Dennis Taylor in the 1985 Embassy World Championship after leading 8–0.

As a teenager at Plumstead Common WMC he was not identified as a potential world beater, promising though he was, but through sober habits, single-mindedness and the intelligence which turns practice and experience into knowledge, this is what he became. He has also become one of television's most familiar faces, not only through playing but through celebrity appearances on chat shows and even the Royal Command Variety performance.

His first television impact was made with his 13–10 defeat of Terry Griffiths, then the defending champion, in the 1980 Embassy World Championship before he lost to Higgins in the quarter-finals. It was three and a half years before Higgins beat him again. The following season, he won the first of his three Coral UK titles and the first of his three world titles.

The mere listing of his chief triumphs below is fearsome enough but some of them – like his 9–0 defeat of Dennis Taylor in the 1981 Jameson International final – were achieved with a combination of skill and ruthlessness which has rarely been approached by other players in the game's modern era.

The challenges of adversity have also sometimes stimulated him to produce a burst of irresistible form, notably when he won the last two frames to beat Higgins in the 1981 Jameson semi-final and the last two to beat Tony Meo in the 1985 Tolly Cobbold English Professional Championship semi-final. Of the 19 matches in his professional career in which he has been taken to a deciding frame, he has won 12.

Even in the 1980–1 season, when his five first prizes brought him only £45 000, his annual income was well into six figures. In the 1983–4 and 1984–5 seasons he earned £115 555 and £182 501·75 respectively merely from prize money, and is one of Britain's highest paid sportsman.

His manager, Barry Hearn, surrogate elder brother though he may be, also brought new dimensions to snooker management, not only in terms of care and attention to detail but in those of commercial exploitation.

Only once, when he lost 10–1 to Tony Knowles in the first round of the 1982 Embassy World Championship, did Davis appear to be unmanageably overloaded with off-the-table commitments. Otherwise, he has been able to play a full part in the media and commercial sideshows of the snooker circus while always remaining fully conscious that his real business is in the lion's cage.

Within the snooker business, he has lucrative endorsing arrangements with the table and equipment firm E. J. Riley, and outside it with John Courage, the brewers, Goya, manufacturers of a range of men's toiletries and, on a shorter-term basis, many other products.

His Anglia instructional video and his 147 maximum in the 1982 Lada Classic, a Granada video, are both in their different ways, lasting reminders not only of his endless quest for perfection but of how he sometimes attains it.

1980 Coral UK Championship
Final v Higgins Won 16–6

1981 Yamaha International Masters
Final v David Taylor Won 9–6

1981 John Courage English Professional Championship
Final v Meo Won 9–3

1981 Embassy World Professional Championship
Final v Mountjoy Won 18–12

1981 Langs Scottish Masters
Semi-final v White Lost 5–6

1981 Jameson International
Final v Dennis Taylor Won 9–0

1981 Northern Ireland Classic
Final v White Lost 9–11

1981 Coral UK Championship
Final v Griffiths Won 16–3

Steve Davis

1982 Lada Classic
Final v Griffiths Lost 8–9

1982 Benson and Hedges Masters
Final v Griffiths Won 9–5

1982 Yamaha International
Final v Griffiths Won 9–7

1982 Tolly Cobbold Classic
Final v Dennis Taylor Won 8–3

1982 Benson and Hedges Irish Masters
Final v Griffiths Lost 5–9

1982 Embassy World Professional Championship
1st round v Knowles Lost 1–10

1982 Langs Scottish Masters
Final v Higgins Won 9–4

1982 Jameson International
Quarter-final v David Taylor Lost 3–5

1982 Coral UK Championship
Quarter-final v Griffiths Lost 6–9

1983 Lada Classic
Final v Werbeniuk Won 9–5

1983 Benson and Hedges Masters
Quarter-final v Mountjoy Lost 4–5

1983 Tolly Cobbold Classic
Final v Griffiths Won 7–5

1983 Benson and Hedges Irish Masters
Final v Reardon Won 9–2

1983 Embassy World Professional Championship
Final v Thorburn Won 18–6

1983 Langs Scottish Masters
Final v Knowles Won 9–6

1983 Jameson International
Final v Thorburn Won 9–4

1983 Professional Players Tournament
2nd round v Hallett Lost 2–5

1983 Coral UK Championship
Final v Higgins Lost 15–16

1984 Lada Classic
Final v Meo Won 9–8

1984 Benson and Hedges Masters
Quarter-final v Stevens Lost 3–5

1984 Benson and Hedges Irish Masters
Final v Griffiths Won 9–1

1984 Tolly Cobbold Classic
Final v Knowles Won 8–2

1984 Embassy World Professional Championship
Final v White Won 18–16

1984 Langs Scottish Masters
Final v White Won 9–5

1984 Jameson International
Final v Knowles Won 9–2

1984 Rothmans Grand Prix
Semi-final v Thorburn Lost 7–9

1984 Coral UK Open
Final v Higgins Won 16–8

1984 Mercantile Credit Classic
Semi-final v Thorne Lost 8–9

1985 Benson and Hedges Masters
1st round v Higgins Lost 4–5

1985 Tolly Cobbold English Professional Championship
Final v Knowles Won 9–2

1985 Dulux British Open
Semi-final v Stevens Lost 7–9

1985 Benson and Hedges Irish Masters
Semi-finals v Higgins Lost 2–6

1985 Embassy World Professional Championship
Final v Dennis Taylor Lost 17–18

Cliff Thorburn
CANADA   1948 –

World ranking: 2
Turned professional: 1973

	World	Ranking tournaments	Other tournaments
First prize	1	–	3
Second prize	2	3	2
Semi-finalist	1	2	4

As Canadian snooker had no competitive structure at the time, and is indeed only acquiring it slowly now, Cliff Thorburn gained his early experience playing cue games for money all over Canada and North America.

It was on the road that he developed his unwavering concentration and determination. Playing non-stop for 54 hours, he once won $1000 – playing for no more than $40 a game – from one Canadian Dick in San Francisco. 'I really knew he had come to play when he laid out three pairs of socks,' Thorburn recalls with his characteristic wry humour.

After George Chenier's death in 1970, Thorburn won the vacant Canadian title which he has held with occasional interruptions ever since. He also saw British professionals, Fred Davis and Rex Williams, for the first time. Discovering how authentic tournament professionals dressed and conducted themselves, he began to cherish an ambition to break into the tournament circuit himself.

In 1971, Thorburn played John Spencer, then the world champion, for three weeks, losing 56–49 in Calgary, 54–43 in Edmonton and 42–33 in Vancouver. He gained a special respect for Spencer's ability and learned from him the practical steps he had to take to become a tournament player.

In 1973, he competed in the world championship for the first time, beating Dennis Taylor 9–8 before losing 16–15 to Rex Williams for a place in the quarter-finals, a very creditable debut in view of the adjustment he had to make from the lighter Vitalite balls then used in Canada to the Super Crystalates used in other parts of the world.

Having gradually enhanced his reputation, he reached the world final for the first time in 1977. He

Cliff Thorburn

Tony Knowles

led Spencer by four frames but the feelings of awe and inferiority which belonged to their first encounters returned to undermine him as he went down 25–21. It did not help him either that his friends in Canada, oblivious to the time difference, constantly disturbed his sleep to wish him well.

His career then hit a marginal recession and he had particular difficulty in clinching winning positions when it mattered most. However, all came right in the 1980 Embassy World Championship when, after trailing 5–9, he beat Alex Higgins 18–16 in a memorable final. He was beaten in the semi-finals by Steve Davis the following year and also in the 1983 final after he had won his three previous matches by single frame margins.

In the first of these struggles, playing against Terry Griffiths, he compiled the first 147 maximum in the history of the event. Their final session lasted 6 hours 25 minutes, a record, and did not finish until 3.51 a.m.

He was two down with three to play before beating both Kirk Stevens and Tony Knowles but he had nothing in reserve for Davis.

Any century break he makes illustrates the outstanding quality and precision of his cue-ball control and among the many examples of his prodigious determination may be included his defeat of Griffiths from three down with four to play in the 1983 Jameson semi-final and a victory over Ray Reardon from four down with five to play in the 1984 Coral UK Open quarter-final.

He has twice in three years won the Benson and Hedges Masters, first in 1983 when he also won the Winfield Australian Masters, and in 1985. During the latter season, he was also runner-up in the Rothmans Grand Prix (scoring in the semi-finals his first victory over Steve Davis since he came to the fore), the Hofmeister World Doubles (with Willie Thorne) and the Mercantile Credit Classic.

Tony Knowles
ENGLAND   1955 –

World ranking: 3
Turned professional: 1980

	World	Ranking tournaments	Other tournaments
First prize	–	2	1
Second prize	–	1	3
Semi-finalist	2	–	4

Though British Junior champion in 1972 and 1974, Tony Knowles did not win any notable amateur titles until the Pontins autumn tournament at Prestatyn in 1979 which was run in conjunction with the Home International Championship and in which he won the 'Player of the Series' award.

He turned professional in February 1980 and achieved his first significant breakthrough by beating Fred Davis and Doug Mountjoy to reach the semi-

finals of the Coral UK Championship in 1981. He became nationally known through his defeat of the defending champion, Steve Davis, in the first round of the 1982 World Professional Championship, in which he went on to reach the quarter-finals before losing to Eddie Charlton.

A few months later, his first prize in the Jameson International represented his second breakthrough and in the 1983 Embassy World Championship he was on the brink of a place in the final before losing to Cliff Thorburn from two up with three to play in their semi-final.

His second first prize in a world ranking tournament was provided by the 1983 Professional Players Tournament but in five attempts he has never scored a second win over Davis. Four of these defeats, though, came in finals and should not be allowed to obscure the many other successes which enabled him to rise to second place in the 1983–4 rankings.

At its best, his game has a natural flair and elegance but after winning the 1984 Winfield Australian Masters his 1984–5 British season was patchy. He did end it by reaching his second world semi-final but he nevertheless dropped one place, to third, in the rankings.

Dennis Taylor
NORTHERN IRELAND   1949 –

World ranking: 4
Turned professional: 1971

	World	Ranking tournaments	Other tournaments
First prize	1	1	4
Second prize	1	1	2
Semi-finalist	3	–	6

It took Dennis Taylor 13 years as a professional to win his first major title, the 1984 Rothmans Grand Prix, but even that emotional triumph paled into insignificance besides his capture of the 1985 Embassy World Championship. His defeat of Steve Davis on the final black of their best of 35 frames final was the stuff of which dreams are made.

Earlier in his career, Taylor had so desperately wanted to prove himself that whenever he found himself at the interface of dream and reality he invariably tried too hard.

His mother's death, which caused him to withdraw from the quarter-finals of the 1984 Jameson International, redefined his perspectives. He had no heart for the next tournament, the Rothmans Grand Prix, but after he had survived a round or two he began producing his very best. His 10–2 slaughter of Cliff Thorburn – who had beaten Davis in the semi-finals – was the performance of a man possessed, perhaps by a wish to unite his large and loving family in joy as they had been in sorrow. 'I don't think I'll ever feel the pressure that I did in the past', he said that night. 'When something like this happens, you realise that snooker comes a poor second to your family.'

Dennis Taylor

In his notable contribution to Ireland's capture of the 1985 Guinness World Cup at Bournemouth, overshadowed as it was by Alex Higgins winning the clinching frames, and the regaining of the Irish Championshi from Higgins in the Ulster Hall, Belfast, two days before he went to Sheffield, he revealed that he was in condition for a serious assault on snooker's Everest.

Convincing victories over Silvino Francisco, Cliff Thorburn and Tony Knowles pitched his camp for the final assault on the title.

He had first reached the semi-finals of the World Professional Championhip in Australia in 1975, and in 1977, the first year it was held at the Crucible, he did so again. Two years later, he reached the final but from 15–15, slid to a 24–16 defeat to Terry Griffiths.

'I wasn't cueing well enough,' said Taylor in the post-match press conference. 'My arm went tense and I couldn't get the cue through properly.' He did not mention then, but did recall years later, that his eyes were 'red raw' from a fortnight's intensive play wearing contact lenses under television lighting.

He tried unassisted eyesight again for a while and then spectacles of various design but it was not until the 1983–4 season that he adopted the 'Joe 90' type of model and truly began to see the light. They are worn so high on his face that he can look down the cue and through the optical centre of the lens rather than downwards through slight distortion. The larger lenses also give better peripheral vision for pots which are not straight or at any rate straightish.

In the 1984 world semi-finals he was within one easy ball of being 7–7 with Davis before losing 16–9, and the snooker world remained convinced that for all his professionalism and popularity he would somehow never manage to pot the balls which win world titles. However, there can never have been more widespread delight in being proved wrong. A recovery from 0–8 against the greatest player of the modern era, probably of all time, required incredible grit. Even to attempt, let alone pot, some of the balls he potted in the epic 68-minute deciding frame, required the premeditated courage which is so much rarer than a spontaneous reaction to danger.

Kirk Stevens
CANADA   1958 –

World ranking: 5
Turned professional: 1978

	World	Ranking tournaments	Other tournaments
First prize	–	–	–
Second prize	–	1	–
Semi-finalist	2	3	3

Having made his first century break at the age of 12 and having gone on the road all over Canada and North America playing for money when he was 15, there has never been any doubt about Kirk Stevens's exceptional ability.

In 1978, he was the youngest-ever world amateur championship semi-finalist and two years later also earned this distinction in the professional event. His break of 136 on the opening day of that championship would have beaten the then championship record of 142 but for failure at the black.

Jimmy White, who in 1980 superseded him as the youngest-ever world amateur semi-finalist before going on to win the title itself, deprived him of his other 'youngest-ever' distinction by beating him in the 1982 Embassy World Championship quarter-final.

Stevens was also beaten in the 1983 Embassy World Championship quarter-finals by Cliff Thorburn, having been two frames ahead with three to play, and in 1984 he was beaten 16–14 in the semi-finals by White, having led 12–10 going into the final session.

This disappointment put his game into reverse gear for most of the 1984–5 season though he did beat Steve Davis to reach the final of the Dulux British Open before losing to Silvino Francisco. This first appearance in a major final followed defeats in four semi-finals including one to White in the 1984 Benson and Hedges Masters when he made a 147 maximum.

Ray Reardon
WALES   1932 –

World ranking: 6
Turned professional: 1967

	World	Ranking tournaments	Other tournaments
First prize	6	1	4
Second prize	1	–	6
Semi-finalist	3	1	9

Ray Reardon was born into a snooker family in Tredegar, South Wales. His father and uncles all played local competitive snooker and he grew up in this atmosphere, even to the extent of playing make-shift games on one of his aunt's kitchen tables with marbles for balls and books for cushions.

He went into the mines when he was 14 and his first significant success was the Welsh amateur when he was 17. This was the first of six consecutive wins, a sequence which was broken only when his family moved to Stoke.

This move also ended a period of intense rivalry with Cliff Wilson, another Tredegar boy, who won the British Junior Championship in 1952 and 1953 and who reached the final of the English Championship in 1954. The pattern of their matches was that Reardon tended to win in the Welsh Championship and Wilson in the English. There were also some raw battles in money matches with the town split into two camps, favouring either Reardon at the Miners Institute or Wilson who reigned at the Lucania billiard hall. Much later, in

Kirk Stevens

Ray Reardon

1978, Tredegar was uniquely supplying both the world professional champion – Reardon – and the world amateur champion – Wilson.

At the Florence Colliery, Stoke, Reardon was buried in a roof fall, unable to move a muscle for three hours. He fought against the impulse to try to move by playing, in his mind, endless frames of snooker or games of marbles with his young brother, a demonstration of his iron calmness and resolve which was to see him through many a crisis on the table.

Outstandingly talented as he was as an amateur, he had to wait until 1964 to win his one and only English amateur title though he had been desperately unlucky in the 1956 final when he led Tommy Gordon 7–3 at the end of the first day only to lose his tip with his first shot on the second day and eventually lose 11–9.

It was at the expense of John Spencer, later a recurring professional adversary, that he won the English amateur title in 1964. This resulted in an amateur tour of South Africa which in turn led to an offer from Ken Shaw of Union Billiards to organise a professional tour for him. On the strength of this, Reardon resigned from the City of Stoke Constabulary, in which he had served since shortly after his mining accident and in which he earned two commendations for bravery.

Having turned professional in 1967, Reardon won the world title at his second attempt in 1970 and in 1973 started a run of four consecutive wins.

His other first prizes have included the 1976 Benson and Hedges Masters, the Welsh Championship (three times), the 1982 Professional Players Tournament, the 1983 Yamaha International Masters and several in smaller events.

Since 1978, though, the status he accrued through his six world titles has remained almost independent of the vicissitudes of form inevitable when a player's peak is past. That peak came a few years too early in the commercial sense and it was perhaps to the detriment of his game that he worked the exhibition circuit so assiduously. Nevertheless, he earned an enviably high reputation for professionalism in every aspect of his career and on the table his innate class was always obvious even when his results were poor. His fighting spirit certainly remained undimmed, not least after the 1984–5 season had proved the worst of his professional career.

Having made an unsuccessful attempt to adjust to wearing spectacles, he reverted to unassisted vision for the Embassy World Championship and courageously reached the semi-finals before losing to Steve Davis. He was awarded the M.B.E. in 1985.

Jimmy White

ENGLAND   1962 –

World ranking: 7
Turned professional: 1980

	World	Ranking tournaments	Other tournaments
First prize	–	–	5
Second prize	1	1	3
Semi-finalist	1	–	3

Jimmy White made his first century break when he was only 13 and spent his early teenage years neglecting his formal education while honing his staggering natural talent for snooker in the billiard halls of South London.

Managed by Bob Davis, a London taxi driver, he played money matches all over the capital, as indeed did his boyhood friend, Tony Meo, before he became, at 16, the youngest-ever English amateur champion.

Two years later, he became the youngest-ever world amateur champion and on turning professional gave Steve Davis his closest match, 10–8, on the latter's way to his first world title.

A few months later, he beat Davis in winning the Langs Scottish Masters to become the youngest-ever winner of a professional tournament and also won the next event on the circuit, the Northern Ireland Classic, again beating Davis.

Davis annihilated him 9–0 in the 1981 Coral UK semi-finals and he has not beaten Davis since though he did come within a frame of reaching the 1982 world final before losing to Alex Higgins from two up with three to play in a marvellous contest.

In the 1982–3 season, he lost to Ray Reardon in two finals, the Professional Players Tournament and the Yamaha International Masters, and in 1983–4 won the Benson and Hedges Masters.

At the end of that season he reached the Embassy World Championship final for the first time with what was his last attempt to become the youngest-ever professional champion.

Inwardly drained by his 16–14 semi-final victory over Kirk Stevens, he functioned poorly on the first day of the final and trailed Davis 12–4 overnight but made a stirring recovery on the second day before conceding defeat at 18–16.

With the quick, fluent, instinctive style, White perhaps falls short of less talented players in day-in, day-out consistency. Neither did he, until the 1984–5 season, appear to study deeply safety and tactical play. The improvement in this aspect of his game, however, was certainly an important factor in him winning the 1985 Benson and Hedges Irish Masters with victories over Tony Knowles and Higgins in the last two rounds, and with Higgins he also won the Hofmeister World Doubles.

Jimmy White

Terry Griffiths
WALES   1947 –

World ranking: 8
Turned professional: 1978

	World	Ranking tournaments	Other tournaments
First prize	1	–	7
Second prize	–	–	10
Semi-finalist	–	1	9

By today's standards, Terry Griffiths developed slowly. Although he won the West Wales Championship at 17, he was 24 before he made his first century break, the year in which he reached the final of the Welsh Amateur Championship at his first attempt.

The Welsh amateur title in 1975 gave him a place in the World Amateur Championship in Johannesburg in 1976. He was beaten in the quarter-finals but returned home to win the English amateur title in 1977 and 1978.

When a quarter-final defeat in the 1978 Welsh Amateur Championship ended his prospects of competing in the 1978 World Amateur, Griffiths turned professional, but his professional tournament debut was a disaster. He led Rex Williams 8–2 in the qualifying section of the Coral UK Championship but was beaten 9–8.

Just before the 1979 Embassy World Championship he was struggling to survive as a full-time professional but in storybook fashion came through the qualifying section and went on to win snooker's most prestigious title at his first attempt.

His 13–12 quarter-final victory over Alex Higgins and his 19–17 semi-final victory over Eddie Charlton were among the most memorable matches the championship has seen. The contrasting styles of his opponents showed Griffith's ability to play both types of game to the highest standards. Cool and positive under pressure, winning countless frames from losing positions with late clearances, Griffiths achieved a degree of concentration and inward harmony that he had never, by his own admission, achieved before.

The quarter-final, in which Higgins made centuries in consecutive frames and Griffiths a break of 107 in the decider, was superb attacking, break-building snooker, one mistake usually being sufficient to cost the frame. Charlton involved him in a gruelling battle of attrition including a 5 hours 25 minute final session which did not finish until 1.40 a.m.

After defeating Dennis Taylor in the final – something of an anti-climax in view of the epic battles which had preceded it – Griffiths was inundated with demands for his services. Managerless as he was at the time, Griffiths coped well with the stress, winning the 1980 Benson and Hedges Masters before his game fell apart at the Embassy World Championship. Defending his title, he lost the first seven frames of his first match with Steve Davis and despite a spirited recovery which

brought him to 10–10 was beaten 13–10.

Davis also beat him 9–0 in the 1980 Coral UK semi-final and it was his rivalry with the player with whom he became a Barry Hearn management stablemate that came almost to obsess him. They met in four consecutive finals in the 1981–2 season (Griffiths winning the Lada Classic and the Benson and Hedges Irish Masters, Davis the Benson and Hedges Masters and Yamaha International) before both lost in the first round of the Embassy World Championship, in which they were confidently expected to meet in the final.

There was a quarter-final win over Davis in the 1982 Coral UK which he went on to win, after twice being runner-up for this title, by beating Alex Higgins 16–15.

In comparison with his early years as a professional, his subsequent career has been disappointing. He has frequently confirmed that he is a player of the highest quality but in some strange way has failed to clinch matches he should have won and tended to follow a good performance with a poor.

Scrutiny of the results of the tournament circuit reveals an infuriating number of losses by the odd frame as he sank down the rankings and it is curious that since his initial world title success he has never progressed beyond the semi-finals of a ranking tournament. This one semi-final place seems incongruous besides his seven first prizes and ten second prizes in non-ranking events.

He won the Welsh professional title for the first time at the end of the 1984–5 season.

Alex Higgins
NORTHERN IRELAND   1949 –

World ranking: 9
Turned professional: 1971

	World	Ranking tournaments	Other tournaments
First prize	2	–	6
Second prize	2	1	8
Semi-finalist	3	3	13

Like George Best, Alex Higgins was born in Belfast, reached the top very quickly at a very early age and had some problems coping with fame and fortune.

He was only ten when he learned to play in a billiard hall called The Jampot which became his second home, living off Coke and Mars bars and learning in a tough school by playing for money. When he was 14 he was apprenticed to Eddie Reavey at Wantage but his career as a jockey foundered on a weight increase and after only one public ride he was back in Belfast where, at 19, he won the Northern Ireland Amateur Championship and almost single-handed took Belfast YMCA to the British amateur team title.

He turned professional armed with a professional's ability but blithely ignorant of the political workings of the snooker scene or of how to organise himself as a true pro, giving exhibitions in clubs and playing public

Terry Griffiths

Alex Higgins

matches instead of impromptu money matches in dingy saloons.

The North of England soon began to hum with tales of four-minute centuries and high living and his career was re-launched under a Blackburn bingo tycoon, John McLoughlin. It was under Dennis Broderick, though, that Higgins, starting in the qualifying competition, came through to win the world professional title at his first attempt in 1972 at the age of 23.

Higgins progressed from folk hero to media personality, the first modern snooker had had; his exploits with wine, women and horses were well publicised; he earned an unenviable reputation for behaving badly under the influence of drink.

An instinctive competitor, he compensated for a deterioration in his potting by improving the tactical side of his game. He remained, through his boldness, flair and anti-hero status, the game's biggest box-office attraction. He enjoyed a measure of success – one quarter-final, two semi-finals and a final – in the world championship between 1973 and 1976 before twice losing in the first round and once in the quarter-finals in 1977–9. Ironically, on each of these three occasions, his skill and personality produced high adrenalin levels not only in the crowd but in his opponents, who each found inspiration from the atmosphere he had engendered. In 1980, he led Cliff Thorburn 9–5 in the world final only to lose 18–16.

Outside the world championship, he won several miscellaneous minor tournaments and made four consecutive appearances in the final of the Benson and Hedges Masters, winning in 1978 and 1981. On his first appearance in the Coral UK final in 1980, he was heavily defeated by Steve Davis 16–6, this instituting a Davis dominance over him which appeared to have a depressive effect.

He was at a low ebb when the 1982 Embassy World Championship came along but with Davis and Terry Griffiths, the two favourites, both losing in the first round, he sensed, opportunist that he is, that the title was there for the taking.

The key to winning it was his recovery from two down with three to play to beat Jimmy White in the semi-finals. His 69 clearance to win the penultimate frame on the black undoubtedly stands as one of the greatest efforts in the history of the event.

From 15–15, he beat Ray Reardon 18–15 in the final and was beaten only by a single frame by Griffiths when he was on the brink of completing the world/UK double later than year.

In his mercurial way, he slid to his lowest in the early part of the 1983–4 season when his marriage appeared to be on the brink of a much publicised disintegration.

However, reconciliation brought an instant return to form during the 1983 Coral UK in which he completed an incredible recovery to beat Steve Davis 16–15 in the final after losing the first seven frames.

The 1984–5 season saw him reach the finals, the Coral UK and the Benson and Hedges Irish Masters.

With Jimmy White he won the Hofmeister World Doubles and with Dennis Taylor and Eugene Hughes he steered Ireland to the Guinness World Cup. He held the Irish Championship from 1972 until 1980 before losing it to Dennis Taylor and regained it once before losing again to Taylor in 1985.

In February 1976, at Leicester YMCA, he became the first player to achieve a public 'sixteen red' clearance, the extra red being of course a free ball after his opponent had left him snookered from a foul with all fifteen reds remaining. Sixteen reds, ten blacks, five pinks, one green and all the colours brought his break to 146 but Higgins himself did not realise that he could relatively easily have taken blacks instead of some of the pinks and thus achieved a higher break than the 147 which is ordinarily regarded as the maximum.

Tony Meo
ENGLAND   1959 –

World ranking: 10
Turned professional: 1979

	World	Ranking tournaments	Other tournaments
First prize	–	–	2
Second prize	–	1	1
Semi-finalist	–	1	6

Tony Meo's membership of the Barry Hearn management stable has placed him in an ambivalent position. Commercially and organisationally, the association has been of immense benefit; on the table, it may have contributed to some sense of inferiority when he has played the two other members of the stable, Steve Davis and Terry Griffiths.

Griffiths has beaten him on all four occasions they have met in major events while his record against Davis is 0–9. Frustratingly, those losses to Davis include some desperately close finishes.

In the 1984 Lada Classic, the only major final he has reached, he needed only a straightforward yellow to pink clearance to win but was distracted on his shot by a shout of 'Come on, Tony' and Davis won 9–8.

He led Davis 7–3 in the second round of the Coral UK in 1984 but opted for safety at a crucial moment when a pot might have been ventured. Davis did not allow him as good a chance again and reeled off five frames to win 9–7.

One up on Davis with two to play in the Tolly Cobbold English Professional Championship semi-final Meo again finished a 9–8 loser.

Outside his own camp, he has beaten virtually every other leading player at one time or another and his rise from 24th in the 1982–3 world rankings to 10th place testifies to his overall consistency. His matches with Jimmy White, with whom he grew up in Tooting, have invariably produced something special and he has twice won the Hofmeister World Doubles with Davis.

Tony Meo

Willie Thorne

Willie Thorne

ENGLAND   1954 –

World ranking: 11
Turned professional: 1975

	World	Ranking tournaments	Other tournaments
Frist prize	–	1	–
Second prize	–	–	1
Semi-finalist	–	1	1

Willie Thorne's capture of the £40 000 first prize in the 1985 Mercantile Credit Classic changed his status from talented but brittle 'Nearly Man' to accepted 'High Achiever'. His 9–8 semi-final victory over Steve Davis may well come to be looked back upon as a turning point in his career and his 13–8 win over Cliff Thorburn in the final involved him taking the last five frames in a gratingly competitive manner at odds with his natural attacking instincts. The title was also compensation for Thorne, if not for Thorburn, for their defeat in partnership a fortnight earlier in the final of the Hofmeister World Doubles.

Ever since his first games as young boy, on holiday at a hotel in Eastbourne and then at Anstey Conservative Club, Leicester where his father was steward, his fluent potting and break building appeared to destine him for the game's glittering prizes.

He was only 16 when he became England's youngest-ever amateur international but his career rarely delivered in full what his ability promised. He was favourite to win the British Junior title three times but won it only once; he was odds-on in the 1975 English amateur final but lost it; and when he turned professional he became notorious for his difficulty in clinching winning positions on big occasions, for losing close finishes and for following a big win with a bad loss. However, with persistence Thorne rose to 12th in the world rankings.

The likeable Thorne has never lacked a corps of supporters, faithful alike through encouraging successes and frustrating defeats. In his early days, they were largely from Osborne's Snooker Hall in down-town Leicester where Thorne invariably preferred to practise amidst people rather than in isolation on his own table at the Shoulder of Mutton, Braunstone, the family pub.

In recent years, his base has been the Willie Thorne Snooker Centre, a family concern, in the city centre.

'Racing Raymond' Winterton, a rotund tic-tac man and student of form, is the ample figure at the core of his non-family support: Gary Lineker, the Leicester City striker, who is probably the best snooker player in the Football League, is his most regular practice opponent. In turn, Thorne is Leicester City's most ardent supporter.

The remainder of his 1984–5 season was an anti-climax and even with his Mercantile first prize he improved his world ranking by only one place to 11th.

Eddie Charlton

AUSTRALIA   1929 –

World ranking: 12   Turned professional: 1960

	World	Ranking tournaments	Other tournaments
First prize	–	–	–
Second prize	2	–	–
Semi-finalist	6	2	5

Eddie Charlton has held the Australian Professional Championship every year, except 1968, since 1964 and for many years dominated the Australian scene not only on the table but through his chairmanship of the Australian Professional Association, his promotions company (who stage tournaments), through his connection with the billiards trade and through his contacts with sponsors and television companies.

Charlton began playing when he was nine and at eleven played billiards exhibitions with Walter Lindrum. He made his first billiards century at 15 and his first snooker century at 17 but spent much of his youth, with some success, playing more robust sports. These included ten years First Grade soccer, the 1950 Australian Surfing Championship with the Swansea Belmont crew, a string of victories in speed roller-skating and competitive cricket, athletics, boxing and tennis. He was one of the carriers of the Olympic torch for the 1956 Olympics in Melbourne and boxed an exhibition bout with Dave Sands, then world middle-weight champion.

He turned professional in 1960 when he was still a miner and gradually began to concentrate on what was, after all, his number one game. He first visited England in 1968 to challenge John Pulman for the world title in the days when the champion defended against any challenger who could make a satisfactory commercial offer. He was beaten 39–34 and did not play in the championship again until it was held in Australia in 1970. He lost surprisingly to his fellow Australian, Warren Simpson, in the semi-finals.

In 1972 he pushed John Spencer very hard to 37–32 in the semi-finals but the highlight of his trip was winning the first of two consecutive *Pot Black* titles, a success which may well have been material in the Australian Broadcasting Corporation's decision to buy the series.

Though he has been very close many times, he has never won the world title or a major tournament in Britain. He led Ray Reardon 7–0 in the 1973 world final but was beaten 38–32; in the 1975 world final he recovered from 8–16 to lead Ray Reardon 28–23 but was beaten 31–30; in 1976 he lost 20–18 to Alex Higgins in the semi-finals; in 1979 he lost an epic semi-final to Terry Griffiths 19–17.

Outside the professional championship, Charlton's successes have included a 31–24 defeat of Reardon in the final of the controversial 'World' Matchplay Championship in Melbourne in 1976; a 23–19 defeat of John

Eddie Charlton

Spencer in the final of the biggest tournament South Africa has ever staged, the Limosin International, in Cape Town, in 1979; and consecutive breaks of 135 and 137, neither opponent having a single shot, in an exhibition at the Kempsey Crescent Head Country Club, New South Wales in 1967.

Inevitably, his place in the top group of players came under threat as he grew older but he still remained admirably consistent until 1984–5 when his worst ever professional season saw him drop from 6th to 12th in the world rankings.

He is also a useful billiards player and lost by only 33 points to Mark Wildman in the 1984 world final.

Silvino Francisco
SOUTH AFRICA   1946 –

World ranking: 13
Turned professional: 1978

	World	Ranking tournaments	Other tournaments
First prize	–	1	–
Second prize	–	–	–
Semi-finalist	–	1	–

Five times South African amateur snooker champion and a losing semi-finalist in the 1976 World Amateur Championship in Johannesburg, Silvino Francisco turned professional in 1978 when it appeared clear that international opposition to his government's apartheid policy would deny South Africans the opportunity to participate in international amateur competition in the foreseeable future.

He entered the Embassy World Professional Championship for the first time in 1982 and did oustandingly well to reach the quarter-finals, beating Dennis Taylor, then the No. 5 seed, in the first round before losing to Ray Reardon in the last eight.

He worked his way up the rankings to 17th before the 1984–5 season saw him break into the elite top 16 in 13th place. After reaching the semi-finals of the Jameson International in early season, he beat Jimmy White, Tony Meo, Alex Higgins and, in the final, Kirk Stevens, to win the £50 000 first prize in the Dulux British Open.

However, during the final, Francisco remonstrated angrily with his opponent when he believed him to be playing under the influence of an illegal stimulant. Francisco's feelings were aired by a newspaper and in a welter of claim, counter claim, disclaimer and counter disclaimer, he was fined £6000, a record, by the WPBSA for causing a damaging statement to be published about a fellow professional. The punishment was considered harsh by the snooker world and did not affect his popularity within it.

Two other members of his family are professionals. His elder brother, Mannie, had an outstanding amateur career in which he won the South African amateur billiards title thirteen times and the snooker five whilst also earning second places in world amateur championships at both games. Mannie has never played the British circuit but his son Peter, who became the third member of the family to win South African titles at both games, earned 59th place in the world rankings in his first season as a professional.

David Taylor
ENGLAND   1943 –

World ranking: 14
Turned professional: 1968

	World	Ranking tournaments	Other tournaments
First prize	–	–	–
Second prize	–	1	3
Semi-finalist	1	–	–

World amateur champion in 1968, David Taylor achieved little in his first ten years as a professional but in 1978 reached the final of the Coral UK Championship, beating Patsy Fagan, the holder, John Virgo and Alex Higgins before losing to Doug Mountjoy in the final.

In the 1980 Embassy World Championship, he beat Ray Reardon in the quarter-finals before losing to Cliff Thorburn. In 1981 he was runner-up to Steve Davis in the Yamaha International at Derby and at the same venue in 1982 he beat Davis in the quarter-finals of the Jameson International before losing to Tony Knowles in the final.

Despite two indifferent seasons, he managed to maintain 14th place in the world rankings at the end of the 1984–5 campaign in which he struggled gamely to adjust to playing in spectacles. This process was not assisted by his wife treading on them just before he was due to play the quarter-finals of the Tolly Cobbold English Professional Championship.

In an exhibition at Butlins, Minehead in 1978, he made three consecutive total clearances, 130, 140 and 139, and made centuries in seven consecutive frames in a witnessed practice session in 1975.

Throughout his career, however, he has only intermittently conveyed the positive approach appropriate to his considerable ability.

Doug Mountjoy
WALES   1942 –

World ranking: 15
Turned professional: 1976

	World	Ranking tournaments	Other tournaments
First prize	–	–	5
Second prize	1	–	6
Semi-finalist	–	–	4

Twice Welsh amateur champion and in 1976 world amateur champion, Doug Mountjoy began his professional career in a blaze of glory through winning

Silvino Francisco

Doug Mountjoy

David Taylor

the Benson and Hedges Masters in 1977, the Coral UK Championship in 1978 and the Woodpecker Welsh Professional Championship in 1980 (beating both Terry Griffiths and Ray Reardon) in what was to be the first of three successes in five years.

Winner of the first event of the 1980–1 British season, the now defunct Champion of Champions, he suffered a worrying attack of Bell's palsy, which paralysed one side of his face and affected the blinking function of one eyelid. In turn, this inevitably affected his performances for most of the season but he returned to form in time to make his best ever world championship showing, beating Wille Thorne, Eddie Charlton, Dennis Taylor and Ray Reardon to reach the final. In this, he lost the first six frames to Steve Davis and was still six frames behind when he was beaten 18–12.

In his 16–10 semi-final defeat of Ray Reardon he compiled what was then a new championship record of 145.

In his early career, his potting and break building was much better than his tactical and safety play. His game is now much more maturely balanced and his dedication and professionalism through good times and bad are exemplary.

In the 1983 Benson and Hedges Masters he scored a fine win over Steve Davis in reaching the semi-finals, and Wembley Conference Centre again provided a happy hunting ground in 1985 when he beat Tony Knowles, Tony Meo and Terry Griffiths to reach the final before losing to Cliff Thorburn.

One of four members of the tiny Abertysswg club to win the Welsh amateur title – Alwyn Lloyd, Des May and the young professional Wayne Jones are the others – Mountjoy lived in Ebbw Vale before moving across the Welsh border to take over the Temple Bar Inn at Ewyas Harold in Herefordshire, a haven and financial hedge from the circuit's competitive pressures.

Joe Johnson
ENGLAND   1952 –

World ranking: 16
Turned professional: 1979

	World	Ranking tournaments	Other tournaments
First prize	–	–	–
Second prize	–	1	–
Semi-finalist	–	1	–

Joe Johnson was runner-up in the English and World Amateur Championships in 1978 and between these events made a break of 140 on Tyne Tees Television which still stands as a world amateur record in competition.

He did not attract many headlines in his first five years as a professional but broke through spectacularly in 1983 by beating Jimmy White, Eddie Charlton, Cliff Thorburn and Tony Meo in reaching the final of the Professional Players Tournament before losing 9–8 to Tony Knowles.

In 1985, he beat Knowles in reaching the semi-finals of the Mercantile Credit Classic and was consistent enough overall to reach 16th in the world rankings. Curiously, he has never won a match in the televised phase of the Embassy World Championship.

Bill Werbeniuk
CANADA   1947 –

World ranking: 17
Turned professional: 1973

	World	Ranking tournaments	Other tournaments
First prize	–	–	–
Second prize	–	1	1
Semi-finalist	–	–	2

Gargantuan in bulk, but with the ability both to play delicately precise position and control shots using extreme power, Bill Werbeniuk is the only player to have compiled two breaks over 140 in the Embassy World Championship, 142 in 1979 and 143 in 1985.

Three times a world quarter-finalist, he looked very much a potential semi-finalist in 1983 when he led Alex Higgins 9–7 going into the final session only to lose 13–11.

This was certainly the most successful season of his career for he reached the final of the Lada Classic with wins over Higgins, Doug Mountjoy and Kirk Stevens before losing to Steve Davis. That summer, he also reached the final of the Winfield Australian Masters by beating Dennis Taylor, Higgins and Tony Knowles before losing to Cliff Thorburn.

From this peak he plummetted to the depths of two desperately disappointing seasons, winning only two matches in 1983–4 and one in 1984–5. This appeared largely due to two interconnected problems. He has an hereditary nervous disease which causes his cue arm to shake at all times. Nervous of the side effects of controlling this with drugs, he found an enormous intake of lager, sometimes 40 pints a day, the best stabiliser though even when he was at his most successful this seemed unlikely to provide a permanent solution.

John Parrott
ENGLAND   1964 –

World ranking: 18
Turned professional: 1983

	World	Ranking tournaments	Other tournaments
First prize	–	–	–
Second prize	–	–	–
Semi-finalist	–	1	–

The first two years of John Parrott's professional career suggested that he was a player for the big occasion. In the televised phase of the 1984 Lada Classic he beat

Joe Johnson

John Parrott

Bill Werbeniuk

Tony Knowles and Alex Higgins before losing only 5–4 in the semi-finals to Steve Davis, and in the Embassy World Championship a few months later he again beat Knowles.

After a disappointing 1984–5 campaign, he again produced the goods under the gaze of the television cameras at the Embassy World Championship by beating John Spencer and Kirk Stevens before losing a desperately close quarter-final to Ray Reardon 13–12.

He took to snooker at the age of 12 when rain ruled out an intended game of bowls with his father. The Liverpool professional George Scott and the Blackpool coach Frank Callan helped him with his game as he won a variety of titles as an amateur, ranging from *Junior Pot Black*, his first experience of television, to two Zimbabwe Opens.

To many professonals it appears of little relevance where they live or even where they were born but Parrott is fervently Liverpudlian in his loyalties and the support which he attracts.

John Virgo
ENGLAND   1946 –

World ranking: 19
Turned professional: 1976

	World	Ranking tournaments	Other tournaments
First prize	–	–	1
Second prize	–	–	1
Semi-finalist	1	2	1

In recent years, John Virgo's fame has rested more on his cabaret impressions of his fellow professionals than on his achievements on the table even though he reached two major semi-finals in late 1982 and has recorded wins over such luminaries as Cliff Thorburn, Tony Knowles, Ray Reardon, Dennis Taylor and Eddie Charlton.

The real John Virgo has occasionally stood up in competition in this way but the future which was promised by reaching the Embassy World Championship semi-final in 1979 and winning both the Coral UK title and a strong international tournament in Bombay later that year has not materialised.

In two one-off events, he was runner-up in the Champion of Champions in 1980 and won the Professional Snooker League in 1984. Ironically, these tournaments were virtually the only serious financial failures of snooker's modern era and in neither case did he receive the advertised prize money.

John Spencer
ENGLAND   1935 –

World ranking: 20
Turned professional: 1967

	World	Ranking tournaments	Other tournaments
First prize	3	–	4
Second prize	–	–	–
Semi-finalist	2	1	4

John Spencer learnt to play on a makeshift home table with 12 nails knocked into a bagatelle board to form pockets and tape tied from one nail to another to form cushions. His first snooker on a more traditional surface was played at the Radcliffe Sunday School Institute where, at the age of 15, less than a year after his first proper game, he made a break of 115, starting with a red and a yellow and followed by 14 reds and 14 blacks.

He played until he was 18 and then retired for ten years until a friend recruited him to a local needle match. A succession of money matches, for sums between £10 and £20 followed. He won 14 in succession and was persuaded to enter the English Amateur Championship, the first tournament in which he ever participated.

He reached the final, lost in the final again the following year but won it in 1966. He represented England in the 1966 World Amateur Championship in Karachi, finishing second, and on his return withdrew from all amateur events after a dispute with the governing body.

With no previous thought of turning professional, he was contacted out of the blue by the National Spastics Society to play some exhibitions on their behalf. A summer engagement at Pontins holiday camp also came his way and when entries were invited for the 1968–9 World Professional Championship, a sympathetic bank manager advanced him the £100 entry fee.

Winning the title in an attractive style in which deadly long potting and prodigious screw shots were prominent elements, Spencer became almost overnight, snooker's biggest name. Even his defeat by Ray Reardon in the March 1970 semi-final did not much interrupt his reign for in November that year he regained the title in spectacular fashion when it was held in Australia for the first time.

When between January 1971 and February 1972 Park Drive sponsored four four-man tournaments, Spencer won three £750 first prizes and £550 second prize. He won *Pot Black* in 1970 and 1971 and when, in February 1972, he was beaten by Alex Higgins in the world final, it was the greatest snooker upset for years.

There was another traumatic reverse in the 1973 world semi-final when he lost 23–22 to Reardon after leading 19–12. He won the Norwich Union Open both in 1973 and 1974 and the inaugural Benson and Hedges Masters in 1975 but his world championship perform-

John Virgo

John Spencer

ances gave him no cause for elation until, having sunk to No. 8 in the world rankings, he won the 1977 title.

He compiled the first ever 147 maximum in tournament play in winning the Holsten tournament at Slough in January 1979 – albeit with the pockets oversized and ITV's cameramen on meal break – but only sporadically regained the inspiration and sparkle of his early professional years.

As his cue action lost its natural straightness and timing, he fell back increasingly on a knowledgeable tactical game. Despite a downward trend in the rankings he was still good enough to record wins over players like Cliff Thorburn and Tony Knowles and take Steve Davis to 5–4 in their semi-final of the 1983 Lada Classic.

For all his efforts, none the easier because of the business pressures of owning a club, Spencers, in Bolton, he was dealt a further blow when persistent double vision almost ended his career altogether in 1984. The condition is now controlled through a permanent daily intake of prescribed steroids.

Eugene Hughes
IRELAND   1955 –

World ranking: 21
Turned professional: 1981

	World	Ranking tournaments	Other tournaments
First prize	–	–	–
Second prize	–	–	–
Semi-finalist	–	1	2

Twice Republic of Ireland amateur champion at both games, Eugene Hughes reached the quarter-finals of the 1983 Professional Players Tournament, beating Terry Griffiths and Bill Werbeniuk, before the 1984–5 season provided him, via wins over Doug Mountjoy, Ray Reardon and Willie Thorne, with his first place in a major semi-final, the Jameson International.

He extended Steve Davis to 5–4 in the quarter-finals of the 1985 Benson and Hedges Irish Masters and lost only 6–5 to Dennis Taylor in their semi-final of the Irish Championship after having a clearcut chance to win when he led 5–2.

With Alex Higgins and Taylor he was involved n Ireland's capture of the Guinness World Cup for the first time in 1985.

Cliff Wilson
WALES   1934 –

World ranking: 22
Turned professional 1979

	World	Ranking tournaments	Other tournaments
First prize	–	–	–
Second prize	–	–	2
Semi-finalist	–	–	3

Welsh amateur champion in 1956 and after a 15-year retirement from the game again in 1977 and 1979, Cliff Wilson won the World Amateur Snooker Championship in Malta in 1978 and turned professional the following year. Partly because of eye trouble he has not recaptured the consistency of his youth but at his best he remains an outstanding potter with a uniquely entertaining style.

His competitive victims include Jimmy White, Tony Knowles, Ray Reardon, Terry Griffiths and Doug Mountjoy. He has twice lost in the final of the Welsh Professional Championship.

Neal Foulds
ENGLAND   1963 –

World ranking: 23
Turned professional: 1983

	World	Ranking tournaments	Other tournaments
First prize	–	–	–
Second prize	–	–	–
Semi-finalist	–	1	–

With a 10–9 win over Alex Higgins in 1984 and a dramatic 10–8 loss to Steve Davis in 1985, Neal Foulds made his mark in the Embassy World Championship in the first two seasons of his professional career. Through wins over Willie Thorne and Tony Knowles he also reached the semi-finals of the Rothmans Grand Prix in 1984. His father, Geoff, also a professional, is an unfailing guide, factotum and friend, though he has also found time to specialise as a technical adviser on plays and films with snooker backgrounds like *Give us a Break* (BBC) and *Billy the Kid and the Green Baize Vampire*.

Cliff Wilson

Neal Foulds

Eugene Hughes

Dean Reynolds

Dean Reynolds

ENGLAND   1963 –

World ranking: 24
Turned professional: 1981

	World	Ranking tournaments	Other tournaments
First prize	–	–	–
Second prize	–	–	–
Semi-finalist	–	–	–

Turning professional at 18 as the inaugural winner of *Junior Pot Black*, Dean Reynolds reached the last 16 of the Embassy World Championship at his first attempt in 1982. Perhaps not surprisingly, he could not maintain this start but in 1984 he reached his first major quarter-final, the Rothmans Grand Prix, by beating Silvino Francisco, and also beat Willie Thorne to reach the quarter-finals of the Tolly Cobbold English Championship.

Mark Wildman

ENGLAND   1936 –

World ranking: 25
Turned professional: 1979

	World	Ranking tournaments	Other tournaments
First prize	–	–	–
Second prize	–	–	–
Semi-finalist	–	1	1

Mark Wildman was 43 when he turned professional but immediately made an impression in the World Professional Billiards Championship by reaching two finals before winning the title itself in 1984.

His outstanding snooker performance was a run to the semi-finals of the Lada Classic in 1984 with wins over John Virgo, Silvino Francisco and Eddie Charlton. He is a member of ITV's commentary team.

Murdo Macleod

SCOTLAND   1947 –

World ranking: 26
Turned professional: 1981

	World	Ranking tournaments	Other tournaments
First prize	–	–	1
Second prize	–	–	–
Semi-finalist	–	–	–

Having turned professional on a slim amateur record, Murdo Macleod has established himself as Scotland's leading professional by winning the Scottish title twice and becoming the highest ranked Scot in the world list. His tournament victories include two over Willie Thorne and one each over David Taylor and Eddie Charlton, but he went into the 1985–6 season without having won a match on television.

Rex Williams

ENGLAND   1933 –

World ranking: 27
Turned professional: 1951

	World	Ranking tournaments	Other tournaments
First prize	–	–	–
Second prize	–	–	–
Semi-finalist	3	–	2

See Billiards, p. 114.

Mike Hallett

ENGLAND   1959 –

World ranking: 28
Turned professional: 1979

	World	Ranking tournament	Other tournaments
First prize	–	–	–
Second prize	–	–	–
Semi-finalist	–	–	–

Mike Hallett's 5–2 second round victory over Steve Davis in the 1983 Professional Players Tournament provided the biggest shock of that season. He subsequently beat Dennis Taylor in the 1984 Lada Classic and Alex Higgins in the Rothmans Grand Prix and further glory seemed nigh when he led Cliff Thorburn 6–1 in the first round of the 1985 Embassy World Championship. However, this match ended in a 10–8 defeat as his career remained for another season one of promise rather than fulfilment.

Dave Martin

ENGLAND   1948 –

World ranking; 29
Turned professional: 1981

	World	Ranking tournaments	Other tournaments
First prize	–	–	–
Second prize	–	–	1
Semi-finalist	–	1	–

Second prize in the 1984 Yamaha International Masters, a sprint-style tournament proceeding by means of a series of three-man round robin groups, was the highlight of the first four years of Dave Martin's professional career.

In his first year on the circuit, however. he did reach the semi-finals of the Jameson International with wins over Bill Werbeniuk, Eddie Charlton and Graham Miles and in 1985 beat Ray Reardon to reach the last 16 of the Dulux British Open.

Rex Williams

Mike Hallett

Mark Wildman with the World Professional Billiards trophy
he won in 1984

Murdo Macleod

Perrie Mans

SOUTH AFRICA   1940 –

World ranking: 30
Turned professional: 1961

	World	Ranking tournaments	Other tournaments
First prize	–	–	1
Second prize	1	–	–
Semi-finalist	1	–	1

Perrie Mans, whose father, Peter, was a World Professional Championship quarter-finalist in 1950, became in 1978 the first South African to reach the world final.

An outstanding single ball potter and a good competitor, with an unorthodox pattern of play which often disconcerted players technically more accomplished, Mans made good the comparative weakness of his positional play and break building in defeating John Spencer, Graham Miles and Fred Davis before losing to Ray Reardon in the final.

South African amateur champion in 1960, at his first and only attempt, Mans won the South African professional title from Freddie van Rensberg in 1965 and retained it until defeated by Derek Mienie in 1979. He regained the title the following year and held it until 1984.

Mans, a left-hander, first competed in the World Professional Championship in 1970 but did not score a notable success until he sensationally beat John Spencer 15–13 in a second round match in 1974. Two years later, he beat Graham Miles and Jim Meadow-croft to reach the semi-finals.

Outside the championship, Mans won *Pot Black* at his first attempt in 1977 and the Benson and Hedges Masters in 1979, beating Cliff Thorburn, Ray Reardon and Alex Higgins.

Since then he has slid steadily down the rankings and did not compete full time on the circuit in 1984–5.

John Campbell

AUSTRALIA   1953 –

World ranking: 31
Turned professional: 1982

	World	Ranking tournaments	Other tournaments
First prize	–	–	–
Second prize	–	–	–
Semi-finalist	–	–	–

Australian amateur champion in 1979, John Campbell has reached one major professional quarter-final, the 1983 Professional Players Tournament, in which he beat Doug Mountjoy, Graham Miles and Dave Martin.

Dene O'Kane

NEW ZEALAND   1963 –

World ranking: 32
Turned professional: 1984

	World	Ranking tournaments	Other tournaments
First prize	–	–	–
Second prize	–	–	–
Semi-finalist	–	–	–

New Zealand amateur champion at the age of 17, Dene O'Kane is certainly the best snooker player his country has produced in the modern era. His high place in the world rankings after only one season as a professional is chiefly attributable to reaching the quarter-finals of the Dulux British Open with wins over John Campbell, Vic Harris and Dave Martin.

Perrie Mans

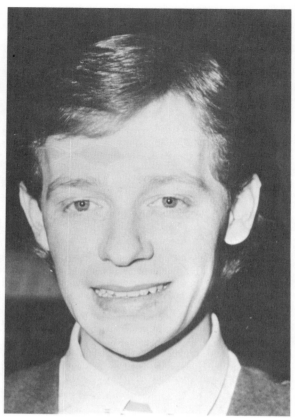

Dene O'Kane

Dave Martin

John Campbell

How snooker started

In 1875 Sir Neville Chamberlain was a young subaltern with the Devonshire Regiment stationed at Jubbulpore. During the rainy season the officers' long afternoons were spent at the mess billiards table where the parent game was less popular than various round games which were more suitable for more than two players and to which it was easier to add a modest gambling element.

Pyramids, perhaps snooker's most obvious forerunner, was a game played with 15 reds, initially placed in a triangle, with the apex red on what is now the pink spot but which was then known as the pyramid spot. Each time a player potted a red, all his opponents paid across the agreed stake money per ball.

In Life pool, each player was given a cue-ball and an object-ball (e.g. white on red, red on yellow) so, for the second player, his object-ball was the first player's cue-ball and so on. The object was to pot one's specified object-ball three times. Each time a player's ball was potted, he lost a life and had to pay an agreed stake. When he had lost three 'lives' he paid an extra sum for a 'star' or extra life and when that was gone he was 'dead'. When only one player remained he scooped the kitty.

Black pool was a development of Life pool in that a black ball was added. When a player had potted his allocated ball, he could attempt the black. If he was successful, each of his opponents paid across an additional sum and he could then attempt the nearest ball. Joe Davis spent many of his youthful hours playing a similar game, pink pool.

Black Pool was the preferred game among the Devonshire officers but it was Chamberlain's inspiration to gradually add other coloured balls so that snooker came to be played with 15 reds, yellow, green, pink and black. Blue and brown were added some years later.

These new colours produced a game whose variety (and variety of monetary forfeits) immediately caught on. The concept of break building was much in the future and even the point values of the balls were not established until a little later; but it was in these casual and almost chance beginnings that the game undoubtedly had its origin.

When Compton Mackenzie, the novelist, interviewed him in 1938, Chamberlain recalled that the Devons one afternoon received a visit from a young subaltern who had been trained at the Royal Military Academy, Woolwich. In the course of conversation, the latter happened to remark that a first-year cadet at Woolwich was referred to as a 'snooker' with the implication that this was the status of the lowest of the low. The original word for a cadet had been the French 'neux' which had been corrupted to 'snooker'.

Chamberlain said: 'The term was a new one to me but I soon had the opportunity of exploiting it when one of our party failed to hole a coloured ball which was close to a corner pocket. I called out to him: "Why, you're a regular snooker"! I had to explain to the company the definition of the word and to soothe the feelings of the culprit I added that we were all, so to speak snookers at the game so it would be very appropriate to call the game snooker. The suggestion was adopted with enthusiasm and the game has been called snooker ever since.'

In 1876, when Chamberlain left the Devons to join the Central India Horse, he took the game with him. After being wounded in the Afghan War, he served with the Commander-in-Chief of the Madras Army and was with him every summer when he moved to the hill station at Ootacamund. Snooker came to be recognised as the speciality of the Ooty Club and the rules of the game were drawn up and posted in the billiards room.

During the 1880s rumours of this new game reached England and when John Roberts went out to India on one of his tours he had it in mind to find out the rules. One evening, in 1885, in Calcutta, Chamberlain was dining with the Maharajah of Cooch Behar when Roberts was introduced to him. Roberts duly brought the game back to England.

It was many a long day before snooker became widely played. Not every hall nor every club could afford a snooker set of 22 balls though it was not long before the manufacturers appreciated snooker's superior commercial possibilities. Even so, billiards remained such a popular game to play that not until the Second World War could a billiard hall risk carrying fewer sets of billiard balls than they had tables.

By 1910 a measure of break building had come into the game and Tom Aiken, the Scottish professional billiards champion, was reported to have made a break of 102 at snooker and Cecil Harverson two. Phil Morris, a Tottenham marker, made a 103 at the Eagle Hotel, Tottenham.

In 1912 the official record, on tables with standard pockets, was 73, held jointly by John Roberts (1907) and James Harris (1908). In 1915 George Hargest, the manager of the Lucania Hall, made a break of 112, a total clearance with Durolite balls, at Blackwood, Monmouthshire. In the same year, William Murray made a 103 at the Collingwood Billiard Hall, Newcastle, of which he was manager. Tom Newman made

Joe Davis in play during the 1946 World Professional Snooker Championship final at the Horticultural Hall, Westminster.

an official break of 89 in 1919.

The rules of snooker, which had been subject to many local variations, were codified in when the Billiards Association and Billiards Control Club amalgamated in 1919. The drawn game was abolished when provision was made for the black to be respotted at the end of a frame if the scores were equal. The free ball was introduced to supersede the BCC rule that if a player was snookered after a foul he could have the snookering ball(s) taken up so that he could play onto the 'nearest ball playable', though, when in hand, a player was judged to be snookered or not from the brown spot only and not any part of the 'D'. The penalty for going in-off a red was still only one, the four point minimum penalty still being a few years away.

The touching ball rule was introduced in 1927.

In the earliest professional matches Fred Lawrence beat Albert Cope 31–27 for the Midland Professional Championship in 1921 and J. S. Nicholls beat W. Davies 1032–777 (the aggregate score of 18 frames) for the Welsh Professional Championship in 1922.

The first week's snooker match at a major London venue was staged as a season curtain-raiser at Burroughes and Watts, Soho Square in September 1922 when Arthur Peall beat Joe Brady 34–14.

George Nelson, a Leeds professional deeply involved in the promotion and trade aspects of the game, was publicly urging the BA & CC to wake up to snooker potentialities and the indefatigable Bill Camkin produced a book of rules. The Midland Counties Billiards Association with whom Camkin was closely associated imposed a minimum penalty of four points for a foul stroke, contrary to the then official rules.

From 1932 to 1936, amateur snooker consolidated its popularity without its leading exponents noticeably improving their skill.

There was an important rule change in 1934 when the so-called crawl stroke, rolling the cue-ball up behind a nominated free ball, was outlawed, first as a six month's experiment but then permanently.

Snooker overtook billiards in popularity because it was a more sociable game to play and a more varied game to watch.

As the top professional billiards players specialised more and more in nursery cannons and gained levels of expertise in break building sequences which, with small variations, were essentially repetitive, the game they played came to bear less and less resemblance to the one which amateurs themselves played or could identify with. As crowds for professional billiards dwindled away it was not long before professionals began to concentrate on snooker.

In 1936, the *Daily Mail* switched its annual sponsorship of a billiards tournament to snooker, the great feature of the event being a 133 break by Sidney Smith, the first ever official 'total clearance' and a new world record.

Tournaments sponsored by the *Daily Mail* and later the *Empire News, News of the World* and *Sporting Record* were to provide the staple fare at Thurston's and, after the war, at Leicester Square Hall: round robin events of three days or week's matches on handicap, involving seven or eight players and lasting at least half the season. It was a long drawn out procedure – in sharp contrast to the much shorter matches in today's major tournaments – and was eventually rejected by the public.

As the professional game contracted, fewer amateurs turned professional. The public tired of the same old players competing endlessly against each other and professional snooker, by the mid fifties, had virtually petered out. Nothing looked less likely for snooker's future than its affluent state today.

Past Masters

JOE DAVIS (1901–78)

If Joe Davis was a Master among Masters at Billiards, appreciably above Newman and McConachy, appreciably below Lindrum, he was indisputably King of Snooker, not only on the table but in all matters pertaining to the game.

In his days managing a billiard hall in Chesterfield, Davis realized at first hand that while billiards remained the championship game, snooker was increasingly becoming the people's game. It was more sociable in that breaks did not take as long and the inferior player did not therefore spend most of his time fielding out. With an appropriate handicap, a poor player could compete with an even chance with a good one. There was skill in the game but there was luck as well, more than there was at billiards, and this too enhanced its attractions as a gambling game.

As a young man, Davis also played a great deal of pink pool, a gambling game which employed 15 reds and the pink. Potting a red entitled the player to an agreed stake from all other players plus a chance, for a higher stake, to attempt the pink. He was so much too good for the local miners that he was made to play left-handed, thus acquiring the skill as a left-handed player which enabled him to deal with many positions at billiards – and even more at snooker – for which he would otherwise require the rest, an implement which he rarely employed with great confidence. (Joe's younger brother Fred later learnt to play left-handed for a similar reason and was also comparatively poor with the rest.)

Another chance factor may well have contributed to Davis's extraordinary consistent and accurate potting. As his right eye was virtually useless, he automatically sighted with his left eye, almost like a marksman, his cue touching his chin beneath his good eye.

The Amateur Snooker Championship had started in 1916; there had been a Midland Professional Championship in 1921 and a Welsh Professional Championship in 1922; but snooker's role in the professional world was chiefly to fill out, with a couple of light-hearted frames, a billiards session which finished early. When it was suggested in 1924 that the BA & CC organise a professional championship their secretary, A. Stanley Thorn, replied: 'The suggestion will receive consideration at an early date but it seems a little doubtful whether snooker as a spectacular game is sufficiently popular to warrant the successful promotion of such a competition'.

Two billiard traders, George Nelson of Leeds and Bill Camkin of Birmingham, both friends of Davis, could see snooker's possibilities, even if the Establishment could not, and brought snooker to the fore whenever they could. Finally, Camkin and Davis drafted a letter to the BA & CC drawing up conditions for a

Steve Davis

Cliff Thorburn

Tony Knowles

Dennis Taylor

Kirk Stevens

Ray Reardon

Alex Higgins

Jimmy White

Terry Griffiths

Tony Meo

Eddie Charlton

Willie Thorne

Joe Davis

professional championship and received this august body's blessings.

There was a five guinea entry fee and five guinea sidestake, half the money to be distributed in a 60–40 ratio between winner and runner-up, the other half to pass to the BA & CC. Gate receipts would be divided equally between the players. The entire organisation fell on Camkin who not only promoted the final but refereed it.

In those days, the prevailing idea was to pot a red or two, a couple of colours and play safe but in the time he could spare from billiards Davis devoted considerable thought and practice to evolving the positional and breakbuilding shots, sequences and techniques which are taken for granted today. In 1925, he made a break of 96 which superseded Tom Newman's official record of 89 which had stood since 1919.

Predictably, Davis won the inaugural 1926–7 championship with ease. His top break was 57 and he pocketed £6 10s 0d. The BA & CC used the players' half of the entry fees to buy a trophy. Few of the early championships were much more remunerative. Even by 1931, it was still held in such low esteem that the final was staged in the back room of a Nottingham pub owned by the other finalist, Tom Dennis.

In January 1928, Davis made his first public snooker century – he never counted anything he did in practice

– against Fred Pugh at Manchester. He inched up the official record to 105 (1930), 109 (1933), 114 (1933), with a 132 on a non-standard table for good measure. His first championship century was 110 in 1935, the first year in which the event became a paying proposition.

Davis, according to his brother, 'a very good player before anyone else knew how to play the game', won the championship as regularly as clockwork each year. Though he never lost a frame on purpose, he was so far superior to his rivals that he could virtually pick his moment to tighten up if he needed to.

Even so, he trailed Dennis 10–14 and 16–19 before beating him 25–21 in the 1931 final. He cut it even finer against Horace Lindrum, the young Australian he had hammered 42–22 in a match for £100 plus all the gate money in Melbourne in 1933. Lindrum led 27–24 in the 1936 final before Davis won 34–27.

Lindrum, who had an exceptionally attractive style and personality was little if at all inferior to Davis in technique but when the chips were really down the Englishman's infinitely superior temperament carried him through. Lindrum never beat Davis level but did so several times when receiving seven. Davis never lost on purpose but it no doubt crossed his mind that the audiences for week's matches between them might fall away if the same player always won.

In 1936, Lindrum equalled Davis's break record of 114 and later that year improved it to 131 though on the same evening as Sidney Smith made a 133. Davis improved his own best to 124, 128 and then regained the record with 135 in 1937 though Lindrum's break of 141 in January 1937 had been denied official status only on a technicality, the table not being tested *before* rather than *after* the match, a condition now abandoned.

On the first of many trips to South Africa, Davis made a 141 break that year which beat the all-comers record of 113 which had been set by Walter Lindrum, who did not take snooker seriously, in 1933. He increased the official record to 137 and three weeks later to 138 in the *Daily Mail* Gold Cup of 1938, the newspaper having switched its annual sponsorship from billiards to snooker in the 1936–7 season. It was also in 1938 that Davis first cleared the table from opening stroke with an effort of 134.

The championship record passed out of his hands but remained within the family as Fred made a 113 in their 1939 semi-final. Joe won narrowly 17–14 and even more narrowly in the 1940 final, clinching his 37–35 victory with a break of 100.

During the war, Davis raised over £125 000 for war charities and made a considerable name for himself on variety stages including the London Palladium, with a trick shot performance involving the use of a large tilted mirror. He married June Malo, the singer.

After the war, he was elected chairman of the resurrected Professional Billiards Players Association and formed a partnership with Sidney Smith and Bob Jelks, a billiard trader, to lease and promote at Leicester

Square Hall (which opened on the old bombed Thurston's site in 1947).

His last title defence culminated in a fabulously successful fortnight's match against Horace Lindrum at the Royal Horticultural Hall, Westminster where crowds of 1200 a session poured £12 000 into the box office. Expenses were high and entertainment tax was reduced from 48 to 33⅓ per cent only the day before the match but each finalist pocketed a hitherto undreamt of £1500 for his efforts. Six century breaks (the two highest of the match, 133 and 136, being in turn championship records) helped Davis retain the title 78–67.

He retired from championship play, having held the world professional snooker title undefeated for 20 years, but like John Roberts before him continued to rule as king in exile. As the best player, the dominant personality, the chairman of the player's body, the man with the biggest say in who played at Leicester Square Hall, the game's showcase, he virtually ran professional snooker. When television came early in the 1950s, it was Joe with whom the BBC negotiated; when a player wished to turn professional he needed Davis's approval or he was frozen out. He had innumerable friends in show business, the professions, the city and the press. He was astute in business though, no matter what deal or conversation might have been occupying him only minutes before, his concentration was absolute when he reached the table. His instructional books, classics of their kind, sold hugely.

That Joe had the interests of the game at heart there is no doubt. With professional players squabbling and an ineffectual governing body there was a desperate need for a strong man to take charge as he did. Neither did anyone begrudge him his legitimate commercial pickings. But his retirement from championship play was soon to devalue the championship itself – just as Roberts's withdrawal had devalued it. In less than ten years, professional snooker was to decline from that peak of the 1946 final almost to the point of extinction.

Outside the world championship, professional tournaments were conducted on a handicap basis. Davis inevitably was the scratch man. Victory confirmed his supremacy, defeat did not threaten him because, of course, his opponent had received a certain number of points per frame. He played only the reigning official champion on level terms. He won the tournament twice in its ten-year history and was invariably near the top. Some players were so much in awe of his dominant personality that they were, literally, afraid to beat him.

It disappointed him that his brother allowed the title to pass outside the family in 1947 to Walter Donaldson, though there was some compensation in the crowds which flocked to Kelvin Hall, Glasgow, to see the king, a Scot himself, play the king in exile. During the week 10 000 spectators attended. Davis won 42–29 and made a new world record of 140.

Davis also made a break of 112 in which he took blacks with the first 14 reds. He could easily have left himself on the blue from the last red and gone on to make 145 but elected to play the red very slowly to stay on the black. It failed to drop and he had to wait until 1955 to achieve snooker's first 147 maximum under standard conditions. (Murt O'Donoghue in 1934, Horace Lindrum in 1941, Leo Levitt in 1948, Clark McConachy in 1952 had previously made witnessed 147's on non-standard tables in practice frames.)

After his brother had beaten Donaldson in the 1948 final, Fred and Joe met in the *Empire News* tournament which ran throughout the 1948–9 season. The brothers played level but as Joe had never lost to anyone he was expected to be conceding two or three frames on the sealed handicap which was revealed at the end of the match.

Fred won a great victory, 36–35, having achieved a winning lead at 36–33, but when the sealed envelope was opened it was revealed that Fred was conceding two frames! The handicapper, Harold Mayes, sports editor of the *Empire News*, for whom Fred was writing a column in opposition to Joe's in the *News of the World*, had evidently thought it one-up to his paper to have 'their' man conceding start to Joe. As it was, this bizarre denouement, which enabled Joe to take the first prize of £450, obscured Fred's victory, which never achieved a sense of reality with the public.

In the 1949–50 season, Davis won the new £1500 *News of the World* tournament from the back mark, conceding 7 to Donaldson and at least 20 to every other competitor. George Chenier, a Canadian whom he had brought over after they had contested a week's match in Bermuda, snatched the world record with 144 but was Davis's opponent when the maestro wrested it back five weeks later with 146, taking a pink after his sixth red.

In 1951 in South Africa and twice in 1954, Davis made century breaks in three consecutive frames. On 22 January 1955, having just made his second 146 in the *News of the World* tournament, Davis achieved his dearly held ambition: against Willie Smith at Leicester Square Hall, only a few weeks before it closed due to the expiry of the lease, he made the first official 147 maximum.

Pettily and short-sightedly the BA & CC refused to recognize the break on the grounds that professionals were playing under their own 'play again' rule though this had not, of course, cropped up in this particular frame. Everyone knew what the break meant, however, and the BA & CC did in fact belatedly recognize it in April 1957, shortly before they themselves adopted the 'play again' rule for amateur play.

The break was the climax of Davis's career. He received the OBE in 1963 and continued to play until 1964. Whenever snooker was on television the formula was Joe *v.* A. N. Other.

In retrospect, the game suffered from revolving too closely round one man. By retiring from the championship (i.e. not risking his reputation) he devalued the game's premier event and, it followed, anyone who won it. No doubt he would have won many more world titles but the chances are that, at least once, he would have lost. His brother, after all, beat him four times on level terms in the fifties, admittedly far fewer times than Joe beat him but enough to constitute a real threat.

The future of professional snooker was not safe-guarded in any way. He had had the vision to build up snooker as a public entertainment but always, quite understandably, in a context which allowed for his personal progress, standing and profit. His determination and that of his immediate colleagues to uplift the game's status had been wholly admirable but their lack of forethought in not only failing to encourage but actually discouraging leading amateurs of the day from turning professional was not in the best interests of the game.

Little was seen of Davis in the first few years of his retirement but as snooker gathered an unstoppable momentum in the late seventies he was regularly seen at big tournaments. Invariably, he received a mighty ovation.

It was tragic, if appropriate, that at the age of 77, he should be taken ill while watching his brother contest the 1978 semi-final against the South African Perrie Mans. He survived a 6½-hour operation but died a few months later from a chest infection while convalescing.

He died with the satisfaction of having seen, at Sheffield and on television, the game which he had pioneered at a peak of popularity and the championship he founded established, with events like Wimbledon and the Open Golf Championship, as one of Britain's great annual sporting spectacles.

FRED DAVIS (1913–)

With any other surname, Fred Davis would have made a very much more substantial impact on the general public than was the case as Joe's younger brother. Eight world titles in ten attempts would in ordinary circumstances have made him the dominant player of his generation but with Joe not playing in the championship, though otherwise pursuing a full playing career, Fred became immovably stuck in the public mind as the perennial number two. Four times (not of course counting short matches and exhibitions) Fred beat Joe on level terms but this affected their relative standings with the public not at all. It was even suggested that Joe had allowed Fred to beat him in order to give his brother a leg-up though anyone who was aware of Joe's intense pride of performance and his ambition to retire undefeated recognized the absurdity of this diagnosis.

Some 12 years the younger, Fred grew up so deeply in Joe's shadow that it was remarkable that he ever emerged from it. He began playing on a miniature table at his home on Wittingham Moor, near Chesterfield. No one as much as told him the rules but he picked up the basics very quickly and at the age of 12 was taken by his father to play at Burroughes Hall, London in the Boys (Under 16) Championship. A semi-final place in competition with older boys did not impress anyone in Chesterfield, least of all his family, who were now accustomed to Joe playing – and usually winning – at the very highest level and he was not even entered for the event for another three years, on which occasion he won it comfortably.

Easygoing, not a glutton for practice, Fred tended to be written off by Joe as not dedicated or ambitious enough. Apart from a forcible suggestion that he should wipe the grin off his face when he was practising, Fred received little advice and certainly no coaching from his elder brother. Through working in his family's billiard hall in Chesterfield he automatically became a professional on his 16th birthday but Joe held such a low opinion of his game that he was most reluctant that he should be allowed to enter the Junior Professional Billiards Championship. In fact, Fred won the event on each of the three occasions it was held.

Professional opportunities, though, were few and far between. There were a few club exhibitions – £1 was the fee for his first – but with professional billiards going out of existence at just the wrong time he did not surface again as a competitor until the 1937 World Professional Snooker Championship.

By this time he was self-consciously keeping to himself that he was suffering from myopia. He could tell the time from the large clock which stood in the family billiard hall only by standing right underneath it. When he played, the balls had a woolly edge. He lost 17–14 in the first round to Bill Withers, a Welshman of no previous or subsequent record.

Joe was furious at this affront to family honour. He berated Fred for losing . . . and beat Withers in the next round 30–1. Fred overcame his self-consciousness sufficiently to consult an optician and thus became the first professional to play with the special swivel joint spectacles which have since become the saviour of many an imperfectly sighted player.

His game improved rapidly. A semi-finalist in 1938, Fred lost only 17–14 to Joe in the 1939 semi-final and in 1940 reached the final, giving Joe his closest-ever championship battle before losing only 37–35. Fred, who had several times been told by Joe that he would never beat him, was thus very near to doing so before the Army spirited him away for almost the full duration of the war.

In the first post-war championship, Fred lost in the semi-final to Horace Lindrum but with Joe then retiring from championship play he was odds-on favourite to beat Walter Donaldson in the 1947 final. Their previous meetings had given Fred no great cause for anxiety but Donaldson, having locked himself away in the loft practising by himself for weeks on end, produced such a deadly mixture of brilliant single ball potting and, at the first semblance of risk, tight safety play that a name other than Davis was inscribed on the trophy for the first time.

Fred Davis

This proved to be the first of eight consecutive world finals that Fred and Donaldson contested. Only once more was Donaldson successful, in 1950, but the matches were invariably hard work. The best tactics against Donaldson were to play him at his own patient, careful game, an approach which lent their contests an attritional aspect at times but which did not, strangely, deter spectators from attending in large numbers. Blackpool Tower Circus, which became established as the venue for the world final, was packed to near its considerable capacity every April.

Public interest would doubtless have been greater if Fred had been playing Joe with the title at stake. Even outside the championship they played some memorable matches. Joe preferred to concede a black start, a handicap which hardly reduced his chances of winning but which safeguarded his reputation and record if he did lose. Nevertheless, on four occasions, Fred defeated Joe on level terms, the only player ever to do so.

Fred's first victory over Joe was in the *Empire News* tournament, a round robin event, with each match lasting a week, which ran through the 1948–9 season at Leicester Square Hall. Fred took a winning lead at 36–33 and won 36–35. However, the tournament was conducted on a sealed handicap basis with the handicapping entrusted to Harold Mayes, sports editor of the *Empire News*, for which Fred was writing a weekly column.

Several judges on the inside of snooker felt that around this time Fred was actually playing better than Joe but the fact remained that Joe had never lost level to anyone. Accordingly, when the sealed handicap revealed Fred to be conceding two frames start, Joe was presented with a 37–36 victory which not only obscured Fred's feat but gave Joe the £450 first prize.

The second victory, 37–34, occurred in a week's challenge match at Leicester Square Hall in 1949, the third, 20–17, in a three day match on level terms in the *News of the World* tournament in 1952 and the fourth, 21–16 in the *News of the World* tournament in 1954. In all fairness, these four close victories have to be set against a great many defeats, some by wide margins. Apart from his two championship defeats by Donaldson, though, Fred did not lose level to any other player before, on the grounds of dwindling financial return, he himself chose not to enter the 1957 championship.

Donaldson's retirement in 1954 had led to Fred meeting John Pulman in the 1955 and 1956 world finals, both of them close matches just as their 1954 semi-final had been. But the advent of television and the failure of professional snooker to provide new names was diminishing public support. Some leading amateurs were vaguely thought to be 'not the right type' so the professional game grew ever more confined to a few familiar names. There was still a living to be earned from the club exhibition circuit but this had little to do with competitive sport. Fred, securely encamped at the Llandudno hotel which was run by his wife, felt less and less inclined to bestir himself.

This remained the position during Pulman's reign as champion from 1957 to 1969. With the championship dormant from 1957 to 1964 and only on a challenge basis from 1964 to 1969, Fred challenged in 1964, in 1965 (when he was within one frame of victory) and in 1966 but, playing so infrequently, his standard inevitably suffered.

It became crystal clear, in 1968–9, when there was at last a new intake of professionals and the championship was restored to a knock-out basis, that the established players had gone soft through lack of exposure to competition.

Ten years in which Fred might otherwise have been in his prime had been frittered away when professional snooker once again began to gather momentum. Calling on his great experience, he beat Ray Reardon, then a new professional, 25–24 after winning five of the last seven frames in a 5 hour 33 minutes final session but lost easily to Gary Owen.

Though snooker's revival rekindled much of Fred's enthusiasm, this was inevitably negated by two heart attacks, in 1970 and 1974.

In the circumstances, it would clearly have been unrealistic to have expected him to recapture his former position in the game. Indeed, for someone born in 1913, it is amazing, so late in his career, that he should still compete so successfully at top level, winning the last three frames to beat Alex Higgins

15–14 in the 1974 world quarter-final, beating John Spencer in the 1975 Watney Open, losing only 11–10 to Ray Reardon in the 1976 Pontins Professional final, reaching the semi-final of the World Championship in 1978 and the quarter-final in 1979.

Though he has always been popular, Fred's efforts have been supported in the last few years by a special warmth. For all his steely determination and coolly analytical mind, his mild manner and ever-present sense of fun communicate an enjoyment of the game which, in an age of temperamental and overpaid superstars, the public find both endearing and refreshing.

Late in his career, Davis returned to billiards, his first love, which he had played only occasionally for more than 40 years as commercial reality had demanded that he concentrate on snooker. On one of his rare excursions into the three ball game he had won the 1951 United Kingdom Championship but declined to play Clark McConachy for the world title because he felt that the first week in September was too early in the season for a match of such importance.

Davis had long since abandoned all thoughts of playing for the Billiards Championship until Jim Williamson, proprietor of the Northern Snooker Centre, Leeds, persuaded Yorkshire Bank to sponsor a four day world title match with Rex Williams in May 1980.

A break of 583, the highest in the championship for 46 years, clinched Davis's convincing victory and enabled him to equal the record of his late brother Joe as the only player to have won the World Professional title both at snooker and billiards. He retained the Championship at Rugby later that year when the event was restored to a tournament basis.

WALTER DONALDSON (1907–73)

Walter Donaldson was the first winner of the British Boys Billiards Championship in 1922. He turned professional the following year and won the Scottish Professional Billiards Championship in 1928.

Combining hard practice with moves to Rotherham and Chesterfield to manage billiard halls, he began to concentrate on snooker and first entered the World Championship in 1932.

Heavily defeated by Joe Davis, he went away for no less than seven years to work on his game until he entered again in 1939, the year in which he established himself by finishing fourth in the *Daily Mail* Gold Cup.

After five years war service in the Eighth Army's desert and Italian campaigns he returned home in 1946 to undertake a relentless programme of solo practice to regain his form.

After Joe Davis's retirement had thrown the 1947 championship wide open, Donaldson shut himself away in a billiard room in a friend's loft for hours on end and to the surprise of the snooker world emerged to beat Fred Davis in the final.

These two were also to meet in the next four finals, Davis winning the first two and the last and Donaldson the other.

Donaldson's strong points were his imperturbability and the general consistency which arose from absolutely plain ball striking for he rarely used side in potting. This helped make his long potting the most consistently accurate the game had yet seen but it limited his positional play and restricted the number of centuries he made.

His dour approach and thrust out determined Scottish chin symbolized his approach to the game and indeed to life. He was a literal kind of man and he played a literal point-by-point type of game, making few concessions to the public. Though an excellent match player he was not in great demand for exhibitions and as professional snooker's appeal dwindled he acted out his disillusionment with the game by turning his billiard room at his Buckinghamshire home into a cowshed and breaking up the slates of his table to pave a path.

JOHN PULMAN (1926–)

John Pulman won the 1946 English Amateur snooker title as a 20-year-old unknown from Exeter and turned professional that year with the backing of a Bristol businessman, Bill Lampard, at whose house he stayed and in whose billiard room he practised intensively every day.

He won £400 in his first professional tournament, the *Empire News* event, but his progress to the championship was gradual. He gave Fred Davis a close match in the 1954 semi-final and another in the 1955 final. Leading 31–29 starting the last day he was on the brink of victory in the final the following year but Davis recovered to beat him and it was not until 1957, when Davis did not enter and when there were only four entries, that Pulman won the world title in Jersey.

He was unable to capitalize fully on his new status as champion as the game was entering an unprecedented depression and the championship became dormant until it was revived on a challenge basis in 1964. Public interest was limited but Pulman proved his qualities as a competitor by defending the title against a variety of opponents in a variety of venues until the championship was restored to a knock-out basis in 1968–9.

When the established players were challenged by a wave of newcomers from the amateur ranks, Pulman stood up to the test better than any of his contemporaries, reaching the world final again in 1970. Thereafter, however, his standard gradually declined. There were, though, glimpses of his former quality and in 1978 he made a great personal effort to achieve his best form for some years in reaching the world semi-final. He has become chiefly known in recent years as an ITV commentator.

The World Professional Snooker Championship

1927

First round: M. Inman beat T. Newman 8–5; T. Carpenter beat N. Butler 8–3.

Second round: T. A. Dennis beat F. Lawrence 8–7; A. Cope beat A. Mann 8–6; J. Davis beat J. Brady 10–5; Carpenter beat Inman 8–3.

Semi-finals: Davis beat Cope 16–7; Dennis beat Carpenter 12–10.

Final: Davis beat Dennis 20–11.

1928

First round: T. Newman beat F. Smith 12–6; A. Mann beat A. Cope 14–9.

Second round: Newman beat T. A. Dennis 12–5; F. Lawrence beat Mann 12–11.

Third round: Lawrence beat Newman 12–7.

Final: J. Davis beat Lawrence 16–13.

1929

First round: F. Lawrence beat A. Mann 13–12.

Semi-finals: J. Davis beat Lawrence 13–10; T. A. Dennis beat K. Prince 14–6.

Final: Davis beat Dennis 19–14.

1930

First round: F. Lawrence beat A. Mann 13–11; N. Butler beat T. Newman 13–11.

Semi-finals: J. Davis beat Lawrence 13–2; T. A. Dennis beat Butler 13–11.

Final: Davis beat Dennis 25–12.

1931

Final: J. Davis beat T. A. Dennis 25–21.

1932

First round: C. McConachy beat T. A. Dennis 13–11.

Final: J. Davis beat McConachy 30–19.

1933

First round: W. Donaldson beat W. Leigh 13–11.

Semi-finals: J. Davis beat Donaldson 13–1; W. Smith beat T. A. Dennis 16–9.

Final: Davis beat Smith 25–18.

1934

Final: J. Davis beat T. Newman 25–23.

1935

First round: W. Smith beat C. Stanbury 13–12.

Semi-finals: Smith beat A. Mann 13–4; J. Davis beat T. Newman 15–10.

Final: Davis beat Smith 25–20.

1936

First round: C. O'Donnell beat S. Lee 16–15; H. Lindrum beat H. Terry 20–11; J. Davis beat T. Newman 29–2; W. Smith beat S. Smith 16–15; C. Stanbury beat A. Mann 22–9.

Second round: Alec Brown beat Stanbury 16–15; Lindrum beat O'Donnell 19–6 (retired); J. Davis beat W. Smith 22–9; S. Newman w.o.

Semi-finals: Davis beat Brown 21–10; Lindrum beat S. Newman 29–2.

Final: Davis beat Lindrum 34–27.

1937

First round: W. A. Withers beat F. Davis 17–14.

Second round: J. Davis beat Withers 30–1; H. Lindrum beat S. Lee 20–11; W. Smith beat T. Newman 16–15; S. Smith beat Alec Brown 18–13.

Semi-finals: Lindrum beat W. Smith 20–11; Davis beat S. Smith 18–13.

Final: Davis beat Lindrum 32–29.

1938

Qualifying

First round: H. Holt beat C. W. Read 21–10.

Second round: F. Davis beat Holt 23–8.

Competition proper

First round: F. Davis beat Alec Brown 14–6 (retired ill); S. Smith beat C. Stanbury 27–4; J. Davis beat S. Lee 24–7; W. Smith beat T. Newman 16–15.

Semi-finals: Davis beat W. Smith (n.r.s.); S. Smith beat F. Davis (n.r.s.).

Final: J. Davis beat S. Smith 37–24.

1939

Qualifying

First round: W. Donaldson beat H. Holt 18–13; H. W. Laws beat S. Newman 19–12.

Second round: Donaldson beat Laws 18–13.

Competition proper

First round: S. Smith beat S. Lee 21–10; W. Donaldson beat C. Falkiner 21–10; T. Newman beat A. Mann 19–12; F. Davis beat C. Stanbury 19–12.

Second round: J. Davis beat W. Smith 19–12; F. Davis beat T. Newman 20–11; Alec Brown beat H. Lindrum 17–14; S. Smith beat Donaldson 16–15.

Semi-finals: J. Davis beat F. Davis 17–14; S. Smith beat Alec Brown 20–11.

Final: J. Davis beat S. Smith 43–30.

1940

Qualifying

H. Holt beat C. Stanbury 18–13.

Competition proper

First round: W. Donaldson beat Holt 24–7; J. Davis beat Alec Brown 20–11; F. Davis beat S. Lee 20–11; S. Smith beat T. Newman 22–9.

Semi-finals: J. Davis beat Donaldson 22–9; F. Davis beat S. Smith 17–14.

Final: J. Davis beat F. Davis 37–36.

1946

Qualifying

First round: K. Kennerley beat F. Lawrence 22–9; C. Stanbury beat J. Barrie 18–13; S. Newman beat W. Leight 16–15.

Second round: Kennerley beat T. Reece 8–2 (retired); S. Newman beat Stanbury 17–14.

Third round: S. Newman beat Kennerley 21–10.

Competition proper

First round: J. Davis beat W. Donaldson 21–10; S. Newman beat S. Lee 19–12; F. Davis beat Alec Brown 24–7; H. Lindrum beat H. Holt 17–14.

Semi-finals: J. Davis beat S. Newman 21–10; Lindrum beat F. Davis 16–12.

Final: J. Davis beat Lindrum 78–67.

1947

Qualifying

First round: Albert Brown beat J. Pulman 21–14; W. Leigh beat H. F. Francis 19–16; S. Lee beat J. Lees 19–16; K. Kennerley beat C. Stanbury 23–12; E. Newman w.o. H. Holt.

Second round: J. Barrie beat F. Lawrence 25–10; Albert Brown beat Newman 28–7; Kennerley beat A. Mann 23–12; Leigh beat Lee 25–10.

Third round: Albert Brown beat Barrie 24–11; Kennerley beat Leigh 21–14.

Fourth round: Albert Brown beat Kennerley 21–14.

Competition proper

First round: H. Lindrum beat Albert Brown 39–34; S. Smith beat Alec Brown 43–28; W. Donaldson beat S. Newman 46–25; F. Davis beat C. McConachy 53–20.

Semi-finals: Donaldson beat Lindrum 39–32; Davis beat Smith 39–32.

Final: Donaldson beat Davis 82–63.

1948

Qualifying

First round: C. Stanbury beat E. Newman 26–9; W. Leigh beat H. Holt 18–17; J. Barrie beat H. F. Francis 19–16; J. Pulman w.o. S. Lee.

Second round: Leigh beat Barrie 21–14; Pulman beat Stanbury 19–16.

Third round: Pulman beat Leigh 18–17.

Competition proper

First round: F. Davis beat Alec Brown 43–28; C. McConachy beat J. Pulman 42–29; Albert Brown beat S. Smith 36–35; W. Donaldson beat K. Kennerley 46–25.

Semi-finals: Davis beat McConachy 43–28; Donaldson beat Alec Brown 40–31.

Final: Davis beat Donaldson 84–61.

1949

Qualifying

First round: C. Stanbury beat H. F. Francis 18–17.

Second round: Stanbury beat J. Rea 18–17.

Third round: Stanbury beat H. Holt 18–17.

Competition proper

First round: W. Donaldson beat Stanbury 58–13; J. Pulman beat Albert Brown 42–29; S. Smith beat Alec Brown 41–30; F. Davis beat K. Kennerley 50–21.

Semi-finals: Donaldson beat Pulman 49–22; Davis beat Smith 42–29.

Final: Davis beat Donaldson 80–65.

1950

Qualifying

First round: W. Smith beat W. A. Withers 28–7; H. Holt beat H. W. Laws 26–9; S. Lee beat C. Stanbury 20–15; K. Kennerley beat J. Barrie 21–14.

Second round: Kennerley beat Smith 22–13; Lee beat Holt 16–8 (retired ill).

Third round: Kennerley beat Lee 21–14.

Competition proper

First round: Albert Brown beat J. Pulman 37–34; W. Donaldson beat K. Kennerley 42–29; G. Chenier beat P. Mans 37–34; F. Davis beat Alec Brown 44–27.

Semi-finals: Donaldson beat Albert Brown 37–34; Davis beat Chenier 43–28.

Final: Donaldson beat Davis 51–46.

1951

Qualifying

First round: J. Barrie beat S. Lee 23–12.

Second round: Barrie beat H. W. Laws 28–7.

Competition proper

First round: F. Davis beat Barrie 42–29; H. Lindrum beat Albert Brown 43–28; W. Donaldson beat K. Kennerley 41–30; J. Pulman beat S. Smith 38–33.

Semi-finals: Donaldson beat Lindrum 41–30; Davis beat Pulman 22–14 (retired ill).

Final: Davis beat Donaldson 58–39.

1952

First round: Alec Brown beat R. Williams 39–22; J. Rea beat J. Lees 38–32; Albert Brown beat J. Pulman 32–27 (records incomplete).

Semi-finals: W. Donaldson beat Albert Brown 31–30.

Final: F. Davis beat Donaldson 38–35.

1953

Qualifying

First round: W. Smith beat J. Lees 21–14; K. Kennerley beat R. Williams 25–12.

Second round: Kennerley beat Smith 42–29.

Competition proper

First round: Albert Brown beat Alec Brown 35–26; J. Pulman beat J. Rea 36–25; W. Donaldson beat Kennerley 42–19; F. Davis beat J. Barrie 32–29.

Semi-finals: Donaldson beat Brown n.r.s.; F. Davis beat Pulman 36–25.

Final: Davis beat Donaldson 37–34.

1954

First round: J. Pulman beat J. Rea 31–30.

Semi-finals: W. Donaldson beat Alec Brown 36–25; F. Davis beat Pulman 32–29.

Final: Davis beat Donaldson 39–21.

1955

First round: J. Pulman beat R. Williams 22–15; J. Rea beat H. Stokes n.r.s.

Semi-finals: F. Davis beat Rea 36–25; Pulman beat Alec Brown n.r.s.

Final: Davis beat Pulman 37–34.

1956

Semi-finals: J. Pulman beat J. Rea 36–25; F. Davis beat R. Williams 35–26.

Final: Davis beat Pulman 38–35.

1957

Semi-finals: J. Pulman beat R. Williams 21–16; J. Rea beat K. Kennerley 25–12.

Final: Pulman beat Rea 39–34.

Through lack of public support no championship was organized between 1957 and 1964. After a truce with the BA & CC a new system was adopted whereby the champion defended his title against a series of single challengers. These matches resulted:

1964

J. Pulman beat F. Davis 19–16.
J. Pulman beat R. Williams 40–33.

1965

J. Pulman beat F. Davis 37–36.
J. Pulman beat R. Williams 25–22 (matches).
J. Pulman beat F. van Rensburg 39–12.

1966

J. Pulman beat F. Davis 5–2 (matches).

1968

J. Pulman beat beat E. Charlton 39–34.

Modern snooker

Professional Tournaments

1969
WORLD PROFESSIONAL CHAMPIONSHIP
Sponsor: Players No 6   *Entries*: 8
Prize money: £3500
First prize: £1300

The eight man draw providentially brought the four established professionals against the four newcomers. The first match, at Wryton Stadium, Bolton, saw the end of Pulman's reign as champion at the hands of John Spencer. Pulman, at one time 11 frames behind, recovered to only three behind but was eventually beaten 25–18. Jack Rea was beaten 25–17 at Stratford Hippodrome by Gary Owen but Rex Williams scored a very comfortable victory over Bernard Bennett, a Southampton player who turned professional without any substantial amateur record, at Southampton. In the last first round match, Fred Davis just overcame Ray Reardon by the odd frame in 49 after several marathon sessions at Tunstall British Legion, Stoke.

There were thus two new and two established professionals remaining in the semi-finals though, at this stage, both newcomers were to record crushing victories, Spencer over Williams at the Co-op Hall, Bolton, and Owen over Davis at Wilstanton Miners Club, Stoke.

Owen, in view of the fact that he had always beaten Spencer in their previous important matches, started favourite for the final, a week's match at the Victoria Hall, London, but Spencer established a psychological ascendancy in the early stages and won very comfortably.
First round: J. Spencer beat J. Pulman 25–18; R. Williams beat B. Bennett 25–4; G. Owen beat J. Rea 25–17; F. Davis beat R. Reardon 25–24.
Semi-finals: Spencer beat Williams 37–12; Owen beat Davis 37–24.
Final: Spencer beat Owen 37–24.

1970 (Apr)
WORLD PROFESSIONAL CHAMPIONSHIP
Sponsor: Players No 6   *Entries*: 9
Prize money: Not known
First prize: £1225

David Taylor, having turned professional after winning the 1968 World Amateur in Sydney, brought about an increase of one on the entry for the previous year. He held Pulman to 12–12 at Grimsby before going down 31–20. Pulman also crushed Owen in a semi-final at Middlesbrough and after trailing 14–27 to Reardon in the final at the Victoria Hall, London recovered to 33–34 before losing 37–33. Controversy attended the other semi-final for which a diabolically difficult table was installed at Bolton. Spencer let the difficulties it presented get the better of him and Reardon, adapting himself better to the conditions, scored a narrow victory to reach the final.
First round: David Taylor beat B. Bennett 11–8.
Quarter-finals: J. Pulman beat David Taylor 31–20; G. Owen beat R. Williams 31–11; R. Reardon beat F. Davis 31–26; J. Spencer beat J. Rea 31–15.
Semi-finals: Pulman beat Owen 37–12; Reardon beat Spencer 37–33.
Final: Reardon beat Pulman 37–33.

1970 (Nov)
WORLD PROFESSIONAL CHAMPIONSHIP
Sponsor: None   *Entries*: 9
Prize money: Not known
First prize: £2333

The championship was organized in Australia for the first time by Frank Holz on behalf of the Lewisham Hospital Sports Medicine Clinic. The four semi-finalists were obtained by means of an incomplete and thus unsatisfactory round robin. Matches were spread round Australia and thus involved competitors in a certain amount of air travel even, in some cases, on the day of a match.

Eddie Charlton, who had domi-nated the Australian scene since winning the Australian professional title in 1964, was expected to reach the final but lost to his compatriot Warren Simpson, a good potter with a deceptively casual and cheerful approach who spent most of his time playing for money in City Tattersall's Club, Sydney. Earlier, Simpson had beaten Pulman and, by a single frame, both Owen and the South African Perrie Mans.

With Spencer in his prime, however, he never looked like losing. The final saw him make three centuries in four frames, the first time this had been done in the championship.
Round robin: J. Spencer beat P. Mans 20–17; beat N. Squire 27–10; beat J. Pulman 23–14. R. Reardon beat Mans 22–15; beat E. Charlton 21–16; beat Spencer 21–16. W. Simpson beat G. Owen 19–18; beat Pulman 21–16; beat Mans 19–18. Charlton beat Squire 27–10; beat Mans 26–11; beat Owen 23–14. Owen beat P. Morgan 26–11; beat Squire 19–18. Pulman beat Morgan 25–12; beat Squire 26–11. Morgan beat Simpson 21–16.
Semi-finals: Spencer beat Reardon 34–15; Simpson beat Charlton 27–22.
Final: Spencer beat Simpson 37–29.

1971
PARK DRIVE £2000

Gallahers first involvement with snooker, which was also that of their sports sponsorship consultants, West and Nally, was in the form of a triple round robin between four invited professionals with matches played over a single evening in 18 club venues. The top two in the final league table contested the final, which was televised by the BBC.

Final placings	P	W	L	*Prize*
John Spencer	9	8	1	£750
Rex Williams	9	5	4	£550
Gary Owen	9	5	4	£400
John Pulman	9	0	9	£300

Play off for first prize: Spencer beat Williams 4–1.

1971

PARK DRIVE £2000

Park Drive repeated in October the tournament they had first staged in January. Reardon, who had been unable to take part in the first event because he was touring South Africa, finished second to Spencer in the round robin section but took the £750 first prize by winning the play-off 4–3 after needing a snooker with only pink and black remaining in the deciding frame.

Final placings
	P	W	L	Prize
John Spencer	9	7	2	£550
Ray Reardon	9	4	5	£750
John Pulman	9	4	5	£400
Rex Williams	9	3	6	£300

Play off for first prize: Reardon beat Spencer 4–3.

1972

PARK DRIVE £2000

The third Park Drive tournament was notable for a break of 146 by Reardon in the round robin section, the highest ever break in competitive play until Spencer's 147 in the 1979 Holsten Lager International. Spencer beat Higgins, playing in his first major professional tournament, 4–3 in the final which was played the day before they commenced their week long final of the 1972 World Professional Championship.

Final placings
	P	W	L	Prize
John Spencer	9	6	3	£750
Alex Higgins	9	5	4	£550
John Pulman	9	4	5	£400
Ray Reardon	9	3	6	£300

Play off for first prize: Spencer beat Higgins 4–3.

1972

WORLD PROFESSIONAL CHAMPIONSHIP

Sponsor: None *Entries*: 16
Prize money: By arrangement with individual promoters.

Running from March 1971 to February 1972 this incredibly long drawn out event began with eight qualifiers being reduced to two to join the eight other entries in the competition proper. Those in the qualifying section included four former amateur champions, Ron Gross, Maurice Parkin, Pat Houlihan and Geoffrey Thompson, who all turned professional when well past their prime, but also Higgins, who was to make history as the first qualifier ever to go on to win the title.

He was not extended until the semi-final when Rex Williams led him by six frames before the Irishman got home in an exciting finish by the odd frame in 61.

The final proceeded on even lines until Higgins struck the front with a 6–0 victory in the Thursday evening session. This created a gap which Spencer was never able to close.

One of the surprises of the championship had come in the quarter-finals when Williams beat Reardon 25–23, the match being contested in five different club venues in Scotland.

Qualifying competition
First round: A. Higgins beat R. Gross 15–6; M. Parkin beat G. Thompson 11–10; J. Dunning beat P. Houlihan 11–10; G. Miles beat B. Bennett 15–6.
Second round: Higgins beat Parkin 11–3; Dunning beat Miles 11–5.
Competition proper
First round: J. Pulman beat Dunning 19–7; Higgins beat J. Rea 19–11.
Quarter-finals: J. Spencer beat F. Davis 31–21; E. Charlton beat David Taylor 31–25; Higgins beat Pulman 31–23; R. Williams beat R. Reardon 25–23.
Semi-finals: Higgins beat Williams 31–30; Spencer beat Charlton 37–32.
Final: Higgins beat Spencer 37–32.

1972

PARK DRIVE £2000

Spencer finished second to Higgins in the round robin section but beat him 5–3 in the play-off in front of a crowd of 2000 at Belle Vue, Manchester, an attendance which sealed Park Drive's decision to enlarge their support from a four man tournament to the world championship itself.

Final placings
	P	W	L	Prize
Alex Higgins	9	7	2	£550
John Spencer	9	6	3	£750
Ray Reardon	9	3	6	£400
John Pulman	9	2	7	£300

Play off for first prize: Spencer beat Higgins 5–3.

1973

PARK DRIVE WORLD CHAMPIONSHIP

Sponsor: Gallaher *Entries*: 23
Prize money: £8000
First prize: £1500

Snooker's box office potentialities, particularly when Higgins was playing, and the benefits it could

offer a sponsor led to West and Nally devising the streamlined modern formula under which, with one or two alterations, the championship is still contested. Instead of dragging on interminably in diverse and often out of the way venues, with little sense of continuity and little or no publicity, the championship was tele-scoped into a fortnight at the City Exhibition Halls, Manchester with play taking place simultaneously, rather like Wimbledon, in eight different arenas. BBC Television covered the latter stages of the final, the first time it had done so. During the fortnight, there were 25 000 spectators. On site, betting was introduced through Ladbrokes, there were many successful trade stands and press coverage increased.

The championships provided one of the greatest recoveries in its history when Reardon, having trailed Spencer 12–19, won their semi-final 23–22. Reardon after losing the first session 0–7, went on to beat Charlton in the final. Higgins beat Davis in a memorable quarter-final but, burnt out by the accumu-lated pressures of the year following his 1972 title win, lost easily to Charlton in the semi-final.

First round: P. Houlihan beat J. Rea 9–2; D. Greaves beat B. Bennett 9–8; G. Miles beat G. Thompson 9–5; P. Mans beat R. Gross 9–2; W. Simpson beat M. Parkin 9–3; C. Thorburn beat Dennis Taylor 9–8; David Taylor beat J. Dunning 9–4.
Second round: F. Davis beat Greaves 16–1; Miles beat J. Pulman 16–10; E. Charlton beat Mans 16–8; G. Owen beat Simpson 16–14; R. Reardon beat J. Meadowcroft 16–10; R. Williams beat Thorburn 16–15; J. Spencer beat David Taylor 16–5; A. Higgins beat Houlihan 16–3.
Quarter-finals: Higgins beat Davis 16–14; Spencer beat Williams 16–7; Charlton beat Miles 16–6; Reardon beat Owen 16–6.
Semi-finals: Charlton beat Higgins 23–9; Reardon beat Spencer 23–22.
Final: Reardon beat Charlton 38–32.

1973

NORWICH UNION OPEN

Sponsor: Norwich Union
Entries: (invited) 24
Prize money: £3500

57

First prize: £1000

Norwich Union, another West and Nally sports sponsorship client, restored big time snooker to London with a tournament featuring both professionals and leading amateurs at the Piccadilly Hotel. This was the first notable Open since the removal of restrictions on amateurs accepting prize money but only one amateur, Sid Hood, with victories over Jack Rea, a professional, and Mannie Francisco, then an amateur, reached the quarter-finals. London Weekend Television covered an exciting final in which Pulman, having trailed 2–6, levelled at 7–7 before missing a vital green in the deciding frame which led to Spencer's 8–7 victory.

First round: *S. Hood beat J. Rea 4–0; *C. Ross beat *M. Owen 4–3; *A. Savur beat D. Greaves 4–1; David Taylor beat J. Karnehm 4–2; Dennis Taylor beat *A. Lloyd 4–1; *J. Barron beat R. Gross 4–2; J. Dunning beat J. Meadowcroft 4–2; P. Houlihan beat *J. Virgo 4–3.

Second round: G. Miles beat Savur 4–1; *R. Edmonds beat Barron 4–3; Hood beat *M. Francisco 4–3; E. Charlton beat Ross 4–0; C. Thorburn beat Houlihan 4–0; A. Higgins beat Dennis Taylor 4–3; J. Spencer beat Dunning 4–3; J. Pulman beat David Taylor 4–3.

Quarter-finals: Spencer beat Edmonds 4–0; Charlton beat Hood 4–0; Higgins beat Thorburn 4–2; Pulman beat Miles 4–3.

Semi-finals: Spencer beat Higgins 8–2; Pulman beat Charlton 8–3.

Final: Spencer beat Pulman 8–7. (*amateur)

1974
PARK DRIVE WORLD CHAMPIONSHIP
Sponsor: Gallaher Entries: 31
Prize money: £10 000
First prize: £2000

Following the euphoria generated by the success of the 1973 championship, the 1974 event at Belle Vue, Manchester was a disappointment. The building was perhaps too reminiscent of a vast aircraft hangar and the pattern of results was a promoter's nightmare. Of the name players, Spencer lost his first match to Perrie Mans, the left-handed South African; Charlton went out to a lifetime best performance by John Dunning, a dour Yorkshireman; and

Higgins lost the last three frames to Davis to lose their quarter-final by the odd frame. Reardon, a comfortable victor over Miles in the final, had his most difficult match in the quarter-final against Marcus Owen, who had turned professional after regaining in 1973 the English amateur title he had won three times between 1958 and 1967.

Qualifying round: J. Dunning beat D. Greaves 8–2; W. Simpson beat J. Rea 8–3; J. Meadowcroft beat P. Houlihan 8–5; C. Thorburn beat A. McDonald 8–3; J. Pulman beat J. Karnehm 8–0; David Taylor beat R. Gross 8–7; M. Owen beat Dennis Taylor 8–1.

First round: B. Bennett beat Simpson 8–2; B. Werbeniuk beat G. Thompson 8–3; Meadowcroft beat K. Kennerley 8–5; M. Owen beat M. Parkin 8–5; P. Mans beat I. Anderson 8–1; Pulman beat S. Lee 8–0; Dunning beat David Taylor 8–6; P. Morgan beat Thorburn 8–4.

Second round: Mans beat J. Spencer 15–13; Dunning beat E. Charlton 15–13; M. Owen beat G. Owen 15–8; A. Higgins beat Bennett 15–4; G. Miles beat Morgan 15–7; R. Williams beat Pulman 15–12; F. Davis beat Werbeniuk 15–5; R. Reardon beat Meadowcroft 15–3.

Quarter-finals: Williams beat Mans 15–4; Miles beat Dunning 15–13; Davis beat Higgins 15–14; Reardon beat M. Owen 15–11.

Semi-finals: Miles beat Williams 15–7; Reardon beat Davis 15–3.

Final: Reardon beat Miles 22–12.

1974
CANADIAN OPEN
The Canadian National Exhibition Centre in Toronto, a large scale trade and entertainment complex, offered for the first time a snooker tournament among its many attractions promoted by Canadian snooker entrepreneur Terry Haddock. The Open tournament was joined in its late stages by a number of professionals with Canada's Cliff Thorburn securing the £1500 first prize, half the total prize money, in an event which was to develop over the next five years into a regular feature of the international circuit. Dennis Taylor, who reached the final, achieved an amazing sequence of 349 points, in pre-tournament practice, without missing a shot. This

consisted of a 103 clearance, a 134 total clearance after fluking a red from the break off and 112 at his first visit in the following frame.

Semi-finals: C. Thorburn beat G. Miles 8–5; Dennis Taylor beat A. Higgins 8–6.

Final: Thorburn beat Taylor 8–6.

1974
NORWICH UNION OPEN
Sponsor: Norwich Union
Entries: (invited) 16
Prize money: £4750 First prize: £1500

Spencer, his cue broken into four pieces in a car accident just before the tournament, had it magically restored by Cliff Curtis of Riley Burwat with 13 plugs and a wood graft and won the tournament with it, both the semi-finals and the final providing first class matches.

First round: C. Thorburn beat F. Davis 5–4; B. Werbeniuk beat J. Dunning 5–1; J. Spencer beat *R. Edmonds 5–0; J. Pulman beat *G. Thomas 5–0; G. Miles beat *E. Sinclair 5–0; R. Williams beat M. Owen 5–3; A. Higgins beat Dennis Taylor 5–1; R. Reardon beat *P. Burke 5–2.

Quarter-finals: Higgins beat Werbeniuk 5–4; Thorburn beat Pulman 5–3; Spencer beat Miles 5–2; Reardon beat Williams 5–2.

Semi-finals: Reardon beat Higgins 9–8; Spencer beat Thorburn 9–7.

Final: Spencer beat Reardon 10–9. (*amateur)

1975
BENSON AND HEDGES MASTERS
Sponsor: Gallaher Entries: (invited) 10
Prize money: £5000
First prize: £2000

Another West and Nally sponsor achieved at the first attempt only a partial success at the West Centre Hotel, Fulham, too far out of town, it seemed, to attract big crowds. Spencer and Reardon contested a final which could not have been closer – though the overall standard, partly because of the ultra-fast table, was disappointing.

First round: J. Pulman beat C. Thorburn 5–3; A. Higgins beat B. Werbeniuk 5–0.

Quarter-finals: E. Charlton beat F. Davis 5–3; J. Spencer beat Pulman 5–3; R. Reardon beat G. Miles 5–3; R. Williams beat Higgins 5–3.

Semi-finals: Spencer beat Charlton 5–2; Reardon beat Williams 5–4.

Final: Spencer beat Reardon 9–8.

1975
WORLD PROFESSIONAL CHAMPIONSHIP
Sponsor: None *Entries*: 27
Prize money: £18 900
First prize: Not known

With Park Drive somehow having slipped away as a sponsor the world championship was awarded to Eddie Charlton Promotions to stage in Australia. The WPBSA's seeding system, which was based only on previous world championships, or rather the promoter's failure to carry it out in full, led to Reardon (no. 1) and Spencer (no. 8) clashing in the quarter-final, a match which many saw as the real final. Dennis Taylor achieved his best championship showing so far to reach the semi-final in the other half before a choppy Sydney to Brisbane plane journey on the morning of his semi-final against Charlton contributed to him making a poor start from which he never recovered.

The final fluctuated amazingly. Reardon led 16–8; Charlton led 29–23; Reardon led 30–29 and after Charlton had levelled took the decider for his 31–30 victory.

Qualifying round: P. Tarrant beat B. Bennett 15–8; L. Condo beat M. Parkin 15–8; D. Greaves beat J. Charlton 15–14.
First round: W. Simpson beat R. Mares 15–5; J. Pulman beat Tarrant 15–5; David Taylor beat R. King 15–8; I. Anderson beat Condo 15–8; Dennis Taylor beat P. Mans 15–12; G. Owen beat Greaves 15–3; B. Werbeniuk beat J. Meadowcroft 15–9; C. Thorburn beat P. Morgan 15–6.
Second round: R. Reardon beat Simpson 15–11; J. Spencer beat Pulman 15–10. A. Higgins beat David Taylor 15–2; R. Williams beat Anderson 15–4; Dennis Taylor beat F. Davis 15–14; Owen beat J. Dunning 15–8; E. Charlton beat Werbeniuk 15–11; Thorburn beat G. Miles 15–2.
Quarter-finals: Reardon beat Spencer 19–17; Higgins beat Williams 19–12; Dennis Taylor beat Owen 19–9; Charlton beat Thorburn 19–12.
Semi-finals: Charlton beat Dennis Taylor 19–12; Reardon beat Higgins 19–14.
Final: Reardon beat Charlton 31–30.

1975
CANADIAN OPEN
With prize money increased to $10 000 in all with $5000 for the winner there was a cascade of big breaks, albeit on sympathetic tables, in which a break of 142 by Cliff Thorburn was the highest of 23 centuries. The big surprise was a 9–7 quarter-final win for Willie Thorne, then an amateur, over Spencer.
Semi-finals: J. Pulman beat W. Thorne 9–6; A. Higgins beat G. Miles 9–5.
Final: Higgins beat Pulman 15–7.

1976
BENSON AND HEDGES MASTERS
Sponsor: Gallaher *Entries*: (invited) 10
Prize money: £5200
First prize: £2000

A new central London venue, the New London Theatre, attracted capacity crowds to its 1500 seat arena and gave the event its distinctive character. Reardon took the £2000 first prize with a comfortable victory over Miles, a surprise semi-final winner over Spencer, though the match of the tournament was Reardon's 5–4 semi-final victory over Charlton.
First round: F. Davis beat C. Thorburn 4–2; J. Pulman beat Dennis Taylor 4–2.
Quarter-finals: G. Miles beat A. Higgins 4–1; R. Reardon beat J. Pulman 4–1; J. Spencer beat Davis 4–0; E. Charlton beat R. Williams 4–1.
Semi-finals: Miles beat Spencer 5–4; Reardon beat Charlton 5–4.
Final: Reardon beat Miles 7–3.

1976
EMBASSY WORLD CHAMPIONSHIP
Sponsor: W. D. and H. O. Wills
Entries: 27
Prize money: £15 300
First prize: £6000

Embassy's first sponsorship of the championship was attended by all sorts of organizational difficulties. 'Q' Promotions, who became defunct shortly afterwards, over-stretched their resources and the decision to play the top half of the draw at Middlesbrough Town Hall with the bottom half and the final at Wythenshawe Forum created all sorts of problems. There was trouble over the pockets on one table not conforming to official standards and in the final the table, the television lighting and the refereeing all attracted initial criticism.

Reardon comfortably retained the title: Perrie Mans reached the semi-final for the first time; and Higgins, as usual, kept the crowd alight by winning three desperately close matches to reach the final. Charlton made a break of 137 against Pulman and Spencer one of 138 against David Taylor.
Qualifying competition
First round: J. Rea beat I. Anderson 8–5; D. Greaves beat J. Charlton 8–5; J. Meadowcroft beat D. Wheelwright 8–1; R. Gross beat M. Parkin 8–5; L. Condo beat M. Owen 8–6.
Second round: Rea beat B. Bennett 8–5; David Taylor beat Greaves 8–1; Meadowcroft beat Gross 8–4; W. Thorne beat Condo 8–3.
Third round: David Taylor beat Rea 8–7, Meadowcroft beat Thorne 8–5.
Competition proper
First round: R. Reardon beat J. Dunning 15–7; Dennis Taylor beat G. Owen 15–9; P. Mans beat G. Miles 15–10; Meadowcroft beat R. Williams 15–7; E. Charlton beat J. Pulman 15–9; F. Davis beat B. Werbeniuk 15–12; A. Higgins beat C. Thorburn 15–14; J. Spencer beat David Taylor 15–5.
Quarter-finals: Reardon beat Dennis Taylor 15–2; Mans beat Meadowcroft 15–8; Charlton beat Davis 15–13; Higgins beat Spencer 15–14.
Semi-finals: Reardon beat Mans 20–10; Higgins beat Charlton 20–18.
Final: Reardon beat Higgins 27–16.

1976
CANADIAN OPEN
Spencer took the $5000 first prize by beating Higgins 17–9 in the final. The match of the tournament was the victory of Bernie Mikkelsen, a 6ft 5in Canadian amateur over John Pulman in the quarter-finals, Mikkelsen making a break of 141 in the deciding frame.
Semi-finals: J. Spencer beat J. Virgo 9–4; A. Higgins beat B. Mikkelsen 9–1.
Final: Spencer beat Higgins 17–9.

1976
WORLD PROFESSIONAL MATCHPLAY CHAMPIONSHIP
A 16-man international tournament

promoted by Eddie Charlton in Melbourne was confusingly given world title recognition by the WPBSA. When Charlton won the event, beating Reardon 31–24 in the final, sections of the uninformed media and public believed that he had won the World Professional Championship. Despite strong criticism of the title of the tournament, the WPBSA sanctioned it twice more, but on both occasions organizational difficulties prevented it from taking place.

1977
BENSON AND HEDGES MASTERS
Sponsor. Gallaher   *Entries:* (invited) 10
Prize money. £5200
First prize: £2000

Doug Mountjoy, brought into his first major professional tournament only as a late replacement, duly won it as the 33/1 outsider.

Having turned professional only a couple of months previously after winning the world amateur title in Johannesburg, Mountjoy confirmed how narrow was the gap between professionals and top amateurs by beating three former world professional champions before defeating the current title holder Ray Reardon in a thrilling finish 7–6 on the final pink.

First round: D. Mountjoy beat J. Pulman 4–2; J. Spencer beat Dennis Taylor 4–2.

Quarter-finals: R. Reardon beat R. Williams 4–1; G. Miles beat Spencer 4–1; A. Higgins beat P. Mans 4–2; Mountjoy beat F. Davis 4.2

Semi-finals: Mountjoy beat Higgins 5–3; Reardon beat Miles 5–2.

Final: Mountjoy beat Reardon 7–6.

1977
EMBASSY WORLD CHAMPIONSHIP
Sponsor. W. D. and H. O. Wills
Entries: 24
Prize money. £17 000 *First prize:* £6000

A new promoter, Mike Watterson, a plush but intimate theatre in the round venue, the Crucible Theatre, Sheffield, and increased television coverage enabled snooker's premier event to take a massive step forward. Record crowds of over 20 000 for the championship fortnight saw some memorable finishes – Mountjoy sinking a daring black down the side cushion to beat Higgins 13–12, Thorburn beating Charlton 13–12 after a

62-minute final frame – and the end of Reardon's reign as champion as he went out tamely to Spencer in the quarter-finals. Spencer did not show the flair and brilliance of his vintage years but grit, determination and a high level of confidence carried him to the title by defeating Thorburn, the first ever Canadian finalist. Spencer was the first player to win the title with a two-piece cue.

Qualifying competition
First round: J. Virgo beat R. Andrewartha 11–1.

Second round: P, Fagan beat J. Meadowcroft 11–9; Virgo beat J. Dunning 11–6; W. Thorne beat B. Bennett 11–4; J. Pulman w.o.; David Taylor beat D. Greaves 11–0; C. Thorburn beat C. Ross 11–0; Dennis Taylor beat J. Karnehm 11–0; D. Mountjoy beat J. Rea 11–9.

Competition proper
First round: R. Reardon beat Fagan 13–7; J. Spencer beat Virgo 13–9; G. Miles beat Thorne 13–4; Pulman beat F. Davis 13–12; E. Charlton beat David Taylor 13–5; Thorburn beat R. Williams 13–6; Dennis Taylor beat P. Mans 13–11; Mountjoy beat A. Higgins 13–12.

Quarter-finals: Spencer beat Reardon 13–6; Pulman beat Miles 13–10; Thorburn beat Charlton 13–12; Dennis Taylor beat Mountjoy 13–11.

Semi-finals: Spencer beat Pulman 18–16; Thorburn beat Dennis Taylor 18–16.

Final: Spencer beat Thorburn 25–21.

1977
CANADIAN OPEN

With the usual permanent building unavailable, the tournament went on in heat wave conditions in a circus tent. Kirk Stevens, subsequently a professional, surfaced for the first time in a major event at the age of eighteen to lead Reardon 5–3 in the last 16 before losing 9–6. Spencer made a break of 146, taking a pink after the 11th red, in beating Kevin Robitaille 9–3 in the quarter-finals after this young Canadian had eliminated Mountjoy 9–8. Higgins won the $6000 first prize with Spencer taking $2000 as runner-up.

Semi-finals: A. Higgins beat R. Reardon 9–7; J. Spencer beat Dennis Taylor 9–6.

Final: Higgins beat Spencer 17–14.

1977
SUPER CRYSTALATE UK
Sponsor. Super Crystalate   *Entries:* 22
Prize money. £7000
First prize: £2000

Fired by his promotional success with the Embassy World Professional Championship, Mike Watterson instituted this new championship with sponsorship from manufacturers of Super Crystalate balls. The venue, Blackpool Tower Circus, had a strong snooker tradition from the April world finals of the fifties but Blackpool in December proved a different proposition and crowds were poor. Partly because matches were short, there were a number of upsets, Reardon going out 5–4 to Jim Meadowcroft in his first match. Only one established player, Higgins, reached the semi-finals and the £2000 first prize went to Patsy Fagan, a London-based Dubliner, a professional for less than a year.

First round: C. Ross beat J. Karnehm 5–4; P. Fagan beat J. Rea 5–1; J. Meadowcroft beat P. Houlihan 5–1; D. Mountjoy beat R. Andrewartha 5–2; W. Thorne beat B. Bennett 5–1; J. Dunning beat M. Parkin 5–4; David Taylor beat D. Greaves 5–4.

Second round: J. Virgo beat Dennis Taylor 5–2; G. Miles beat Ross 5–1; Fagan beat F. Davis 5–0; Meadowcroft beat R. Reardon 5–4; Mountjoy beat J. Spencer 5–3; Thorne beat R. Williams 5–4; Dunning w.o.; A. Higgins beat David Taylor 5–4.

Quarter-finals: Virgo beat Miles 5–2; Fagan beat Meadowcroft 5–4; Mountjoy beat Thorne 5–4; Higgins beat Dunning 5–0.

Semi-finals: Fagan beat Virgo 9–8; Mountjoy beat Higgins 9–2.

Final: Fagan beat Mountjoy 12–9.

1977
DRY BLACKTHORN CUP

Wembley Conference Centre was used for snooker for the first time as Mike Barrett, best known for his boxing promotions, ventured into snooker for the first time with a one-day event covered by London Weekend Television which offered a £2000 first prize. Fagan beat Spencer 4–2 and Higgins 4–2 to double the money he had won a couple of weeks previously at the UK Championship.

1978
BENSON AND HEDGES MASTERS

Sponsor: Gallaher   *Entries:* (invited) 10
Prize money: £8000
First prize: £3000

Higgins, straight from a successful defence of his Irish professional title against Dennis Taylor, won the title for the first time with a 5–1 semi-final win over Reardon as the highlight of the week.

First round: J. Pulman beat P. Fagan 4–2; G. Miles beat F. Davis 4–3.

Quarter-finals: J. Spencer beat Pulman 4–2; A. Higgins beat Dennis Taylor 4–3; C. Thorburn beat D. Mountjoy 4–2; R. Reardon beat Miles 4–1.

Semi-finals: Higgins beat Reardon 5–1; Thorburn beat Spencer 5–3.

Final: Higgins beat Thorburn 7–5.

1978
BENSON AND HEDGES IRISH MASTERS

The beautifully appointed sales ring at Goffs, Kill provided an unusual setting for the inaugural Benson and Hedges Irish Masters, John Spencer taking the £1000 first prize with a 5–3 final victory over Doug Mountjoy.

1978
EMBASSY WORLD CHAMPIONSHIP

Sponsor: W. D. and H. O. Wills
Entries: 28
Prize money: £24 000   *First prize:* £7500

Through the championship's daily coverage snooker became a front rank television sport. A five million audience on the first day built to seven million by the end of the fortnight. Reardon won the championship for the fifth time in six years; Mans became the first ever South African finalist by defeating Fred Davis in a semi-final so gripping that the nervous tension precipitated the collapse of Joe Davis, a highly involved spectator, and in turn led to his fatal illness. Reardon's hardest match was in his 18–14 semi-final defeat of Charlton after the Australian had led 12–9. Charlton had earlier won the last four frames to beat Willie Thorne 13–12 and the last five to beat Thorburn 13–12.

Qualifying competition

First round: M. Parkin beat B. Bennett 9–4; R. Andrewartha beat J. Karnehm 9–0; J. Barrie beat D. Greaves 9–3; P. Houlihan beat C. Ross 9–1.

Second round: D. Mountjoy beat Andrewartha 9–3; P. Fagan beat J. Dunning 9–5; W. Thorne beat R. Williams 9–3; B. Werbeniuk beat Parkin 9–2; P. Mans beat Barrie 9–6; David Taylor beat P. Morgan 9–7; Houilhan beat J. Meadowcroft 9–6; F. Davis beat J. Virgo 9–8.

Competition proper

First round: Mans beat J. Spencer 13–8; G. Miles beat David Taylor 13–10; Fagan beat A. Higgins 13–12; Davis beat Dennis Taylor 13–9; E. Charlton beat Thorne 13–12; C. Thorburn beat Houlihan 13–8; Werbeniuk beat J. Pulman 13–4; R. Reardon beat Mountjoy 13–9.

Quarter-finals: Mans beat Miles 13–7; Davis beat Fagan 13–10; Charlton beat Thorburn 13–12; Reardon beat Werbeniuk 13–6.

Semi-finals: Mans beat Davis 18–16; Reardon beat Charlton 18–14.

Final: Reardon beat Mans 25–18.

1978
CANADIAN OPEN

Cliff Thorburn recovered from 6–10 overnight arrears to beat Tony Meo 17–15 for the $6000 first prize. Meo was the outstanding personality of the tournament, achieving a 9–7 semi-final win over Higgins as he took $2000 as runner-up.

Semi-finals: C. Thorburn beat K. Robitaille 9–5; T. Meo beat A. Higgins 9–7.

Final: Thorburn beat Meo 17–15.

1978
CORAL UK CHAMPIONSHIP

Sponsor: Coral Racing   *Entries:* 24
Prize money: £12 500
First prize: £3500

An impressive new venue, Preston Guildhall, and a new sponsor, Coral Racing, transformed the status of this championship in its second year and ensured its continuance.

The most dramatic match came in the qualifying section when Terry Griffiths, only a few months later to win the world professional title, was beaten 9–8 by Rex Williams after leading 8–2.

The championship proper also provided plenty of surprises. Fagan, the holder, went out 9–7 in the first round to David Taylor who, after a decade in the professional ranks, reached his first major final by beating Higgins 9–5 in the semi. In the other half, Roy Andrewartha

beat Spencer 9–8 and Willie Thorne beat Reardon 9–6 only to collapse 9–1 against Miles, whose 139 break set a tournament record. In the semi-finals it was Miles's turn to collapse 9–1 to Mountjoy who, keeping his best till last, clinched his final victory over Taylor with a break of 120.

Qualifying competition

W. Thorne beat B. Bennett 9–4; R. Andrewartha beat P. Houlihan 9–3; D. Mountjoy beat J. Barrie 9–5; R. Williams beat T. Griffiths 9–8; J. Dunning beat D. Greaves 9–3; J. Virgo beat R. Edmonds 9–4; David Taylor beat M. Parkin 9–2; J. Meadowcroft beat J. Rea 9–5.

Competition proper

First round: David Taylor beat Fagan 9–7; Virgo beat J. Pulman 9–3; F. Davis beat Dunning 9–2; A. Higgins beat Meadowcroft 9–6; Thorne beat R. Reardon 9–6; G. Miles beat Williams 9–8; Mountjoy beat Dennis Taylor 9–4; Andrewartha beat J. Spencer 9–8.

Quarter-finals: David Taylor beat Virgo 9–2; Higgins beat Davis 9–4; Miles beat Thorne 9–1; Mountjoy beat Andrewartha 9–4.

Semi-finals: David Taylor beat Higgins 9–5; Mountjoy beat Miles 9–1.

Final: Mountjoy beat David Taylor 15–9.

1979
FORWARD CHEMICALS £10 000 TOURNAMENT

The Park Drive 2000 format which had launched snooker's modern era was resurrected with Reardon, Spencer, Mountjoy and Higgins each playing each other three times with the top two from the round robin contesting the final. Reardon won six matches, Spencer five, Mountjoy four and Higgins three with Reardon going on to beat Spencer 9–6 in the final at the Royal Exchange Theatre, Manchester. Reardon took £3000 and Spencer £2300.

1979
HOLSTEN LAGER INTERNATIONAL

Spencer made history at the Fulcrum Centre, Slough by compiling the first ever 147 maximum in tournament play, albeit on a table whose pockets were more generous than standard and which thus prevented the break being recognized as an official record. Ironically, the cameras of Thames Television, who covered the last three days of the four day tournament, were idle when the break was made. Union agreements within the television industry over hours and meal breaks were such that without two complete production crews not every frame of the day's play could be recorded.

Spencer and Thorburn arrived late for their quarter-final and the decision was taken to rest the crew then rather than later. The public, believing the match had been deferred, drifted out so only a handful of spectators saw Spencer win the first three frames 106–1, 147–0, 119–0.

The tournament departed from normal practice in that all matches except the semi-final were decided on aggregate score. Under this system, there were some amazing recoveries. Spencer, in the first round, trailed Fagan by 91 with only one frame remaining but took victory with a break of 109; Williams, in the second round, was 97 behind early in the last frame against Reardon before, with the aid of 72 break, he won on the final black. The semi-finals and final were comparatively straightforward though Spencer did raise hopes of a second maximum when he reached 96 by dint of 12 reds and 12 blacks in the penultimate frame of his 11–7 final victory over Miles. The tournament contained one final irony: at a time when many events were starting to offer a jackpot prize of £5000 or more for a 147 this one did not do so.

Semi-finals: J. Spencer beat R. Williams 6–2; G. Miles beat A. Higgins 6–3.
Final: Spencer beat Miles 11–7.

1979
BENSON AND HEDGES MASTERS
Sponsor: Gallaher *Entries*: (invited) 10
Prize money: £8000
First prize: £3000

Perrie Mans, having survived a five hour 5–4 struggle with Thorburn, went on to beat Reardon and Higgins to win the first Masters to be staged at Wembley Conference Centre. Curiously, he failed to make a 50 break in any match but he once again proved, with his awkward style, a difficult man to beat. Higgins's break of 132 against Charlton was a tournament record.

First round: D. Mountjoy beat F. Davis 5–2; David Taylor beat P. Fagan 5–4.
Quarter-finals: A. Higgins beat E. Charlton 5–2; P. Mans beat C. Thorburn 5–4; Mountjoy beat J. Spencer 5–0; R. Reardon beat Taylor 5–2.
Semi-finals: Higgins beat Mountjoy 5–1; Mans beat Reardon 5–3.
Final: Mans beat Higgins 8–4.

1979
BENSON AND HEDGES IRISH MASTERS
Doug Mountjoy recovered from 0–3 and 3–5 to beat Ray Reardon 6–5 for the £2000 first prize, Reardon missing an easy brown which would have given him a 6–4 victory.

1979
BOMBAY INTERNATIONAL
The easing of foreign exchange regulations gave India a chance to stage its most ambitious ever professional tournament, a six man round robin in which Spencer won four of his five matches to take the £2000 first prize. Dennis Taylor, second with three wins, took £1200.

1979
TOLLY COBBOLD CLASSIC
After the initial four man round robin had put Higgins and Reardon through to the final, Higgins snatched the £600 first prize with a 63 clearance which gave him his 5–4 victory on the final black. The event was covered in its entirety from the Corn Exchange, Ipswich by Anglia Television.

1979
EMBASSY WORLD CHAMPIONSHIP
Sponsor: W. D. and H. O. Wills
Entries: 35
Prize money: £35 000
First prize: £10 000

That Terry Griffiths won the title at his first attempt (as only Joe Davis, John Spencer and Alex Higgins had done before him) was not only an amazing personal success story but confirmation that the old order was changing. Two memorable if radically different matches were the key to his success, his 13–12 quarter-final win over Higgins and his 19–17 semi-final victory over Charlton.

The first four frames of the Higgins match took only 46 minutes, Griffiths winning the first and fourth on the black with 61 and 63 clear-

ances, Higgins the second and third with consecutive centuries of 105 and 112. When Higgins went on to lead 6–2 at the first interval he hardly looked beatable but Griffiths levelled at 8–8 at close of play and after a gripping final session won the deciding frame with a break of 107.

Griffiths led Charlton 10–4 but lost the first six frames of the third session and led only 11–10 overnight. A gruelling fourth session with Charlton slowing the tempo with long bouts of safety and taking no risks ended with Griffiths leading 15–13 but Charlton led for the first time at 16–15 and again at 17–16.

The Welshman led 18–17 but the match seemed certain to go the full distance when Charlton led 48–0 in what was scheduled to be the penultimate frame. One mistake, though, was all the encouragement Griffiths needed to steady himself to compile a winning 97 clearance. The final session, which ended at 1.40 a.m., occupied 5 hours 25 minutes.

The final, against Dennis Taylor, was something of an anti-climax. Level at 15–15 starting the final day, Griffiths raised his game when the winning post came in sight to clinch the title by taking nine of the next ten frames.

Taylor had earlier distinguished himself by ousting Reardon, the holder, 13–8 in the quarter-final and John Virgo, appearing in his first semi-final, 19–12. The bulky Canadian, Bill Werbeniuk, eliminated Spencer in the first round and in the quarter-final equalled the 142 championship record set by Rex Williams in 1965 before losing 13–9 to Virgo.

Qualifying competition
First round: D. Mountjoy beat D. Mienie 9–1; T. Griffiths beat B. Bennett 9–2; P. Houlihan beat J. Barrie 9–5; W. Thorne beat J. Charlton 9–3; J. Virgo beat M. Parkin 9–0; J. Dunning beat J. Rea 9–5; R. Williams beat D. Greaves 9–2; J. Meadowcroft beat J. van Rensburg 9–7; R. Andrewartha beat R. Edmonds 9–8; S. Davis beat I. Anderson 9–1; K. Stevens beat R. Amdor 9–1.
Second round: Virgo beat Thorne 9–8; B. Werbeniuk beat Andrewartha 9–2; David Taylor beat Dunning 9–8; Mountjoy beat Houlihan 9–6; S. Davis beat P. Fagan 9–2; Griffiths beat

62

Meadowcroft 9–6; Stevens beat J. Pulman 9–0; G. Miles beat Williams 9–5.

Competition proper
First round: E. Charlton beat Mountjoy 13–6; Werbeniuk beat J. Spencer 13–11; Virgo beat C. Thorburn 13–10; F. Davis beat Stevens 13–8; Dennis Taylor beat S. Davis 13–11; A. Higgins beat David Taylor 13–5; Griffiths beat P. Mans 13–8; R. Reardon beat Miles 13–8.
Quarter-finals: Charlton beat F. Davis 13–4; Dennis Taylor beat Reardon 13–8; Virgo beat Werbeniuk 13–9; Griffiths beat Higgins 13–12.
Semi-finals: Griffiths beat Charlton 19–17; Dennis Taylor beat Virgo 19–12.
Final: Griffiths beat Dennis Taylor 24–16.

1979
LIMOSIN INTERNATIONAL
South Africa's most valuable ever professional tournament, staged at the Good Hope Centre, Capetown, saw Charlton carry off the R5000 (£2747) first prize by beating Spencer 23–19, his first victory over Spencer in a long distance match. Charlton went on to beat Reardon 7–4 to win the R2500 first prize in the Kronenbrau 1308 Classic in Johannesburg the following week.

1979
CANADIAN OPEN
Thorburn won the event for the third time by beating Griffiths 17–16 in a desperate finish after leading 10–3. In the semi-finals Thorburn had made consecutive centuries, 108 and 116, in beating Higgins 9–6 but Griffiths scraped home only 9–8 over Kirk Stevens after the young Canadian had failed to clinch several good chances for victory.

The pick of the remaining matches was a 9–8 win for Jim Wych, another talented young Canadian, over Meo. Wych led 6–2 but Meo with a 142 total clearance levelled at 8–8 before refereeing blunders in the decider effectively cost him the match.
Semi-finals: C. Thorburn beat A. Higgins 9–6; T. Griffiths beat K. Stevens 9–8.
Final: Thorburn beat Griffiths 17–16.

1979
STATE EXPRESS WORLD CUP
Sponsor: British American Tobacco
Entries: six teams
Prize money: £27 500
First prize: £7500
Any doubts that a world team championship might not command the interest of snooker followers or television audiences were triumphantly set at rest at Haden Hill Leisure Centre, near Birmingham. Mike Watterson, promoter of the Embassy World Professional Championship and the Coral United Kingdom Championship, thus completed a notable hat-trick.

Six three-man teams were drawn into two groups of three with the winners contesting the final. Professionals, some of whom had never played team matches even as amateurs, found themselves coping with new pressures and many of the matches were close and tense. The final, however, provided an overwhelming 14–3 victory for Wales (Terry Griffiths, Ray Reardon and Doug Mountjoy) over England (Fred Davis, John Spencer, Graham Miles).
Group 'A': England beat Rest of the World 8–7; England beat Northern Ireland 8–7; Northern Ireland beat Rest of the World 8–7.
Group 'B': Wales beat Canada 9–6; Wales beat Australia 9–6; Australia beat Canada 8–7.
Final: Wales beat England 14–3.

1979
CORAL UK CHAMPIONSHIP
Sponsor: Coral Racing   *Entries*: 27
Prize money: £15 000
First prize: £4500
John Virgo, 33, confounded those who doubted his ability to win on the big occasion by defeating Griffiths, the reigning world champion, by the odd frame of a final chiefly notable for the award of two frames to Griffiths to penalize Virgo's late arrival for the deciding session.

The general pattern of results indicated a new generation about to emerge to take over from most of the players who had dominated the seventies. Of the quarter-finalists, only Ray Edmonds, was over 35.
First round: J. Rea beat B. Bennett 9–8; M. Hallett beat M. Parkin 9–1; J. Dunning beat D. Greaves 9–8.

Second round: W. Thorne beat R. Andrewartha 9–4; P. Houlihan beat Rea 9–3; S. Davis beat Dunning 9–3; P. Fagan beat Hallett 9–4; B. Werbeniuk beat J. Johnson 9–3; R. Edmonds beat J. Meadowcroft 9–3; T. Meo beat David Taylor 9–7; C. Wilson beat J. Pulman 9–7.
Third round: S. Davis beat D. Mountjoy 9–5; T. Griffiths beat Wilson 9–4; A. Higgins beat Houlihan 9–3; Fagan beat G. Miles 9–5; Werbeniuk beat J. Spencer 9–8; Dennis Taylor beat Thorne 9–8; J. Virgo beat Meo 9–6; Edmonds beat F. Davis 9–6.
Quarter-finals: Werbeniuk beat Edmonds 9–8; Dennis Taylor beat Fagan 9–6; Virgo beat S. Davis 9–7; Griffiths beat Higgins 9–7.
Semi-finals: Virgo beat Dennis Taylor 9–4; Griffiths beat Werbeniuk 9–3.
Final: Virgo beat Griffiths 14–13.

1980
BOMBAY INTERNATIONAL
John Virgo beat Cliff Thorburn 13–7 to take the £3000 first prize. Thorburn, who had beaten Virgo 6–1 in the qualifying round robin took £2200 as runner-up and £500 for the highest break, 123. The tournament could not be repeated in 1981 because of currency difficulties.

1980
PADMORE/SUPER CRYSTALATE INTERNATIONAL
The original promoters, though armed with the promise of seven ATV slots, failed to produce a sponsor to guarantee the £15 000 prize money the players were expecting. The tournament was rescued from cancellation at the eleventh hour by world championship promoter Mike Watterson and two trade interests, Padmore's and Super Crystalate, who between them guaranteed £5000 prize money and £3000 towards the costs of staging the event at the Gala Baths, West Bromwich.

Higgins despite being rushed to hospital with a painful ear infection on the first night of the tournament survived a deciding frame with Willie Thorne in the semi-final before taking the £2000 first prize with a 4–2 victory over Perrie Mans in the final.

63

1980
WILSONS CLASSIC

John Spencer took the £3000 first prize, a record for a two day tournament, by beating Alex Higgins 4–3 in the final of an eight man event recorded at the New Century Hall, Manchester by Granada Television and shown in the North West in seven Wednesday night programmes. Higgins took £1500 as runner-up.

1980
BENSON AND HEDGES MASTERS

Sponsor: Gallaher *Entries:* (invited) 10
Prize money: £14 000
First prize: £4500

A crowd of 2323, a record for Britain, saw Terry Griffiths clinch his 9–5 final victory over Higgins with a superb total clearance of 131.
First round: C. Thorburn beat J. Virgo 5–3; A. Higgins beat F. Davis 5–1.
Quarter-finals: R. Reardon beat Dennis Taylor 5–3; T. Griffiths beat Thorburn 5–3; J. Spencer beat E. Charlton 5–2; Higgins beat P. Mans 5–1.
Semi-finals: Griffiths beat Spencer 5–0; Higgins beat Reardon 5–2.
Final: Griffiths beat Higgins 9–5.

1980
WOODPECKER WELSH CHAMPIONSHIP

With the media expecting a confrontation in the final between Terry Griffiths, reigning world champion, and Ray Reardon six times world champion, Doug Mountjoy scored victories over both at Ebbw Vale Leisure Centre to take the £2250 first prize. Reardon had held the Welsh professional title since beating Mountjoy, then the only other Welsh professional, 12–8 at Caerphilly under the sponsorship of William Hill in 1977.
Semi-finals: D. Mountjoy beat T. Griffiths 9–6; R. Reardon beat C. Wilson 9–3.
Final: Mountjoy beat Reardon 9–6.

1980
BENSON AND HEDGES IRISH MASTERS

Terry Griffiths, having led 6–3, 7–4 and 8–5, beat Doug Mountjoy 9–8 for the £2500 first prize.

1980
BRITISH GOLD CUP

A new event at Derby Assembly Rooms, jointly sponsored by three companies in the billiard trade, E. J. Riley, Composition Billiard Ball Supply and Strachan's, was conducted initially through four round robin groups with a knock-out semi-final and final.

Higgins provided a memorable conclusion to his group when, needing to beat Griffiths 3–0 to qualify, he achieved his target with consecutive breaks of 135 and 134.

He also played brilliantly to beat Tony Meo 4–0 in the semi-final and Ray Reardon, with a break of 132, 5–1 in the final to take the £4000 first prize. Reardon, who beat Dennis Taylor 4–3 in the other semi-final, took £3000 as runner-up.

1980
TOLLY COBBOLD CLASSIC

Between his group matches in the British Gold Cup and the semi-finals and final, Higgins won another first prize, this time of £1500, by beating Dennis Taylor 5–4 at the Corn Exchange, Ipswich. An incident in the final, added to others in which he had been involved in other tournaments, led to Higgins subsequently being fined £200 for 'foul and abusive language to referees and bringing the game into disrepute'.

1980
EMBASSY WORLD CHAMPIONSHIP

Sponsor: W. D. and H. O. Wills
Entries: 49
Prize money: £60 000
First prize: £15 000

The title left Britain for the first time when Thorburn scored a dramatic 18–16 victory over Higgins in the final after the Irishman, leading 9–5, had lost the last four frames of the first day.

Higgins, who had had to win the last two frames to beat Tony Meo 10–9 in the first round, came within the last five colours of a 147 maximum in beating Steve Davis 13–9 in the quarter-finals before loss of position on the green ended his hopes of a £10 000 jackpot.

Kirk Stevens gave the tournament a dramatic start with a break of 136 in his 10–3 first round win over Graham Miles, failing at the final black which would have given him a new championship record.

Stevens, with some fearless potting, then eliminated two seasoned campaigners, John Spencer and Eddie Charlton, before losing to Higgins 16–13 in an exciting semi-final.

Jim Wych, at his first attempt, gave Canada a third representative in the last eight and Steve Davis made his name by beating the defending champion Terry Griffiths 13–10 in their second round match before losing to Higgins.

The climax of the final attracted 14.5 million viewers. There was 70 hours of television coverage.

Qualifying competition
Group 1: J. Rea beat B. Bennett 9–1; W. Thorne beat K. Robitaille 9–4; Thorne beat Rea 9–1.
Group 2: S. Davis beat C. Ross 9–3; P. Morgan beat P. Thornley 9–4; S. Davis beat Morgan 9–0.
Group 3: M. Hallett beat K. Kennerley 9–2; K. Stevens beat D. Greaves 9–3; Stevens beat Hallett 9–3.
Group 4: J. Johnson beat R. Andrewartha 9–5; P. Houlihan beat Johnson 9–6; T. Meo beat J. van Rensburg 9–1; Meo beat Houlihan 9–1.
Group 5: R. Amdor beat B. Mikkelsen 9–7; R. Williams beat Amdor 9–4; J. Wych beat J. Bear 9–5; Wych beat Williams 9–7.
Group 6: F. Jonik beat M. Wildman 9–7; C. Wilson beat Jonik 9–6.
Group 7: R. Edmonds beat M. Parkin 9–2; S. Hood beat J. Dunning 9–7; Edmonds beat Hood 9–6.
Group 8: E. Sinclair beat M. Morra 9–5; Sinclair beat D. Mienie 9–7; J. Meadowcroft beat Sinclair 9–1.
Competition proper
First round: S. Davis beat P. Fagan 10–6; A. Higgins beat Meo 10–9; D. Mountjoy beat Wilson 10–6; Wych beat J. Pulman 10–5; J. Virgo beat Meadowcroft 10–2; Stevens beat G. Miles 10–3; David Taylor beat Edmonds 10–3; B. Werbeniuk beat Thorne 10–9.
Second round: S. Davis beat T. Griffiths 13–10; Higgins beat P. Mans 13–6; Stevens beat J. Spencer 13–8; E. Charlton beat Virgo 13–12; C. Thorburn beat Mountjoy 13–10; Wych beat Dennis Taylor 13–10; R. Reardon beat Werbeniuk 13–6; David Taylor beat F. Davis 13–5.
Quarter-finals: David Taylor beat Reardon 13–11; Thornburn beat Wych 13–6; Stevens beat Charlton

13–7; Higgins beat S. Davis 13–9.
Semi-finals: Thorburn beat David Taylor 16–7; Higgins beat Stevens 16–13.
Final: Thorburn beat Higgins 18–16.

1980
CANADIAN NATIONAL EXHIBITION OPEN

Television, new to Canadian tournaments, made a fiasco of the first day of the final by installing lighting so glaring and dazzling that the players could not give of their best.

Cliff Thorburn, who had been less impressive than Terry Griffiths (winner over both Steve Davis and Alex Higgins) in the earlier rounds, maintained his concentration and will to win more single-mindedly in taking a commanding 13–3 lead by the end of the first day's play.
Semi-finals: C. Thorburn beat K. Stevens 9–5; T. Griffiths beat A. Higgins 9–6.
Final: Thorburn beat Griffiths 17–10.

1980
CHAMPION OF CHAMPIONS

Snooker returned to the New London Theatre (home of the Benson and Hedges Masters until 1978) with an ambitious ten-man event, split initially into two round robin sections, but without television coverage or sponsorship the event was financially disastrous. Doug Mountjoy beat John Virgo 10–8 in the final to take the £5000 first prize but the tournament itself made an estimated loss of £30 000.

1980
STATE EXPRESS WORLD CUP
Sponsor: British American Tobacco
Entries: 6 teams
Prize money: £31 555
First prize: £9000

Wales, again represented by Ray Reardon, Terry Griffiths and Doug Mountjoy, retained the title though Reardon needed a 50 break, in which he displayed all his old icy calm, to take his last frame against Alex Higgins to give his team an 8–7 semi-final win over Ireland, this year represented by Higgins and Dennis Taylor from the North and the Dubliner Patsy Fagan. Wales also trailed Canada 4–5 in the final before taking the next four frames for victory.
Group 'A': Wales beat Canada 10–5; Canada beat Rest of World 9–6; Wales beat Rest of World 13–2.

Group 'B': England beat Ireland 11–4; Australia beat England 8–7; Ireland beat Australia 10–5.
Semi-finals: Wales beat Ireland 8–7; Canada beat England 8–5.
Final: Wales beat Canada 8–5.

1980
CORAL UK CHAMPIONSHIP
Sponsor: Coral Racing   *Entries*: 32
Prize money: £22 500
First prize: £6000

With television coverage increased to eight days the championship was the most successful in its four year history. Steve Davis took his first major professional title in the most convincing style imaginable, annihilating Terry Griffiths in the semi-final and disposing of Alex Higgins in the final with almost equal comfort.
Preliminary round: M. Hallett beat B. Bennett 9–4; S. Hood beat C. Ross 9–3.
Qualifying round: Hallett beat R. Edmonds 9–8; E. Sinclair beat K. Kennerley 9–1; M. Wildman beat C. Wilson 9–8; J. Meadowcroft beat D. Greaves 9–1; R. Andrewartha beat A. Knowles 9–8; R. Williams beat J. Barrie 9–1; J. Johnson beat J. Dunning 9–6; T. Meo beat Hood 9–5.
Competition proper
First round: Meo beat P. Houlihan 9–1; S. Davis beat Hallett 9–1; P. Fagan beat Johnson 9–4; Sinclair beat G. Miles 9–5; W. Thorne beat Meadowcroft 9–1; Wildman beat J. Spencer 9–7; Williams beat D. Mountjoy 9–8; Andrewartha beat Pulman 9–6.
Second round: Meo beat J. Virgo 9–1; S. Davis beat B. Werbeniuk 9–3; Dennis Taylor beat Sinclair 9–6; T. Griffiths beat Fagan 9–8; A. Higgins beat Thorne 9–7; F. Davis beat Wildman 9–6; Reardon beat Andrewartha 9–3; Williams beat David Taylor 9–7.
Quarter-finals: S. Davis beat Meo 9–5; Griffiths beat Dennis Taylor 9–2; Higgins beat F. Davis 9–6; Reardon beat Williams 9–4.
Semi-finals: S. Davis beat Griffiths 9–0; Higgins beat Reardon 9–7.
Final: S. Davis beat Higgins 16–6.

1980
WILSON CLASSIC

Steve Davis took his second first prize within a week, this time of £5000, by beating Dennis Taylor 4–1 in the final at Blighty's, Farnworth.

1981
BENSON AND HEDGES MASTERS
Sponsor: Gallahers
Entries: (invited) 12
Prize money: £20 500
First prize: £6000

Alex Higgins, having trailed 1–5, extraordinarily beat Cliff Thorburn 6–5 to reach his fourth consecutive Masters final and reversed the result of the 1980 final against Terry Griffiths, who had himself made a dramatic recovery to beat John Spencer 6–5 in the semi-finals after trailing 2–5 and needing two snookers in the eighth frame. Griffiths set a new tournament record break of 136 in the final. The tournament attracted 18 742 spectators in its six days including a new British tournament record of 2422 for the final session.
First round: P. Mans beat S. Davis 5–2; D. Mountjoy beat E. Charlton 5–0; F. Davis beat K. Stevens 5–4; J. Spencer beat Dennis Taylor 5–2.
Quarter-finals: A. Higgins beat Mountjoy 5–1; C. Thorburn beat Mans 5–4; Spencer beat R. Reardon 5–1; T. Griffiths beat F. Davis 5–2.
Semi-finals: Higgins beat Thorburn 6–5; Griffiths beat Spencer 6–5.
Final: Higgins beat Griffiths 9–6.

1981
WOODPECKER WELSH CHAMPIONSHIP

Ray Reardon, two and a half years after winning his last major event, regained his national title by beating Cliff Wilson, with whom he grew up in Tredegar, for the £3000 first prize.
Semi-finals: R. Reardon beat T. Griffiths 9–6; C. Wilson beat D. Mountjoy 9–6.
Final: Reardon beat Wilson 9–6.

1981
BENSON AND HEDGES IRISH MASTERS

The round robin system which had previously been favoured for the early stages was abandoned in favour of a straight knock-out. Terry Griffiths retained the title and took the £5000 for so doing by beating Cliff Thorburn 6–5 in the semi-finals, winning the last two frames with breaks of 93 and 91, and Ray Reardon 9–7 in the final. Reardon, who took £2500 as runner-up, beat Alex Higgins 6–5 in the other semi-final.

Steve Davis wins the Embassy World Championship for the first time – 1981.

1981
TOLLY COBBOLD CLASSIC

Graham Miles took the £2000 first prize by beating Cliff Thorburn 5–1 in the final.

1981
YAMAHA ORGANS TROPHY

Sponsor: Yamaha Organs   *Entries*: 28
Prize money: £30 000
First prize: £10 000

Taking over the date, venue and playing format of 1980's British Gold Cup, this became the first major tournament to be extensively covered on the ITV network with each day's action shown later that night. Its four days coverage produced viewing figures so impressive that they seemed likely to mark a turning point in ITV's attitude to snooker.

Three of the four groups ended in exciting finishes but Steve Davis won his group with comfort and went on to score decisive victories in both semi-final and final to take his third major first prize of the season.

Semi-finals: David Taylor beat K. Stevens 5–3; S. Davis beat Dennis Taylor 5–2.

Final: S. Davis beat David Taylor 9–6

1981
JOHN COURAGE ENGLISH CHAMPIONSHIP

Steve Davis enriched himself by a further £4000 in becoming the inaugural title holder. The event was staged at Haden Hill Leisure Centre, Sandwell.

Semi-finals: S. Davis beat R. Edmonds 9–0; T. Meo beat W. Thorne 9–8.

Final: S. Davis beat Meo 9–3.

1981
EMBASSY WORLD CHAMPIONSHIP

Sponsor: W. D. and H. O. Wills
Entries: 46
Prize money: £75 000
First prize: £20 000

Steve Davis, winner of four major first prizes earlier in the season, triumphantly justified his status as favourite by beating five tough opponents to take the title.

After leading 8–4, he was only one frame in front of Jimmy White at 9–8 before winning 10–8 and after leading Alex Higgins 6–2 he was pulled back to 9–7 before going away to win 13–8. Both matches revealed the young Londoner's ability to respond with his best when he came under the most severe pressure.

From 4–4 against Terry Griffiths in the quarter-final, Davis led 9–5 after so protracted a second session that it had to be curtailed two frames early and went on to clinch victory at 13–9.

Davis's semi-final against Cliff Thorburn was even more arduous. A three hours, 34 minutes first session saw Davis 4–3 ahead but Thorburn appeared to be right on top when, with his opponent's concentration apparently broken, he led 8–6 at the end of the session. That evening, though, Davis's concentration was amazingly restored and when the session ended at 12.58 a.m. he led 12–10. The first four frames the following morning gave him his place in the final.

Although he won the first six frames against Doug Mountjoy, Davis had to withstand a determined recovery which four times brought the Welshman to within two frames. From 14–12 at the start of the final session, however, Davis won four frames in succession to assure himself of snooker's record cheque of £20 000.

Mountjoy added to his £10 000 runner's-up prize one of £5000 for his new world championship record break of 145 in beating Ray Reardon 16–10 in the semi-final. This break also earned him the tournament break of £1200.

Qualifying:
Group A: W. Thorne beat M. Morra 9–5; D. Greaves beat M. Parkin 9–5; Thorne beat Greaves 9–3.
Group B: J. White beat B. Mikkelsen 9–4; White beat J. Meadowcroft 9–8.
Group C: R. Edmonds beat M. Wildman 9–3; R. Williams beat S. Hood 9–4; Edmonds beat Williams 9–7.
Group D: T. Meo beat J. Johnson 9–8; M. Hallett beat F. Jonik 9–1; Meo beat Hallett 9–4.
Group E: J. Dunning beat B. Bennett 9–6; Dunning beat P. Fagan 9–7.
Group F: D. Martin beat I. Anderson 9–3; Martin beat J. Pulman 9–2.
Group G: C. Wilson beat R. Andrewartha 9–4; E. Sinclair beat P. Morgan 9–8; Wilson beat Sinclair 9–4.
Group H: T. Knowles beat C. Ross 7–0 (retired); Knowles beat J. Wych 9–3.
First round: G. Miles beat Knowles 10–8; David Taylor beat Wilson 10–6; D. Mountjoy beat Thorne 10–6; K. Stevens beat Dunning 10–4; Meo beat J. Virgo 16–6; S. Davis beat White 10–8; B. Werbeniuk beat Martin 10–4; J. Spencer beat Edmonds 10–9.
Second round: C. Thorburn beat Miles 13–2; David Taylor beat F. Davis 13–3; T. Griffiths beat Meo 13–6; S. Davis beat A. Higgins 13–8; Mountjoy beat E. Charlton 13–7; Dennis Taylor beat Stevens 13–11; Werbeniuk beat P. Mans 13–5; R. Reardon beat Spencer 13–11.
Quarter-finals: Thorburn beat David Taylor 13–6; S. Davis beat Griffiths 13–9; Mountjoy beat Dennis Taylor 13–8; Reardon beat Werbeniuk 13–10.
Semi-finals: S. Davis beat Thorburn 16–10; Mountjoy beat Reardon 16–10.
Final: S. Davis beat Mountjoy 18–12.

1981
JAMESON INTERNATIONAL
Sponsor: Irish Distillers   *Entries*: 59
Prize money: £66 500
First prize: £20 000

Offering the same prize money as the previous Embassy World Professional Championship, this new tournament provided a strong send-off to the new season. ITV networked the last seven days play from Derby Assembly Rooms, the most sustained coverage of Snooker it had ever undertaken.

On the debit side, the direct clash of dates led to the cancellation of the Canadian Open, Canada's only major international event.

Steve Davis lived dangerously against Alex Higgins in the semi-final. Up early to catch a 6.00 a.m. flight from Jersey, where he had crammed in an exhibition engagement following his quarter-final, Davis was below par for most of the day but summoned the adrenalin to make a 95 break in the decider to win 9–8.

The final saw Davis produce a flawless performance, including breaks of 135 and 105 in consecutive frames, as he whitewashed Dennis Taylor 9–0.

Dave Martin, in his first full season as a professional, did very well to beat three players ranked in the world's top 16, Bill Werbeniuk, Eddie Charlton and Graham Miles, to earn £5000 as a semi-finalist before going out 9–1 to Taylor.

Second round: G. Miles beat J. Johnson 5–3; D. Martin beat B. Werbeniuk 5–2; R. Williams beat F. Davis 5–0; A. Higgins beat P. Fagan 5–3; J. Spencer beat R. Edmonds 5–3; J. Virgo beat A. Knowles 5–2; K. Stevens beat J. Meadowcroft 5–1; P. Mans beat T. Meo 5–3.
Third round: Miles beat C. Thorburn 5–0; Martin beat E. Charlton 5–2; Virgo beat R. Reardon 5–3; David Taylor beat Stevens 5–0; Dennis Taylor beat Williams 5–1; Higgins beat D. Mountjoy 5–1; T. Griffiths beat Spencer 5–2; S. Davis beat Mans 5–3.
Quarter-finals: Martin beat Miles 5–1; Higgins beat Griffiths 5–2; Dennis Taylor beat Virgo 5–2; S. Davis beat David Taylor 5–1.
Semi-finals: Dennis Taylor beat Martin 9–1; S. Davis beat Higgins 9–8.
Final: S. Davis beat Dennis Taylor 9–0.

1981
LANGS SUPREME SCOTTISH MASTERS
Sponsor: Langs   *Entries*: (invited) 9
Prize money: £20 500
First prize: £8000

Jimmy White, 19, became the youngest ever winner of a major professional tournament by beating three either past or present world champions in the massive but – for this tournament – rarely half-full Kelvin Hall, Glasgow.

Scotland's most ambitious ever professional tournament, which received some television coverage from BBC Scotland, did not offer the standard of organization elsewhere taken for granted for a professional event.

In particular, its failure to provide an official to keep a running written record of the score led to a major row in the semi-finals in which Cliff Thorburn beat Alex Higgins.
Qualifying match: V. Harris beat I. Black 4–0.
First round: J. White beat R. Reardon 5–4; S. Davis beat D. Mountjoy 5–0; C. Thorburn beat K. Stevens 5–1; A. Higgins beat Harris 5–3.

Semi-finals: White beat Davis 6–5; Thorburn beat Higgins 6–2.
Final: White beat Thorburn 9–4.

1981
STATE EXPRESS WORLD TEAM CLASSIC
Sponsor: British American Tobacco
Entries: 7 teams
Prize money: £40 000
First prize: £12 000

Steve Davis anchored England to a 4–3 victory in the final to end Wales's unbeaten record in this event, albeit re-named from the title under which it had operated for the two previous years.

Davis won single frame tie-breakers against both Australia (Eddie Charlton), Northern Ireland (Dennis Taylor) and in the final, Wales (Ray Reardon).

A new venue, the Hexagon Theatre, Reading, added greatly to the success of the event. Additions to the professional ranks enabled the Republic of Ireland and Northern Ireland to field separate teams and Scotland to enter for the first time.

Qualifying: Republic of Ireland beat Scotland 4–2.
Group 'A': England beat Australia 4–3; Northern Ireland beat Australia 4–1; England beat Northern Ireland 4–3.
Group 'B': Wales beat Canada 4–2; Wales beat Republic of Ireland 4–0; Canada beat Republic of Ireland 4–2.
Semi-finals: England beat Canada 4–2; Wales beat Northern Ireland 4–3.
Final: England beat Wales 4–3.

1981
NORTHERN IRELAND CLASSIC
Sponsor: none *Entries*: (invited) 8
Prize money: £20 000
First prize: £5000

Jimmy White not only pocketed his second first prize of the season but scored a second victory over Steve Davis, this time by taking the last four frames of the final of this new event in the Ulster Hall, Belfast to win 11–9.

First round: D. Mountjoy beat Dennis Taylor 5–4; J. White beat C. Thorburn 5–2; T. Griffiths beat K. Stevens 5–0; S. Davis beat A. Higgins 5–2.
Semi-finals: White beat Mountjoy 9–8; Davis beat Griffiths 9–6.
Final: White beat Davis 11–9.

1981
CORAL UK CHAMPIONSHIP
Sponsor: Coral Racing *Entries*: 49
Prize money: £40 000
First prize: £10 000

Steve Davis retained the first of his major titles by demolishing Terry Griffiths 16–3 in the final at Preston Guildhall. Jimmy White, fresh from his successes in the Langs Scottish Masters and Northern Ireland Classic, beat John Virgo, Dennis Taylor and, in the match of the tournament, Ray Reardon, in reaching the semi-finals at his first attempt but then collapsed against a relentless Davis.

Two other young players, Tony Knowles and Tony Meo, also enhanced their reputations, Knowles by beating Fred Davis and Doug Mountjoy in reaching the quarter-finals and Meo by beating Rex Williams, Cliff Thorburn and Alex Higgins in reaching the semis.

Group 1: P. Medati beat E. McLaughlin 9–5; Medati beat J. Donnelly 9–7.
Group 2: M. Hallett beat V. Harris 9–4; Hallett beat D. Hughes 9–6.
Group 3: M. Gibson beat J. Fitzmaurice 9–6; C. Everton beat Gibson 9–7.
Group 4: J. Johnson beat T. Murphy 9–1; M. Watterson beat B. Bennett 9–4; Johnson beat Watterson 9–3.
Group 5: P. Houlihan beat K. Kennerley 9–1; Houlihan beat I. Black 9–4.
Group 6: G. Foulds beat W. Kelly 9–7.
Group 7: E. Sinclair beat M. Wildman 9–8; Sinclair beat S. Hood 9–0.
Group 8: R. Williams beat D. French 9–3; C. Roscoe beat M. McLeod 9–7; Williams beat Roscoe 9–4.

First round: W. Thorne beat Medati 9–6; Hallett beat P. Fagan 9–5; J. White beat Everton 9–4; Johnson beat C. Wilson 9–5; Houlihan beat J. Meadowcroft 9–4; A. Knowles beat Foulds 9–1; D. Martin beat Sinclair 9–7; Williams beat J. Dunning 9–4.
Second round: Thorne beat R. Edmonds 9–4; K. Stevens beat Hallett 9–4; White beat J. Virgo 9–6; Johnson beat J. Spencer 9–5; G. Miles beat Houlihan 9–5; Knowles beat F. Davis 9–6; A. Higgins beat Martin 9–7;

T. Meo beat R. Williams 9–8.
Third round: S. Davis beat Thorne 9–2; B. Werbeniuk beat Stevens 9–7; White beat Dennis Taylor 9–5; R. Reardon beat Johnson 9–7; T. Griffiths beat Miles 9–4; Knowles beat D. Mountjoy 9–6; Higgins beat David Taylor 9–5; Meo beat C. Thorburn 9–6.
Quarter-finals: Davis beat Werbeniuk 9–5; White beat Reardon 9–8; Griffiths beat Knowles 9–5; Meo beat Higgins 9–4.
Semi-finals: Davis beat White 9–0; Griffiths beat Meo 9–3.
Final: Davis beat Griffiths 16–3.

1982
LADA CLASSIC
Sponsor: Lada Cars *Entries*: (invited) 8
Prize money: £15 000
First prize: £5000

Taking the slot in the circuit hitherto filled by the Wilsons Classic and moving to a new venue, Oldham Civic Centre, the new sponsors struck extraordinarily lucky as Steve Davis immortalized the event by becoming the first professional to compile a 147 maximum in a bona fide tournament on a table whose pockets conformed to the official B. & SCC templates.

Davis was scarcely programmed for a maximum. A nine-day round the world trip, returning only the day before the tournament, left him severely jet-lagged but when an opportunity for a maximum occurred in his first match against John Spencer he found the inspiration to take it.

He recovered from 2–4 to beat Ray Reardon 5–4 with the aid of a 105 break in the deciding frame of their semi-final and from 3–8 recovered to 8–8 in the final against Terry Griffiths. He had first shot at a difficult long black for what would have been an amazing victory before Griffiths sank the deciding ball for the 9–8 win which gave him the £5000 first prize.

Lada, who had agreed a scale of prize money appropriate to television exposure only in the Granada area, as in previous years, profited from late interest from companies in other regions and the final was nationally networked on ITV's Midweek Sports Special. With Granada also putting together a special half hour package on the Davis 147, television exposure alone provided the sponsorship bargain of the year.

First round: T. Griffiths beat C. Thorburn 5–1; A. Higgins beat Dennis Taylor 5–1; R. Reardon beat David Taylor 5–1; S. Davis beat J. Spencer 5–2.

Semi-finals: Griffiths beat Higgins 5–1; Davis beat Reardon 5–4.

Final: Griffiths beat Davis 9–8.

1982
BENSON AND HEDGES MASTERS
Sponsor: Gallahers
Entries: (invited) 12
Prize money: £27 000
First prize: £8000

Steve Davis's 9–5 final victory enabled the World, United Kingdom and English champion to complete his uniquely comprehensive collection of snooker's major titles. His cheque for £8000 took his earnings from major first prizes along to £83 000 since the first of his two Coral UK titles 14 months previously.

Tony Meo, who made a new tournament record break of 136 in his 5–0 quarter-final defeat of Cliff Thorburn, spiritedly pulled up from 0–5 to 4–5 before losing his semi-final to Davis 6–4. The other semi-final also ended dramatically with Alex Higgins having two chances of 5–5 before Terry Griffiths closed him out 6–4.

First round: R. Reardon beat Dennis Taylor 5–3; D. Mountjoy beat J. Spencer 5–4; T. Meo beat David Taylor 5–2; E. Charlton beat J. White 5–4.

Quarter-finals: Meo beat C. Thorburn 5–0; S. Davis beat Mountjoy 5–2; A. Higgins beat Charlton 5–1; T. Griffiths beat Reardon 5–3.

Semi-finals: Davis beat Meo 6–4; Griffiths beat Higgins 6–4.

Final: Davis beat Griffiths 9–5.

1982
TOLLY COBBOLD CLASSIC

Extended from two days to three and from four players to eight, the tournament provided another first prize, albeit a modest £2000, for Steve Davis, who beat Dennis Taylor 8–3 in the final after leading 6–0 at the interval.

First round: G. Miles beat T. Meo 3–0; T. Knowles beat David Taylor 3–0; Dennis Taylor beat J. White 3–1; S. Davis beat W. Thorne 3–0.

Semi-finals: Davis beat Miles 5–2;

Dennis Taylor beat Knowles 5–2.

Final: Davis beat Dennis Taylor 8–3.

1982
WOODPECKER WELSH CHAMPIONSHIP

Doug Mountjoy took the last two frames to beat Terry Griffiths 9–8 to take the title for the second time in three years. A record number of eight Welsh professionals competed at Ebbw Vale Leisure Centre for a prize fund of £12 000 of which £5000 went to the winner.

First round: C. Wilson beat M. Owen 6–0; T. Griffiths beat C. Roscoe 6–2; R. Reardon beat C. Everton 6–1; D. Mountjoy beat R. Andrewartha 6–3.

Semi-finals: Griffiths beat Wilson 9–6; Mountjoy beat Reardon 9–7.

Final: Mountjoy beat Griffiths 9–8.

1982
YAMAHA ORGANS TROPHY
Sponsor: Yamaha Organs   *Entries*: 37
Prize money: £38 000
First prize: £10 000

Short matches are traditionally a great leveller but Steve Davis and Terry Griffiths emphasized their standing as snooker's two leading players by negotiating a minefield of best of three frame matches to reach the final.

The final itself was a splendid contest with Davis clinching victory at 9–7 with a tournament record break of 135.

Semi-final groups

Group 'A': S. Davis beat J. Virgo 2–0; Virgo beat R. Edmonds 2–0; Edmonds beat Dennis Taylor 2–1; Virgo beat Dennis Taylor 2–0; Davis beat Dennis Taylor 2–1; Davis beat Edmonds 2–0.

Group 'B': T. Griffiths beat David Taylor 2–0; Griffiths beat C. Thorburn 2–1; Thorburn beat G. Miles 2–1; Griffiths beat Miles 2–0; Miles beat David Taylor 2–0; Thorburn beat David Taylor 2–1.

Final: Davis beat Griffiths 9–7.

1982
IRISH CHAMPIONSHIP

The championship was organized not on the challenge basis on which it had existed since its inception but with a tournament format which allowed all eight Irish professionals to compete at the Riverside Theatre, Coleraine.

Alex Higgins had second thoughts about his original decision to withdraw – for reasons never fully made

clear – but trailed throughout the final against Dennis Taylor, the defending champion.

Higgins made a great effort to save the match, winning five frames in succession from 8–14 before Taylor reaffirmed his status, which in the two years he has held the title had never really sunk in with the snooker public, as Ireland's number 1.

Taylor took £3300 as the winner with Higgins taking £2200 as the runner-up. The total prize found was £8500.

First round: E. Hughes beat D. Sheehan 6–1; T. Murphy beat B. Kelly 6–1.

Quarter-finals: Hughes beat J. Rea 6–0; Murphy beat P. Fagan 6–2.

Semi-finals: Dennis Taylor beat Murphy 6–0; A. Higgins beat Hughes 6–2.

Final: Dennis Taylor beat Higgins 16–13.

1982
SCOTTISH CHAMPIONSHIP

Eddie Sinclair regained the Scottish Professional Championship by beating the defending champion, Ian Black, 11–7 in the final of the three day tournament at the Glen Pavilion, Dunfermline.

Sinclair won the title in a challenge match with Chris Ross, then Scotland's only other professional, when the championship was revived in 1980 on a challenge basis.

Sponsorship from the *Daily Record* and Tartan Bitter provided a prize fund of £3100 of which £1000 went to the winner.

First round: M. Macleod beat J. Donnelly 6–5.

Quarter-finals: C. Ross beat B. Dermco 6–5; M. Gibson beat E. McLaughlin 6–3; I. Black beat Macleod 6–0; E. Sinclair beat J. Phillips 6–3.

Semi-finals: Black beat Ross 6–4; Sinclair beat Gibson 6–2.

Final: Sinclair beat Black 11–7.

1982
BENSON AND HEDGES IRISH MASTERS
Sponsor: Benson and Hedges
Entries: (invited) 12
Prize money: £22 500
First prize: £6666

Terry Griffiths scored his second victory in the five major finals they had contested during the season when Steve Davis fell away after the first session of the final had been split 4–4.

Davis's break of 128 in his 5–2 quarter-final defeat of Mountjoy was a new tournament record.

Alex Higgins made an amazing recovery to beat Cliff Thorburn 5–4 in his quarter-final after Thorburn had won the first four frames.

First round: Dennis Taylor beat D. Sheehan 5–3; T. Meo beat J. Spencer 5–3; A. Higgins beat J. Wych 5–3; D. Mountjoy beat E. Hughes 5–4.

Quarter-finals: T. Griffiths beat Meo 5–3; R. Reardon beat Dennis Taylor 5–4; S. Davis beat Mountjoy 5–2; Higgins beat C. Thorburn 5–4.

Semi-finals: Griffiths beat Reardon 6–3; Davis beat Higgins 6–2.

Final: Griffiths beat Davis 9–5.

1982
HIGHLAND MASTERS

This new event at the Eden Court Theatre, Inverness provided an astonishing 6–0 whitewash for Ray Reardon over Steve Davis in the semi-final, a stage at which John Spencer also whitewashed Alex Higgins 6–0. Reardon went on to take the £5000 first prize by beating Spencer 11–4 in the final.

1982
EMBASSY WORLD CHAMPIONSHIP
Sponsor: W. D. and H. O. Wills
Entries: 67 *Prize money*: £125 000
First prize: £25 000

In view of their domination of the circuit for the whole of the season, Steve Davis and Terry Griffiths were confidently expected to meet in the final but, in the event, neither survived the first round.

Davis, his skill eventually giving way under the weight of the incessant travelling, commercial commitments and public appearances which enabled him to accrue £600 000 in his year as champion, was eliminated 10–1 by Knowles; Griffiths, automatically installed as favourite after Davis's exit, was beaten 10–6 by Willie Thorne.

Dennis Taylor, another player whose chances were increased by Davis's defeat, also missed the boat, beaten 10–7 by Silvino Francisco, a South African competing in the event for the first time. Cliff Thorburn the 1980 champion, who had experienced a poor season, was another first round loser, 10–4 to Jimmy White.

Emotional scenes with his wife Lynn and baby daughter Lauren, as Alex Higgins wins the 1982 Embassy World Championship.

All four giantkillers made further progress. Indeed, White four years earlier the youngest ever English Amateur champion and two years earlier the youngest ever World Amateur champion, added to his collection of 'youngest evers' by becoming the youngest ever professional championship semi-finalist and reaching the very verge of the final itself.

White led Alex Higgins 15–13 in their semi-final but, trailing 14–15 and by 0–59 in the thirtieth frame, Higgins produced an inspired death or glory clearance of 69 to level the match and provide the springboard for his memorable 16–15 victory.

Knowles looked an odds-on favourite to reach the semi-finals too when he led Eddie Charlton 11–6 but wilted when the veteran Australian put him under pressure and lost seven frames in succession to go down 13–11.

Thorne, who had never previously won a match at the Crucible in his six-year professional career, was a 13–10 quarter-final loser to Higgins but had the consolation of making a break of 143, which earned the £2500 highest break prize.

Francisco reached the quarter-finals at the expense of Dean Rey-nolds, 19, survivor of a first round match with Fred Davis, 68, which provided the widest age gap a world championship match has ever produced.

Ray Reardon, displaying his most consistent form since his world title win four years previously, ended Francisco's progress in the quarter-finals and went on to beat his old rival Charlton 16–11 in the semi-finals after the final session had begun with the scores level at 11–11.

Higgins, having experienced the least successful season of his professional career, had not, prior to the championship, been considered in the game's inner circles to have a realistic prospect of regaining the world title he had won at his first attempt in 1972 but the defeat of Davis and Griffiths gave him a new lease of life.

He survived a desperate 13–12 finish against Doug Mountjoy in the second round and an even more desperate 16–15 semi-final against White but once he had overturned his 3–5 first session arrears he was never behind Reardon in the final.

Three times his three frames lead was reduced to one and Reardon even managed to level the match at 15–15 after needing a snooker with only the last four colours remaining in the thirtieth frame.

Higgins had resources enough, though, to produce a decisive finishing burst. He won two frames by wide margins to go two in front with three to play and rounded off the championship with the appropriate flourish of a total clearance of 135.

Qualifying:

Group 1: J. Bear beat F. Jonik 9–4; Bear beat J. Wych 9–4.

Group 2: D. Hughes beat C. Everton 9–4; T. Meo beat Hughes 9–4.

Group 3: D. Reynolds beat D. Sheehan 9–5; Reynolds beat R. Edmonds 9–6.

Group 4: E. Hughes w.o. D. Mienie scr.; A. Knowles beat Hughes 9–7.

Group 5: M. Wildman beat G. Foulds 9–8; J. White beat Wildman 9–4.

Group 6: C. Roscoe beat B. Mikkelsen 9–6; W. Thorne beat Roscoe 9–1.

Group 7: P. Medati beat J. Phillips 9–3; C. Wilson beat Medati 9–5.

Group 8: P. Houlihan beat I. Anderson 9–5; D. Martin beat Houlihan 9–3.

Group 9: M. Mcleod beat E. McLaughlin 9–8; J. Dunning beat Macleod 9–4.

Group 10: M. Watterson beat B. Demarco 9–6; J. Meadowcroft beat Watterson 9–7.

Group 11: D. French beat B. Bennett 9–3; P. Fagan beat French 9–6.

Group 12: I. Black beat M. Parkin 9–6; R. Williams beat Black 9–2.

Group 13: J. Johnson beat V. Harris 9–4; M. Hallett beat Johnson 9–8.

Group 14: J. Donnelly beat M. Gibson 9–8; E. Sinclair beat W. Kelly 9–8; Donnelly beat Sinclair 9–8.

Group 15: P. Morgan beat D. Greaves 9–2; S. Francisco beat C. Ross 9–0; Francisco beat Morgan 9–1.

Group 16: M. Morra beat T. Murphy 9–5; J. Fitzmaurice w.o. J. Pulman scr.; Fitzmaurice beat Morra 9–7.

First round: Knowles beat S. Davis 10–1; G. Miles beat Martin 10–5; B. Werbeniuk beat Bear 10–7; E. Charlton beat Wilson 10–5; Francisco beat Dennis Taylor 10–7; Reynolds beat F. Davis 19–7; J. Virgo beat Hallett 10–4;

R. Reardon beat Donnelly 10–5; Thorne beat T. Griffiths 10–6; J. Spencer beat Dunning 10–4; A. Higgins beat Meadowcroft 10–5; D. Mountjoy beat Williams 10–3; Fagan beat David Taylor 10–9; K. Stevens beat Fitzmaurice 10–4; P. Mans beat Meo 10–8; White beat C. Thorburn 10–4.

Second round: Knowles beat Miles 13–7; Charlton beat Werbeniuk 13–5; Francisco beat Reynolds 13–8; Reardon beat Virgo 13–8; Thorne beat Spencer 13–5; Higgins beat Mountjoy 13–12; Stevens beat Fagan 13–7; White beat Mans 13–6.

Quarter-finals: Charlton beat Knowles 13–11; Reardon beat Francisco 13–8; Higgins beat Thorne 13–10; White beat Stevens 13–9.

Semi-finals: Reardon beat Charlton 16–11; Higgins beat White 16–15.

Final: Higgins beat Reardon 18–15.

1982
LANGS SUPREME SCOTTISH MASTERS
Sponsor: Langs
Entries: (invited) 8
Prize money: £23 000
First prize: £9000

Steve Davis had to take the last three frames to beat Tony Knowles 5–4 to avenge the 10–1 defeat Knowles had inflicted upon him in the first round of the Embassy World Championship in the previous spring but then beat Dennis Taylor and Alex Higgins much more comfortably to take the title. The move from the cavernous Kelvin Hall to Glasgow's Holiday Inn enabled the tournament to establish itself more securely in the league of major tournaments.

First round: Dennis Taylor beat J. White 5–4; S. Davis beat T. Knowles 5–4; T. Griffiths beat R. Reardon 5–3; A. Higgins beat E. Sinclair 5–1.

Semi-finals: Davis beat Taylor 6–1; Higgins beat Griffiths 6–5.

Final: Davis beat Higgins 9–4.

1982
JAMESON INTERNATIONAL
Sponsor: Irish Distillers
Entries: 32
Prize money: £75 000
First prize: £22 000

Tony Knowles won his first major title in the first tournament apart from the Embassy World Championship, in which world ranking points

were awarded. Previously, only results in the last three world championships had counted for this purpose but at the commencement of the 1982/3 season the WPBSA decided that the Jameson and the new PPT event would carry ranking points and the Embassy World Championship double ranking points.

David Taylor, who lost to Knowles in the final, pulled off the surprise of the tournament by beating Steve Davis 5–3 in the quarter-finals.

First round: T. Knowles beat E. Sinclair 5–2; D. Reynolds beat W. Thorne 5–3; S. Davis beat C. Roscoe 5–0; B. Weberniuk beat J. Wych 5–3; David Taylor beat M. Fisher 5–1; K. Stevens beat M. Watterson 5–3; T. Griffiths beat R. Williams 5–2; J. Spencer beat R. Edmonds 5–2; Dennis Taylor beat M. Wildman 5–2; J. Virgo beat E. Charlton 5–4; P. Mans beat L. Dodd 5–3; J. White beat J. Meadowcroft 5–1; R. Reardon beat E. Hughes 5–3; C. Thorburn beat G. Scott 5–1; A. Higgins beat B. Kelly 5–3; C. Wilson beat D. Mountjoy 5–4.

Second round: Davis beat Reynolds 5–0; David Taylor beat Weberniuk 5–2; Stevens beat Mans 5–2; Griffiths beat Higgins 5–2; Dennis Taylor beat Thorburn 5–2; Wilson beat White 5–2; Virgo beat Spencer 5–4; Knowles beat Reardon 5–2.

Quarter-finals: Virgo beat Dennis Taylor 5–3; David Taylor beat Davis 5–3; Knowles beat Wilson 5–4; Stevens beat Griffiths 5–3.

Semi-finals: Knowles beat Stevens 9–3; David Taylor beat Virgo 9–5.

Final: Knowles beat David Taylor 9–6.

1982
PROFESSIONAL PLAYERS TOURNAMENT
Sponsor: none *Entries*: 56
Prize money: £32 000
First prize: £5000

Ray Reardon won his first major tournament since his 1978 world title but the event itself was not a commercial success. It was staged in the match arenas of two Birmingham snooker centres at Sutton Coldfield and Aston but without sponsorship and television coverage the public did not respond to it.

Steve Davis withdrew in order to concentrate on exhibition engagements and without any seeding in the conventional sense Ray Reardon and Alex Higgins met as early as the second round.

There was one curious second round result in that Willie Thorne made breaks of 94, 109 and 135 only to lose 5–4 to Murdo Macleod, and Jimmy White beat the Canadian Jim Wych 5–0 in an hour with five breaks between 57 and 73.

The event was financed entirely by the WPBSA who were keen to re-distribute, in the form of prize money, to its members, substantial income from television contracts which they would otherwise have had to pay away in tax.

First round: E. Sinclair beat F. Davis 5–2; J. Meadowcroft beat B. Bennett 5–4; M. Watterson beat J. Donnelly 5–4; T. Griffiths beat C. Roscoe 5–1; A. Higgins beat D. French 5–3; R. Reardon beat T. Murphy 5–0; B. Werbeniuk beat P. Morgan 5–3; C. Everton beat P. Medati 5–1; David Taylor beat I. Anderson 5–1; Dennis Taylor beat R. Edmonds 5–4; J. Wych beat B. Kelly 5–0; R. Williams beat C. Ross 5–0; P. Mans beat E. McLaughlin 5–2; W. Thorne beat B. Demarco 5–3; M. Wildman beat J. Dunning 5–4; J. Johnson beat G. Miles 5–1; E. Charlton beat D. Hughes 5–2; F. Jonik beat D. Mountjoy 5–3; K. Stevens beat E. Hughes 5–2; T. Meo beat M. Owen 5–4; C. Wilson beat M. Morra 5–2; T. Knowles beat P. Houlihan 5–4; J. Virgo beat I. Black 5–2; M. Hallett beat V. Harris 5–3; D. Martin beat M. Gibson 5–2; J. Fitzmaurice beat D. Sheehan 5–1; J. Spencer beat G. Foulds 5–1; M. Macleod w.o. S. Davis scr.

Second round: Werbeniuk beat J. Rea 5–2; Sinclair beat Meadowcroft 5–3; Thorburn beat Everton 5–2; Griffiths beat Watterson 5–2; Reardon beat Higgins 5–2; Dennis Taylor beat David Taylor 5–1; Wildman beat Mans 5–4; Charlton beat Williams 5–2; Macleod beat Thorne 5–4; White beat Wych 5–0; Johnson beat Stevens 5–1; Meo beat Jonik 5–0; Wilson beat Knowles 5–4; Virgo beat Hallett 5–2; Spencer beat Martin 5–3;

Reynolds beat Fitzmaurice 5–0.
Third round: Werbeniuk beat Thorburn 5–2; Johnson beat Wildman 5–4; Reynolds beat Wilson 5–1; Virgo beat Spencer 5–1; Charlton beat Meo 5–3; White beat Dennis Taylor 5–3; Griffiths beat Sinclair 5–3; Reardon beat Macleod 5–2.
Quarter-finals: White beat Griffiths 5–2; Virgo beat Johnson 5–1; Reardon beat Werbeniuk 5–3; Charlton beat Reynolds 5–2.
Semi-finals: White beat Virgo 10–4; Reardon beat Charlton 10–7.
Final: Reardon beat White 10–5.

1982
STATE EXPRESS WORLD TEAM CLASSIC
Sponsor. British American Tobacco
Entries: 6 teams
Prize money: £50 555
First prize: £16 500

Canada won the event for the first time through its trio of Cliff Thorburn, Bill Werbeniuk and Kirk Stevens. Thorburn and Werbeniuk each lost only one match in the entire competition and both beat Steve Davis in Canada's 4–2 win over England in the final.

Group A: England beat Northern Ireland 4–3; Scotland beat Northern Ireland 4–1; England beat Scotland 4–1.
Group B: Canada beat Wales 4–3; Canada beat Australia 4–0; Wales beat Australia 4–1.
Semi-finals: England beat Wales 4–2; Canada beat Scotland 4–0.
Final: Canada beat England 4–2.

1982
CORAL UK CHAMPIONSHIP
Sponsor. Coral Racing
Entries: 56
Prize money: £50 000
First prize: £11 000

Terry Griffiths frustrated Steve Davis's hopes of a hat-trick of Coral UK titles by eliminating him 9–6 in the quarter-finals.

From 7–7 he beat Tony Meo 9–7 in the semi-finals and from two down with three to play beat Alex Higgins for the title.

The deciding frame registered high for drama for Griffiths, after leading 52–0, led by only 33 with one red remaining but Higgins, failed at a black from its spot in attempting to force the cue ball into position for the yellow and thus the colours clearance he needed to complete the world/UK title double.

Earlier, Higgins had trailed Dean Reynolds 1–5 in the second round before winning 9–8 and Ray Reardon prevailed in two consecutive 9–8 finishes over Mike Hallett and Jimmy White before losing 9–6 to Higgins in the semi.

Qualifying round: T. Meo beat G. Scott 9–5; C. Wilson beat E. Mclaughlin 9–6; D. Martin beat M. Macleod 9–6; J. Meadowcroft beat D. Hughes 9–8; K. J. Donnelly beat C. Ross 9–5; P. Houlihan w.o. J. Dunning; M. Hallett beat B. Demarco 9–1; B. Kelly beat J. Fitzmaurice 9–0; G. Foulds beat M. Gibson 9–3; R. Williams beat Foulds 9–7; V. Harris beat M. Owen 9–4; J. Johnson beat Harris 9–8; T. Murphy beat C. Everton 9–4; E. Sinclair beat Murphy 9–5; B. Harris beat G. Cripsey 9–6; Harris beat M. Watterson; M. Fisher beat I. Black 9–3; Fisher beat R. Edmonds 9–8; L. Dodd beat I. Williamson 9–1; Dodd beat D. French 9–7; B. Bennett w.o. J. Phillips scr.; P. Medati beat Bennett 9–1; C. Roscoe beat J. Rea 9–6; M. Wildman beat C. Roscoe 9–4.

First round: S. Davis beat Williams 9–6; P. Fagan beat B. Harris 9–6; T. Griffiths beat J. Johnson 9–1; Dennis Taylor beat J. Meadowcroft 9–7; David Taylor beat Dodd 9–7; Meo beat G. Miles 9–4; J. Virgo beat Kelly 9–2; D. Mountjoy beat Houlihan 9–3; R. Reardon beat Wildman 9–5; Hallett beat F. Davis 9–7; Wilson beat W. Thorne 9–7; J. White beat Medati 9–7; J. Spencer beat Sinclair 9–8; T. Knowles beat Donnelly 9–6; D. Reynolds beat Fisher 9–6; A. Higgins beat Martin 9–7.

Second round: S. Davis beat Fagan 9–3; Griffiths beat Dennis Taylor 9–7; Meo beat David Taylor 9–6; Virgo beat Mountjoy 9–5; Reardon beat Hallett 9–8; White beat Wilson 9–5; Spencer beat Knowles 9–6; Higgins beat Reynolds 9–8.

Quarter-finals: Griffiths beat Davis 9–6; Meo beat Virgo 9–6; Reardon beat White 9–8; Higgins beat Spencer 9–5.
Semi-finals: Griffiths beat Meo 9–7; Higgins beat Reardon 9–6.
Final: Griffiths beat Higgins 16–15.

1982
HOFMEISTER WORLD DOUBLES
Sponsor: Courage
Entries: 29 pairs
Prize money: £60 000
First prize: £24 000

Snooker's first ever professional doubles championship experienced some teething problems, chiefly relating to the deficiencies of the chosen venue, the National Sports Centre at Crystal Palace. Cold, cavernous and empty, it was completely lacking in atmosphere and long before the end of the week it was apparent that the event could not return there.

Tony Meo won his first major title, albeit in partnership with Steve Davis by defeating Terry Griffiths and Doug Mountjoy with a session to spare in the final.

Qualifying:

Group 1: J. Johnson and C. Wilson w.o. M. Morra and F. Jonik; Johnson and Wilson beat R. Edmonds and J. Meadowcroft 6–4; R. Reardon and J. Spencer beat Johnson and Wilson 6–2.

Group 2: D. Martin and Dennis Taylor beat L. Dodd and D. French 6–2; T. Griffiths and D. Mountjoy beat Martin and Dennis Taylor 6–0.

Group 3: F. Davis and P. Medati beat J. Dunning and B. Demarco 6–0; A. Higgins and E. Charlton beat F. Davis and Medati 6–3.

Group 4: P. Houlihan and B. Bennett beat E. Sinclair and I. Black 6–2; D. Reynolds and M. Watterson beat Houlihan and Bennett 6–3; S. Davis and T. Meo beat Reynolds and Watterson 6–3.

Group 5: M. Hallett and G. Cripsey beat M. Macleod and E. McLaughlin 6–3; Hallett and Cripsey beat P. Fagan and G. Foulds 6–2; K. Stevens and J. Wych beat Hallett and Cripsey 6–4.

Group 6: V. Harris and I. Williamson beat T. Murphy and E. Hughes 6–1; R. Williams and J. Fitzmaurice beat V. Harris and Williamson 6–1; G. Miles and B. Werbeniuk beat Williams and Fitzmaurice 6–5.

Group 7: J. White and T. Knowles beat G. Scott and D. Hughes 6–2; White and Knowles beat David Taylor and W. Thorne 6–1.

Group 8: M. Fisher and M. Wildman beat C. Everton and C. Roscoe 6–3; Fisher and Wildman beat J. Donnelly and M. Gibson 6–5; C. Thorburn and J. Virgo beat Fisher and Wildman 6–2.

Quarter-finals: Griffiths and Mountjoy beat Stevens and Wych 6–1; S. Davis and Meo beat Thorburn and Virgo 6–2; White and Knowles beat Reardon and Spencer 6–2; Higgins and Charlton beat Miles and Werbeniuk 6–3.

Semi-finals: Griffiths and Mountjoy beat Higgins and Charlton 10–7; S. Davis and Meo beat White and Knowles 10–5.

Final: S. Davis and Meo beat Griffiths and Mountjoy 13–2.

1983
LADA CLASSIC
Sponsor: Lada Cars
Entries: (invited) 16
Prize money: £65 000
First prize: £16 000

With the field extended to 16 players the event moved to a splendid new venue, The Spectrum Arena, Warrington.

The whole event was televised by ITV and Steve Davis made up for losing 9–8 on the final black to Terry Griffiths in the 1982 final by winning the £16 000 first prize.

Davis survived two 5–4 finishes, against Eddie Charlton in the quarter-finals and against John Spencer, who led him by two frames with three to play in their semi-final.

Bill Werbeniuk enjoyed the best tournament of his professional career by reaching the final and holding Davis to 5–5 before Davis took the next four frames for the match.

First round: E. Charlton beat J. Virgo 5–2; J. Spencer beat R. Reardon 5–3; C. Thorburn beat C. Wilson 5–3; D. Mountjoy beat T. Griffiths 5–1; David Taylor beat J. White 5–3; B. Werbeniuk beat A. Higgins 5–4; K. Stevens beat T. Knowles 5–0; S. Davis beat Dennis Taylor 5–2.

Quarter-finals: Spencer beat David Taylor 5–2; Werbeniuk beat Mountjoy 5–2; Stevens beat Thorburn 5–3; Davis beat Charlton 5–4.

Semi-finals: Davis beat Spencer 5–4; Werbeniuk beat Stevens 5–2.

Final: Davis beat Werbeniuk 9–5.

1983
BENSON AND HEDGES MASTERS
Sponsor: Gallaher
Entries: (invited) 16
Prize money: £55 250
First prize: £16 000

Cliff Thorburn recorded his first major success since his 1980 world title by clinching a 9–7 final victory over Ray Reardon after the Welshman had recovered threateningly from 4–8 to 7–8.

The first round brought a thrilling 5–4 victory for Bill Werbeniuk over Alex Higgins after trailing by two frames with three to play and the quarter-finals a similar recovery for Doug Mountjoy at the expense of the odds-on favourite, Steve Davis.

There was an even more notable recovery in the semi-finals in which Thorburn beat Eddie Charlton 6–5 from three down with four to play in a marathon which required five hours, ten minutes playing time.

First round: R. Reardon beat D. Reynolds 5–1; J. White beat David Taylor 5–2; C. Thorburn beat J. Johnson 5–2; T. Griffiths beat K. Stevens 5–3; E. Charlton beat T. Meo 5–3; S. Davis beat M. Wildman 5–2; D. Mountjoy beat J. Virgo 5–1; B. Werbeniuk beat A. Higgins 5–4.

Quarter-finals: Thorburn beat Griffiths 5–3; Reardon beat White 5–2; Charlton beat Werbeniuk 5–3; Mountjoy beat Davis 5–4.

Semi-finals: Thorburn beat Charlton 6–5; Reardon beat Mountjoy 6–3.

Final: Thorburn beat Reardon 9–7.

1983
WOODPECKER WELSH CHAMPIONSHIP

Ray Reardon regained the title with the greatest of ease, both in his 9–1 final victory over Doug Mountjoy and in his 9–4 semi-final success over Terry Griffiths.

Quarter-finals: T. Griffiths beat C. Everton 6–1; R. Reardon beat R. Andrewartha 6–2; C. Wilson beat C. Roscoe 6–4; D. Mountjoy beat M. Owen 6–0.

Semi-finals: Reardon beat Griffiths 9–4; Mountjoy beat Wilson 9–3.

Final: Reardon beat Mountjoy 9–1.

1983
TOLLY COBBOLD CLASSIC

Steve Davis and Terry Griffiths carried their final far into the night until Davis clinched his 7–5 win at 1.50 a.m.

This late finish caused some heart-ache at ITV since they are obliged to pay their crews time and a half for working between midnight and 1.00 a.m. and double time between 1.00 a.m. and 2.00 a.m. If the match had run its full distance, triple time would have come into force after 2.00 a.m.

These circumstances led the WPBSA to work more closely with the television authorities to reduce a possible repetition of this situation.

First round: B. Werbeniuk beat D. Mountjoy 4–2; T. Griffiths beat R. Reardon 4–2; S. Davis beat J. White 4–3; Dennis Taylor beat A. Higgins 4–2.

Semi-finals: Griffiths beat Werbeniuk 5–3; Davis beat Taylor 5–1.

Final: Davis beat Griffiths 7–5.

1983
YAMAHA INTERNATIONAL MASTERS
Sponsor: Yamaha Organs
Entries: (invited) 16
Prize money: £47 550
First prize: £12 000

Ray Reardon dashed Steve Davis's hopes of a hat-trick of titles by beating him 2–1 in the last match decider of their semi-final group. As before, the tournament proceeded by means of four man groups until the straight head to head final in which Reardon beat Jimmy White 9–6.

Semi-finals:

Group A: T. Griffiths beat J. White 2–0; Griffiths beat David Taylor 2–1; Taylor beat D. Mountjoy 2–0; Mountjoy beat Griffiths 2–0; White beat Mountjoy 2–0; White beat Taylor 2–0.

Group B: W. Thorne beat R. Reardon 2–1; S. Davis beat Thorne 2–0; Davis beat E. Charlton 2–1; Thorne beat Charlton 3–2; Reardon beat Charlton 2–0; Reardon beat Davis 2–1.

Final: Reardon beat White 9–6.

1983
IRISH CHAMPIONSHIP

Alex Higgins regained the title by carrying his 12–10 lead going into the final session to a 16–11 victory over Dennis Taylor at Maysfield Leisure Centre, Belfast.

Quarter-finals: Dennis Taylor beat B. Kelly 6–0; P. Fagan beat T. Murphy 6–4; A. Higgins beat

Jack Rea 6–3; E. Hughes beat P. Burke 6–2.

Semi-finals: Taylor beat Fagan 6–1; Higgins beat Hughes 6–2.

Final: Higgins beat Taylor 16–11.

1983
BENSON AND HEDGES IRISH MASTERS
Sponsor: Benson and Hedges
Entries: (invited) 12
Prize money: IR£35 000
First prize: IR£12 000

Steve Davis took his fourth first prize of the season with a comfortable 9–2 final victory over Ray Reardon, who had battled manfully all week against the emotional aftermath of his father's death.

First round: J. White beat Dennis Taylor 5–4; T. Meo beat P. Burke 5–0; E. Charlton beat David Taylor 5–4.

Quarter-finals: R. Reardon beat Meo 5–4; A. Higgins beat White 5–2; S. Davis beat Charlton 5–1; T. Griffiths beat Mountjoy 5–4.

Semi-finals: Reardon beat Higgins 6–3; Davis beat Griffiths 6–2.

Final: Davis beat Reardon 9–2.

Ray Reardon with the Yamaha International Masters trophy he won in 1983.

1983
EMBASSY WORLD CHAMPIONSHIP

Sponsor: W. D. and H. O. Wills
Entries: 74 *Prize money:* £130 000
First prize: £30 000

Steve Davis became the first player to win the title twice at the Crucible Theatre, Sheffield, with an emphatic 18–6 final victory over Cliff Thorburn.

Thorburn, though, was as much the man of the championship as anyone can be without actually winning the title. His 147 break in his second round match against Terry Griffiths was the first maximum in the history of the championship and his desperate late night victories over Griffiths, 13–12, Kirk Stevens, 13–12, and Tony Knowles, 16–15, were monumental efforts of grit, application and sheer unwillingness to lose.

Thorburn's final session against Griffiths lasted 6 hours 25 minutes, a record, and finished only at 3.51 a.m. It is the only match in which the BBC were compelled to cease recording since they began covering the championship. His quarter-final against Kirk Stevens did not finish until 2.12 a.m. after a final session of 6 hours, 11 minutes. Thorburn had to recover from two down with three to play, just as he did against Knowles in the semi-finals, but the accumulation of his efforts left him so drained for the final that he was able to offer only token resistance.

Alex Higgins made a curiously tame 16–5 semi-final exit to Davis after coming from behind to beat Bill Werbeniuk in the quarters.

Group 1: B. Kelly beat B. Demarco 10–4; S. Francisco beat Kelly 10–5.
Group 2: P. Morgan beat P. Burke 10–9; G. Miles beat Morgan 10–6.
Group 3: T. Murphy beat P. Houlihan 10–9; J. Virgo beat Murphy 10–8.
Group 4: R. Williams beat M. Darrington 10–0; Williams beat F. Davis 10–1.
Group 5: M. Wildman beat B. Harris 10–7; Wildman w.o. J. Wych scr.
Group 6: R. Edmonds beat F. Jonik 10–4; D. Reynolds beat Edmonds 10–6.
Group 7: M. Fisher beat P. Fagan 10–8; E. McLaughlin beat D. Greaves 10–7; Fisher beat McLaughlin 10–9.
Group 8: T. Meo beat V. Harris 10–0; G. Foulds beat M. Gibson 10–6; Meo beat Foulds 10–4.
Group 9: I. Black beat M. Morra 10–9; P. Medati beat John Bear 10–7; Black beat Medati 10–4.
Group 10: C. Wilson beat C. Everton 10–1; J. Johnson beat P. Watchorn 10–0; Wilson beat Johnson 10–8.
Group 11: M. Macleod beat M. Owen 10–5; D. Martin beat M. Parkin 10–1; Martin beat Macleod 10–7.
Group 12: J. Meadowcroft beat B. Bennett 10–3; G. Cripsey beat D. Hughes 10–2; Meadowcroft beat Cripsey 10–6.
Group 13: J. Donnelly beat D. Sheehan 10–6; J. Campbell beat M. Watterson 10–6; Campbell beat Donnelly 10–2.
Group 14: L. Dodd w.o. J. Dunning scr.; I. Williamson beat D. French 10–8; Dodd beat Williamson 10–9.
Group 15: M. Hallett beat R. Andrewartha 10–7; W. King beat I. Anderson 10–6; Hallett beat King 10–6.
Group 16: E. Hughes beat J. Fitzmaurice 10–7; E. Sinclair beat C. Roscoe 10–2; Hughes beat Sinclair 10–8.
First round: A. Higgins beat Reynolds 10–4; W. Thorne beat Virgo 10–3; B. Werbeniuk beat Martin 10–4; David Taylor beat Meadowcroft 10–2; E. Charlton beat Dodd 10–7; J. Spencer beat Hallett 10–7; Dennis Taylor beat S. Francisco 10–9; S. Davis beat Williams 10–4; C. Thorburn beat Campbell 10–5; T. Griffiths beat Wildman 10–8; P. Mans beat Black 10–3; K. Stevens beat Fisher 10–2; Mountjoy beat Wilson 10–2; Meo beat J. White 10–8; T. Knowles beat Miles 10–3; R. Reardon beat E. Hughes 10–7.
Second round: Higgins beat Thorne 13–8; Werbeniuk beat David Taylor 13–10; Charlton beat Spencer 13–11; Davis beat Dennis Taylor 13–11; Thorburn beat Griffiths 13–12; Meo beat Mountjoy 13–11; Knowles beat Reardon 13–12; Stevens beat Mans 13–3.
Quarter-finals: Higgins beat Werbeniuk 13–11; Davis beat Charlton 13–5; Thorburn beat Stevens 13–12; Knowles beat Meo 13–9;
Semi-finals: Davis beat Higgins 16–5; Thorburn beat Knowles 16–15.
Final: Davis beat Thorburn 18–6.

1983
WINFIELD MASTERS

Having existed for four years as a sprint style Australian version of Pot Black, the event adopted a proper tournament format, albeit with matches still no longer than best of five frames in the first round.

Channel 10 were agreeably surprised by the high viewing figures the tournament attracted although the snooker world itself retained some reservations about the entire event being conducted in a television studio.

Cliff Thorburn displayed some of his best form to take the title by disposing of two fellow Canadians, Kirk Stevens and Bill Werbeniuk, in his last two matches.

First round: C. Thorburn beat W. King 3–1; J. White beat I. Anderson 3–2; K. Stevens beat D. Mountjoy 3–1; E. Charlton beat P. Morgan 3–2; A. Higgins beat J. Spencer 3–2; B. Werbeniuk beat Dennis Taylor 3–2; T. Meo beat David Taylor 3–0; T. Knowles beat J. Campbell 3–1.
Quarter-finals: Thorburn beat White 4–2; Stevens beat Charlton 4–1; Werbeniuk beat Higgins 4–0; Knowles beat Meo 4–3.
Semi-finals: Thorburn beat Stevens 5–2; Werbeniuk beat Knowles 5–0.
Final: Thorburn beat Werbeniuk 7–3.

1983
CAMUS HONG KONG MASTERS

Hong Kong's first taste of top class competitive snooker proved highly popular both with the crowds and local television.

Terry Griffiths made a break of 140, the highest ever made in the colony, but was beaten 4–3 in the final by Doug Mountjoy.

The tour also included two sprint style tournaments in Thailand, both won by Tony Meo.

First round: D. Mountjoy beat C. Chi-Ming 2–1; T. Meo beat S. Leung 2–1.
Semi-finals: Mountjoy beat S. Davis 3–0; T. Griffiths beat Meo 3–2.
Final: Mountjoy beat Griffiths 4–3.

1983
SCOTTISH CHAMPIONSHIP

Although Murdo Macleod earned only £2000 for winning the Scottish professional title for the first time at Glasgow University Students Union, his success also gave him the place in the eight man Langs Scottish Masters kept open for the Scottish champion.

First round: J. Donnelly beat B. Demarco 6–4; I. Black beat E. McLaughlin 6–4; M. Macleod beat M. Gibson.

Semi-finals: E. Sinclair beat Donnelly 6–5; Macleod beat Black 6–2.

Final: Macleod beat Sinclair 11–9.

1983
LANGS SUPREME SCOTTISH MASTERS

Sponsor: Langs
Entries: (invited) 8
Prize money: £25 500
First prize: £10 000

Steve Davis made good the loss of the first three frames to beat Tony Knowles 9–6 to retain the title. He also set a new break record for the event, 137, in completing his 5–1 first round victory over Murdo Macleod.

The most dramatic match of the tournament was also in the first round when Knowles was on the brink of defeat against Tony Meo at 2–4 only to go on to clinch his victory with a break of 92 in the deciding frame.

First round: C. Thorburn beat T. Griffiths 5–1; S. Davis beat M. Macleod 5–1; T. Knowles beat T. Meo 5–4; A. Higgins beat J. White 5–3.

Semi-finals: Knowles beat Thorburn 6–2; S. Davis beat Higgins 6–2.

Final: S. Davis beat Knowles 9–6.

1983
CANADIAN CHAMPIONSHIP

Kirk Stevens earned the most prestigious title of his professional career by beating Jim Bear and Frank Jonik, both by 9–8 margins, to win the Canadian Professional Championship held during the Canadian National Exhibition fortnight in Toronto.

The surprise of the tournament was Jonik's 9–6 semi-final defeat of Cliff Thorburn.

First round: G. Rigitano beat M. Gauvreau 9–6; R. Chaperon beat G. Watson 9–5; J. Cagianello beat W. Sanderson 9–5.

Second round: B. Mikkelsen beat Rigitano 9–4; F. Jonik beat Chaperon 9–4; Jim Bear beat M. Morra 9–8; Cagianello beat P. Thornley 9–7.

Quarter-finals: C. Thorburn beat Mikkelsen 9–2; Jonik beat J. Wych 9–5; Jim Bear beat John Bear 9–5; K. Stevens beat Cagianello 9–0.

Semi-finals: Jonik beat Thorburn 9–6; Stevens beat Jim Bear 9–8.

Final: Stevens beat Jonik 9–8.

1983
JAMESON INTERNATIONAL

Sponsor: Irish Distillers
Entries: 69 *Prize money*: £85 000
First prize: £24 000

Steve Davis regained the title in ruthlessly efficient style at a new venue, Eldon Square Recreation Centre, Newcastle, dropping only seven frames in four matches.

The match of the tournament was the semi-final in which Cliff Thorburn beat Terry Griffiths from three down with four to play after Griffiths had beaten John Spencer from two down with three to play in the quarters.

These recoveries were the continuation of a trend set in the first round proper when Spencer recovered from two down with three to play to beat Tony Knowles, the defending title holder.

Qualifying:

Group 1: M. Watterson beat B. Demarco 5–3; Watterson beat P. Mans 5–1.

Group 2: T. Murphy beat D. Sheehan 5–2; W. Thorne beat Murphy 5–2.

Group 3: R. Williams beat D. French 5–1; D. Reynolds beat Williams 5–3.

Group 4: J. Donnelly beat B. Bennett 5–1; Donnelly beat C. Wilson 5–1.

Group 5: M. Darrington beat I. Williamson 5–3; S. Francisco beat Darrington 5–2.

Group 6: W. King beat I. Black 5–3; G. Miles beat King 5–3.

Group 7: D. Hughes beat M. Parkin 5–0; J. Johnson beat Hughes 5–1.

Group 8: B. Harris beat J. Dunning 5–3; M. Wildman beat Harris 5–2.

Group 9: D. Martin beat D. Greaves 5–1; Martin beat P. Fagan 5–0.

Group 10: R. Andrewartha beat C. Everton 5–1; E. Sinclair beat Andrewartha 5–4.

Group 11: P. Medati beat V. Harris 5–0; M. Macleod beat Medati 5–3.

Group 12: F. Davis beat B. Kelly 5–1; P. Morgan beat J. Fitzmaurice 5–4; Morgan beat Davis 5–3.

Group 13: M. Hallett beat C. Roscoe 5–2; M. Morra beat P. Watchorn 5–3; Morra beat Hallett 5–3.

Group 14: G. Foulds beat P. Burke 5–2; E. Hughes beat M. Fisher 5–4; Hughes beat Foulds 5–1.

Group 15: M. Gibson beat L. Dodd 5–1; G. Scott beat P. Houlihan 5–0; Scott beat Gibson 5–3.

Group 16: E. McLaughlin beat J. Campbell 5–2; R. Edmonds beat J. Rea 5–1; Edmonds beat McLaughlin 5–1.

Qualifying round: Dennis Taylor beat Reynolds 5–3; R. Reardon beat Macleod 5–2; Thorne beat J. Virgo 5–2; Morra beat J. White 5–3; D. Mountjoy beat Wildman 5–4; Martin beat A. Higgins 5–2; Watterson beat T. Meo 5–3; Scott beat B. Werbeniuk 5–3; T. Griffiths beat Miles 5–2; S. Davis beat E. Hughes 5–1; Donnelly beat David Taylor 5–3; Francisco w.o. K. Stevens scr.; E. Charlton beat Johnson 5–2; C. Thorburn beat Sinclair 5–0; J. Spencer beat Morgan 5–1; T. Knowles beat Edmonds 5–1.

First round: Griffiths beat Scott 5–0; Spencer beat Knowles 5–4; Thorburn beat Dennis Taylor 5–3; Mountjoy beat Martin 5–0; Charlton beat Morra 5–3; Thorne beat Reardon 5–0; Francisco beat Donnelly 5–1; Davis beat Watterson 5–0.

Quarter-finals: Griffiths beat Spencer 5–4; Thorburn beat Mountjoy 5–2; Charlton beat Thorne 5–0; Davis beat Francisco 5–1.

Semi-finals: Thorburn beat Griffiths 9–8; Davis beat Charlton 9–2.

Final: Davis beat Thorburn 9–4.

1983
PROFESSIONAL PLAYERS TOURNAMENT

Sponsor: none
Entries: 80 *Prize money*: £60 000
First prize: £12 500

Tony Knowles won his second world ranking tournament at the Redwood Lodge Country Club, Bristol with a 9–8 final victory over Joe Johnson after the Yorkshireman had beaten

Jimmy White, Eddie Charlton, Cliff Thorburn and Tony Meo, players all ranked well above him, to reach his first major final.

Johnson also made a great fight of the final after trailing 1–6. The highest break of the tournament, 135, enabled him to win the last frame of the afternoon and after being three down with four to play he levelled at 8–8 before Knowles scraped home.

Mike Hallett's 5–2 second round win over Steve Davis was to remain the upset of the season.

Qualifying: G. Ganim jr. beat G. Cripsey 5–4; S. Duggan beat M. Darrington 5–4; T. Jones beat B. Oliver 5–2; D. French beat N. Foulds 5–2; B. Bennett beat B. Dermarco 5–4; P. Burke beat G. Foulds 5–4; V. Harris w.o. P. Mifsud scr.; P. Medati beat D. Hughes 5–1; T. Murphy beat P. Browne 5–2; J. Parrott beat P. Watchorn 5–0; D. Sheehan beat P. Houlihan 5–2; M. Morra beat J. Hargreaves 5–0; D. Greaves beat R. Andrewartha 5–2; W. King beat B. Harris 5–3; P. Morgan beat M. Gibson 5–4.

First round: R. Reardon beat Ganim jr. 5–4; C. Thorburn beat V. Harris 5–1; J. Meadowcroft beat C. Roscoe 5–4; Duggan beat J. Dunning 5–2; J. Virgo beat French 5–4; J. Spencer beat I. Black 5–2; W. Thorne beat C. Everton 5–1; C. Wilson beat Bennett 5–1; T. Griffiths beat L. Dodd 5–3; J. White beat I. Williamson 5–2; Parrott beat P. Fagan 5–2; J. Johnson beat Burke 5–3; E. Hughes beat E. Sinclair 5–4; M. Fisher beat F. Davis 5–4; B. Werbeniuk beat T. Jones 5–4; E. Charlton beat E. McLaughlin 5–0; M. Watterson beat A. Higgins 5–2; K. Stevens beat R. Edmonds 5–1; D. Martin beat J. Fitzmaurice 5–0; Murphy beat M. Macleod 5–0; J. Campbell beat D. Mountjoy 5–3; David Taylor beat Morgan 5–3; G. Miles beat M. Gauvreau 5–3; M. Wildman beat F. Jonik 5–4; G. Scott beat Dennis Taylor 5–4; T. Meo beat W. King 5–2; S. Francisco beat M. Morra 5–3; D. Reynolds beat Greaves 5–1; M. Hallett beat B. Kelly 5–0; T. Knowles beat Medati 5–1; S. Davis beat J. Donnelly 5–1.

Second round: Reardon beat Duggan 5–2; Thorburn beat Meadowcroft 5–1; Thorne beat Spencer 5–1; Wilson beat Virgo 5–2; Griffiths beat Parrott 5–1; Johnson beat White 5–3; Hughes beat Werbeniuk 5–0; Charlton beat Fisher 5–4; Stevens beat Murphy 5–1; Martin beat Watterson 5–4; Wildman beat David Taylor 5–3; Campbell beat Miles 5–2; Meo beat Reynolds 5–0; S. Francisco beat Scott 5–1; Knowles beat Williams 5–4; Hallett beat Davis 5–2;

Third round: Thorne beat Reardon 5–3; Thorburn beat Wilson 5–3; Hughes beat Griffiths 5–2; Johnson beat Charlton 5–0; Stevens beat Wildman 5–0; Campbell beat Martin 5–0; Knowles beat Francisco 5–0; Meo beat Hallett 5–3.

Quarter-finals: Johnson beat Thorburn 5–1; Thorne beat Hughes 5–1; Meo beat Stevens 5–3; Knowles beat Campbell 5–3.

Semi-finals: Knowles beat Thorne 9–7; Johnson beat Meo 9–6.

Final: Knowles beat Johnson 9–8.

1983
STATE EXPRESS WORLD TEAM CLASSIC
Sponsor: British American Tobacco
Entries: 6 teams *Prize money:* £60 000
First prize: £20 000

England, represented by Steve Davis, Tony Knowles and Tony Meo, won the event for the second time in three years, albeit amidst a feeling that nine days television coverage was now excessive for it. With six days expended on reducing the field from 16 to 4 there was a general view that the event was being unnaturally expanded to fill the television slot. With State Express announcing their withdrawal from all sports sponsorship, the WPBSA decided to re-schedule the event for a later slot in the calendar the following season with a new sponsor and reduce television exposure.

Group A: Wales beat Canada 4–3; Canada beat Australia 4–2; Wales beat Australia 4–0.

Group B: England beat Northern Ireland 4–1; Northern Ireland beat Scotland 4–3; England beat Scotland 4–0.

Semi-finals: Wales beat Northern Ireland 4–1; England beat Canada 4–2.

Final: England beat Wales 4–2.

1983
CORAL UK CHAMPIONSHIP
Sponsor: Coral Racing
Entries: 60 *Prize money:* £60 000
First prize: £12 000

Alex Higgins completed one of the most amazing recoveries snooker has ever known to beat Steve Davis 16–15 in the final after being white-washed 7–0 in the opening session.

Overwhelming superiority sometimes crushes the will to resist so firmly that the victim participates in his own self-destruction by missing shots which should always be well within his ability but Higgins, at first contained Davis and then accrued one frame after another until, incredibly, victory started to look possible.

Higgins won seven of the eight frames in the second session and was level at 11–11 by the end of the third. He fell one behind with two to play but went to 77–0 in the decider and forced Davis to concede.

Prior to the tournament, Higgins had been in poor form and his wife was threatening to sue for divorce. He trailed Murdo Macleod 0–4 in the opening round but there was a hint of reconciliation in the air as his wife attended the evening session which saw him get through 9–6. Wins over Paul Medati, Tony Knowles and Terry Griffiths then set up his amazing final.

Tony Meo equalled the championship break record of 139. Geoff and Neal Foulds made professional tournament history by becoming the first father and son combination to qualify for the final phase of a major professional event.

Qualifying:

Group 1: J. Johnson beat M. Gibson 9–6.

Group 2: T. Jones beat E. Sinclair 9–3.

Group 3: M. Wildman beat D. Greaves 9–5.

Group 4: M. Macleod beat B. Bennett 9–0.

Group 5: M. Watterson beat C. Everton 9–6; Watterson beat F. Davis 9–6.

Group 6: M. Darrington beat G. Cripsey 9–3; M. Hallett beat Darrington 9–1.

Group 7: N. Foulds beat C. Roscoe 9–2; Foulds beat J. Meadowcroft 9–2.

Group 8: V. Harris beat P. Houlihan 9–6; R. Williams beat Harris 9–6.

Group 9: D. French beat J. Rea 9–5; D. Martin beat French 9–3.

Group 10: G. Foulds beat S. Duggan 9–8; Foulds beat L. Dodd 9–7.

Group 11: J. Parrott beat G. Scott 9–7; Parrott beat M. Fisher 9–0.

Group 12: R. Andrewartha beat B. Oliver 9–1; J. Dunning beat Andrewartha 9–2.

Group 13: T. Murphy beat B. Demarco 9–4; Murphy beat J. Donnelly 9–4.

Group 14: P. Medati beat D. Hughes 9–3; Medati beat R. Edmonds 9–7.

Group 15: B. Harris beat E. McLaughlin 9–8; Harris beat J. Fitzmaurice 9–3.

Group 16: I. Williamson beat J. Hargreaves 9–4; I. Black beat Williamson 9–6.

First round: T. Griffiths beat Martin 9–4; Hallett beat G. Miles 9–4; Johnson beat J. Virgo 9–6; David Taylor beat N. Foulds 9–4; C. Wilson beat Williams 9–4; R. Reardon beat B. Harris 9–7; Dennis Taylor beat Murphy 9–6; J. White beat Black 9–1; J. Spencer beat Dunning 9–7; T. Meo beat Parrott 9–7; W. Thorne beat Wildman 9–5; S. Davis beat G. Foulds 9–1; A. Higgins beat Macleod 9–6.

Second round: Griffiths beat Hallett 9–5; Johnson beat David Taylor 9–3; Knowles beat Mountjoy 9–5; Higgins beat Medati 9–1; Reardon beat Wilson 9–4; White beat Dennis Taylor 9–4; Meo beat Spencer 9–5; Davis beat Thorne 9–3.

Quarter-finals: White beat Reardon 9–4; Griffiths beat Johnson 9–2; Higgins beat Knowles 9–5; Davis beat Meo 9–4.

Semi-finals: Higgins beat Griffiths 9–4; Davis beat White 9–4.

Final: Higgins beat Davis 16–15.

1983

HOFMEISTER WORLD DOUBLES

Sponsor: Courage   *Entries*: 37 pairs
Prize money: £75000 *First prize*: £25 000

A change of venue from the National Sports Centre, Crystal Palace to the modern, theatrical setting of the Derngate Centre, Northampton transformed the appearance and atmosphere of the Hofmeister World Doubles.

Steve Davis and Tony Meo were never pressed in retaining the title. They also won an unusual prize, the highest combined break, when Davis made a break of 140 and Meo won a 56 in their 9–1 semi-final victory over Eddie Charlton and Bill Werbeniuk.

Their margin of victory over Tony Knowles and Jimmy White in the final was equally convincing, 10–2, Knowles and White having benefited in their semi against Cliff Thorburn and John Virgo from an unusual incident which occurred at 7–7.

Knowles committed a foul and was asked by Virgo, who was due to play next, to play again. This in some way confused the Virgo/Thorburn partnership as Thorburn erroneously came to the table next.

He potted a red and disturbed not only the black but several more reds into pottable positions only for the referee to award a foul for playing out of order. White took advantage of the position to make a frame-winning 74.

Pre-Qualifying: B. Bennett and P. Houlihan beat M. Gibson and M. Macleod 5–2; S. Duggan and J. Hargreaves beat B. Oliver and P. Browne 5–1; G. Scott and J. Parrott beat G. Foulds and N. Foulds 5–4; B. Harris and M. Morra beat D. Sheehan and E. McLaughlin 5–2.

Qualifying: T. Murphy and P. Morgan beat P. Burke and D. Martin 5–4; J. Fitzmaurice and V. Harris beat Bennett and Houlihan 5–4; J. Donnelly and C. Roscoe beat W. King and J. Campbell 5–3; Duggan and Hargreaves beat D. Hughes and B. Kelly 5–0; J. Dunning and B. Demarco beat M. Hallett and G. Cripsey 5–4; R. Edmonds and J. Meadowcroft beat C. Everton and D. French 5–2; E. Hughes and L. Dodd beat Scott and Parrott 5–2; B. Harris and Morra beat M. Darrington and I. Williamson 5–1.

First round: Murphy and Morgan beat I. Black and E. Sinclair 5–1; Dennis Taylor and R. Williams beat Fitzmaurice and V. Harris 5–1; T. Jones and S. Francisco beat Donnelly and Roscoe 5–2; G. Miles and G. Ganim beat Duggan and Hargreaves 5–3; F. Davis and M. Watterson beat Dunning and Demarco 5–3; D. Reynolds and P. Fagan beat Edmonds and Meadowcroft 5–0; E. Hughes and Dodd beat C. Wilson and J. Johnson 5–1; B. Harris and Morra beat M. Fisher and M. Wildman 5–2.

Second round: S. Davis and T. Meo beat Murphy and Morgan 5–2; David Taylor and W. Thorne beat Dennis Taylor and Williams 5–4; E. Charlton and B. Werbeniuk beat T. Jones and S. Francisco 5–3; A. Higgins and K. Stevens w.o. Miles and Ganim scr.; R. Reardon and J. Spencer beat F. Davis and Watterson 5–2; J. Virgo and C. Thorburn beat Reynolds and Fagan 5–2; D. Mountjoy and T. Griffiths beat E. Hughes and Dodd 5–3; T. Knowles and J. White beat B. Harris and Morra 5–4.

Quarter-finals: Davis and Meo beat Taylor and Thorne 5–3; Charlton and Werbeniuk beat Higgins and Stevens 5–1; Virgo and Thorburn beat Reardon and Spencer 5–0; Knowles and White beat Griffiths and Mountjoy 5–0.

Semi-finals: Davis and Meo beat Charlton and Werbeniuk 9–1; Knowles and White beat Virgo and Thorburn 9–7.

Final: Davis and Meo beat Knowles and White 10–2.

1984

BENSON AND HEDGES MASTERS

Sponsor: Gallaher   *Entries*: (invited) 16
Prize money: £115 000
First prize: £35 000

Jimmy White beat Terry Griffiths 9–5 to take the title but the match of the tournament was his 6–4 semi-final win over Kirk Stevens.

The latter part of the match belonged in the realm of fantasy as it brought three centuries in five frames, including a maximum.

Aided by a break of 113, White went two up with three to play before Stevens made the 147 which earned him the £10 000 jackpot prize plus £1500 for a new tournament record. Undeterred, White ran 119 to clinch the match in the following frame.

The quarter-finals had brought Stevens a 5–3 victory over Steve Davis. The first round saw John Spencer eliminate the defending title holder Cliff Thorburn 5–4 from two down with three to play before Spencer himself suffered this fate against Griffiths in the next round.

First round: T. Knowles beat Dennis Taylor 5–2; R. Reardon beat J. Virgo 5–3; J. Spencer beat C. Thorburn 5–4; T. Griffiths beat B. Werbeniuk 5–1; J. White beat E. Charlton 5–2; A. Higgins beat D. Mountjoy 5–2; K. Stevens beat David Taylor 5–1; S. Davis beat T. Meo 5–0.

Quarter-finals: Griffiths beat Spencer 5–4; Knowles beat Higgins 5–1; White beat Reardon 5–3; Stevens beat Davis 5–3.

Semi-finals: White beat Stevens 6–4; Griffiths beat Knowles 6–4.

Final: White beat Griffiths 9–5.

1984
LADA CLASSIC

Sponsor: Lada Cars   *Entries*: 80
Prize money: £75 000
First prize: £18 000

Steve Davis retained the title but only after a desperately close 9–8 finish with Tony Meo, whose concentration was critically broken on the crucial yellow in the deciding frame by a spectator's untimely shout of 'Come on Tony'.

Davis was also taken to a deciding frame in the semi-finals by John Parrott, a 20–year-old Liverpudlian in his first professional season who had delighted his army of Merseyside supporters at the Spectrum Arena, Warrington, by scoring wins over Alex Higgins and Tony Knowles in the two previous rounds.

Mark Wildman reached his first major professional semi-final at the age of 47 with a 5–4 win over Eddie Charlton which occupied 4 hours 52 minutes.

Qualifying first round: G. Foulds beat M. Gauvreau 5–2; B. Demarco beat M. Gibson 5–2; N. Foulds beat P. Houlihan 5–3; M. Morra beat P. Burke 5–2; G. Ganim jr. beat D. Hughes 5–2; I. Williamson beat D. French 5–1; J. Hargreaves beat W. King 5–3; P. Morgan beat M. Darrington 5–3; T. Jones beat P. Mifsud 5–3; G. Cripsey beat V. Harris 5–4; J. Parrott beat B. Bennett 5–0; P. Browne beat D. Greaves 5–2; P. Watchorn beat R. Andrewartha 5–2; S. Duggan beat B. Harris 5–2; P. Medati beat T. Murphy 5–4.

Qualifying second round:
E. McLaughlin beat G. Foulds 5–1; G. Scott beat Demarco 5–2; N. Foulds beat J. Rea 5–1; Morra beat C. Everton 5–0; C. Roscoe beat Ganim 5–3; F. Jonik beat Williamson 5–1; Hargreaves beat B. Kelly 5–4; Oliver beat J. Donnelly 5–4; Morgan beat

M. Watterson 5–3; Jones beat I. Black 5–0; J. Campbell beat Cripsey 5–3; Parrott beat J. Fitzmaurice 5–2; R. Edmonds beat Browne 5–1; M. Fisher beat Watchorn 5–4; L. Dodd beat Duggan 5–2; E. Hughes beat Medati 5–1.

Qualifying third round: McLaughlin beat W. Thorne 5–3; D. Reynolds beat Scott 5–3; C. Wilson beat N. Foulds 5–4; S. Francisco beat Morra 5–1; Roscoe beat G. Miles 5–2; J. Johnson beat Jonik 5–2; M. Wildman beat Hargreaves 5–1; P. Fagan beat Oliver 5–1; E. Sinclair beat Morgan 5–2; M. Macleod beat Jones 5–2; Campbell beat F. Davis 5–0; Parrott beat D. Martin 5–1; R. Williams beat Edmonds 5–1; J. Meadowcroft beat Fisher 5–0; M. Hallett beat Dodd 5–1; E. Hughes beat J. Dunning 5–4.

First round: K. Stevens beat McLaughlin 5–4; T. Griffiths beat Reynolds 5–2; E. Charlton beat Wilson 5–0; Francisco beat C. Thorburn 5–1; Roscoe beat B. Werbeniuk 5–4; J. Spencer beat Johnson 5–4; Wildman beat J. Virgo 5–2; A. Higgins beat Fagan 5–3; S. Davis beat Sinclair 5–2; Macleod beat David Taylor 5–4; J. White beat Campbell 5–1; Parrott beat D. Mountjoy 5–4; Williams beat R. Reardon 5–4; T. Meo beat Meadowcroft 5–1; Hallett beat Dennis Taylor 5–4; T. Knowles beat E. Hughes 5–1.

Second round: Davis beat Spencer 5–1; Charlton beat White 5–3; Wildman beat Francisco 5–1; Knowles beat Hallett 5–3; Stevens beat Macleod 5–1; Griffiths beat Roscoe 5–2; Meo beat Williams 5–3; Parrott beat Higgins 5–2.

Quarter-finals: Wildman beat Charlton 5–4; Davis beat Griffiths 5–4; Meo beat Stevens 5–2; Parrott beat Knowles 5–1.

Semi-finals: Meo beat Wildman 5–3; Davis beat Parrott 5–4.

Final: Davis beat Meo 9–8.

1984
TOLLY COBBOLD CLASSIC

Steve Davis disposed very comfortably of Tony Knowles in the final but was within a shot of defeat against Kirk Stevens in the semi-final, the Canadian failing to double the deciding black in the ninth frame after a 12 shot safety duel.

First round: C. Thorburn beat

T. Meo 5–4; T. Knowles beat J. White 5–1; K. Stevens beat E. Charlton 5–3; S. Davis beat W. Thorne 5–2.

Semi-finals: Knowles beat Thorburn 5–3; Davis beat Stevens 5–4.

Final: Davis beat Knowles 8–2.

1984
STRONGBOW WELSH CHAMPIONSHIP

Doug Mountjoy won the title for the third time in five years but the most memorable feature of the tournament was Cliff Wilson's semi-final victory over Ray Reardon, the first he had enjoyed since they were growing up together in Tredegar as the two leading Welsh amateurs of the early fifties.

First round: D. Mountjoy beat C. Everton 6–1; T. Griffiths beat R. Andrewartha 6–1; R. Reardon beat M. Owen 6–1; C. Wilson beat C. Roscoe 6–2.

Semi-finals: Mountjoy beat Griffiths 9–5; Wilson beat Reardon 9–4.

Final: Mountjoy beat Wilson 9–3.

1984
YAMAHA INTERNATIONAL MASTERS

Sponsor: Yamaha Organs
Entries: 27 *Prize money*: £65 000
First prize: £12 000

In the interests of sharper competition, the event was re-vamped so that it proceeded by means of three-man groups with a three way final. Steve Davis won the title for the third time in four years but veteran John Dunning, 56, and Dave Martin excelled themselves by qualifying for the final day's play.

Semi-finals:

Group 1: W. King beat J. Dunning 2–1; Dunning beat T. Griffiths 2–0; Griffiths beat King 2–1.

Group 2: E. Charlton beat R. Reardon 2–0; D. Martin beat Reardon 2–0; Martin beat Charlton 2–1.

Group 3: S. Davis beat W. Thorne 2–1; Thorne beat D. French 2–0; Davis beat French 2–0.

Final: Martin beat Dunning 3–2; Davis beat Dunning 4–1; Davis beat Martin 3–0.

1984
BENSON AND HEDGES IRISH MASTERS

Sponsor: Benson and Hedges
Entries: (invited) 12
Prize money: IR£45 000
First prize: IR£15 000

Steve Davis swamped Terry Griffiths 9–1 in the final but was held to 4–4 before beating Alex Higgins 6–4 in the semi and was taken to a ninth frame decider by Tony Meo in the quarters.

First round: T. Griffiths beat B. Werbeniuk 5–2; Dennis Taylor beat E. Hughes 5–1; T. Meo beat J. White 5–4; A. Higgins beat E. Charlton 5–2.

Quarter-finals: Taylor beat C. Thorburn 5–2; Griffiths beat T. Knowles 5–0; Higgins beat R. Reardon 5–2; S. Davis beat Meo 5–4.

Semi-finals: Griffiths beat Taylor 6–5; Davis beat Higgins 6–4.

Final: Davis beat Griffiths 9–1.

1984
EMBASSY WORLD CHAMPIONSHIP
Sponsor: W. D. and H. O. Wills
Entries: 84
Prize money: £200 000
First prize: £44 000

Steve Davis became the first champion to make a successful title defence at the Crucible by beating Jimmy White 18–16 in what became a marvellous final as White recovered from his 4–12 overnight arrears to trail by only one frame at 15–16.

The first round brought a notable 10–9 victory for Neal Foulds over Alex Higgins and John Parrott eliminated Tony Knowles 10–7, Knowles perhaps contributing to his own demise by involving himself in a tawdry three part series of sexual reminiscences in The Sun which led to him being fined £5000 by the WPBSA for bringing the game into disrepute.

Parrott also pressed Dennis Taylor to a 13–11 scoreline in the second round after being five down with six to play as the Irishman continued his progress towards his fourth world semi-final.

Taylor's progress was halted by Davis, not quite with a session to spare but by a comfortable enough margin to give the champion time to prepare himself mentally for the final the following day.

This proved to be important since that evening Jimmy White had to overcome a 10–12 deficit going into the final session before he beat Kirk Stevens 16–14.

Snooker proved to be the factor which enabled BBC to claim a bigger audience share than ITV over the 17 day spread at the event. At peak time figures were generally between 5.5 million and 6.1 million and rose during the final itself to 12.8 million and 13.1 million for the last two 15 minute segments of the match.

Group 1: J. Parrott beat D. Hughes 10–3; Parrott beat C. Everton 10–2; Parrott beat P. Mans 10–0.

Group 2: B. Mikkelsen beat P. Medati 10–8; Mikkelsen beat F. Jonik 10–9; W. Thorne beat Mikkelsen 10–3.

Group 3: M. Morra beat G. Foulds 10–2; T. Murphy beat J. Fitzmaurice 10–8; Morra beat Murphy 10–5; Morra beat D. Reynolds 10–7.

Group 4: W. Sanderson beat P. Morgan 10–8; P. Mifsud beat E. Hughes 10–5; Mifsud beat Sanderson 10–5; Mifsud beat C. Wilson 10–8.

Group 5: J. Van Rensberg beat V. Harris 10–7; R. Edmonds beat D. Greaves 10–0; Van Rensberg beat Edmonds 10–9; S. Francisco beat Van Rensberg 10–3.

Group 6: I. Williamson beat P.Houlihan 10–5; M. Hines beat I. Black 10–5; Williamson beat Hines 10–6; G. Miles beat Williamson 10–6.

Group 7: M. Gibson beat G. Rigitano 10–7; M. Fisher beat P. Thornley 10–8; Gibson beat Fisher 10–7; J. Johnson beat Gibson 10–3.

Group 8: E. McLaughlin beat J. Hargreaves 10–5; R. Andrewartha w.o. J. Bear scr.; Andrewartha beat McLaughlin 10–8; Andrewartha beat M. Wildman 10–9.

Group 9: J. Wych beat G. Ganim jr. 10–1; G. Scott beat L. Heywood 10–7; Wych beat Scott 10–6; Wych beat P. Fagan 10–3.

Group 10: P. Browne beat S. Duggan 10–9; C. Roscoe beat B. Demarco 10–7; Browne beat Roscoe 10–4; E. Sinclair beat Browne 10–1.

Group 11: M. Gauvreau beat J. Campbell 10–7; G. Cripsey beat M. Parkin 10–4; Gauvreau beat Cripsey 10–1; Gauvreau beat M. Macleod 10–6.

Group 12: I. Anderson beat G. Watson 10–4; J. Donnelly beat P. Watchorn 10–7; Donnelly beat Anderson 10–6; F. Davis beat Donnelly 10–5.

Group 13: W. King beat T. Jones 10–9; M. Watterson beat B. Bennett 10–5; King beat Watterson 10–8; King beat D. Martin 10–8.

Group 14: J. Caggianello beat M. Darrington 10–7; B. Oliver beat J. Dunning 10–3; Oliver beat Caggianello 10–7; R. Williams beat Oliver 10–8.

Group 15: N. Foulds beat D. French 10–5; L. Dodd beat J. Giannaros 10–1; Foulds beat Dodd 10–4; Foulds beat J. Meadowcroft 10–2.

Group 16: B. Harris beat D. Sheehan 10–3; P. Burke beat B. Kelly 10–7; Burke beat Harris 10–4; M. Hallett beat Burke 10–5.

First round: S. Davis beat King 10–3; J. Spencer beat Miles 10–3; T. Griffiths beat Mifsud 10–2; B. Werbeniuk beat F. Davis 10–4; N. Foulds beat A. Higgins 10–9; D. Mountjoy beat Hallett 10–4; Dennis Taylor beat Johnson 10–1; Parrott beat T. Knowles 10–7; C. Thorburn beat Morra 10–3; W. Thorne beat J. Virgo 10–9; J. White beat Williams 10–6; E. Charlton beat Andrewartha 10–4; K. Stevens beat E. Sinclair 10–1; David Taylor beat Gauvreau 10–5; S. Francisco beat T. Meo 10–5; R. Reardon beat Wych 10–7.

Second round: Davis beat Spencer 13–5; Griffiths beat Werbeniuk 13–5; Mountjoy beat Foulds 13–6; Dennis Taylor beat Parrott 13–11; Thorburn beat Thorne 13–11; White beat Charlton 12–7; Stevens beat David Taylor 13–10; Reardon beat Francisco 13–8.

Quarter-finals: Davis beat Griffiths 13–10; Dennis Taylor beat Mountjoy 13–8; White beat Thorburn 13–8; Stevens beat Reardon 13–2.

Semi-finals: Davis beat Dennis Taylor 16–9; White beat Stevens 16–14.

Final: Davis beat White 18–16.

1984
WINFIELD AUSTRALIAN MASTERS

Tony Knowles made up in part for his Embassy World Championship disappointment by taking the Winfield Australian Masters in Channel 10's 300 seat auditorium in Sydney. Each day's play was televised nationally for two hours from 10.40 p.m. as the attempt to strengthen the tripartite relationship

David Taylor

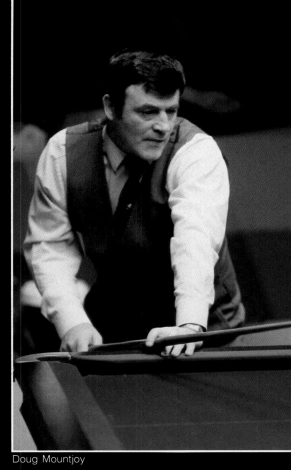

Doug Mountjoy

Eugene Hughes *left*, Alex Higgins and Dennis Taylor, Ireland's winning trio in the 1985 Guinness World Cup.

Dennis Taylor with the Embassy World Championship
Trophy in 1985.

Tony Meo about to play a shot in his 1984 Lada Classic
final against Steve Davis.

Silvino Francisco with his trophy for the 1985 Dulux British

Steve Davis in play against Alex Higgins in their 1983 Cora

Jimmy White plays a length of the table shot in his 1982 Embassy World Championship semi-final against Alex Higgins.

between game, sponsor and television continued.

First round: W. Thorne beat C. Thorburn 4–1; J. Virgo beat D. Mountjoy 4–1; T. Meo beat B. Werbeniuk 4–0; K. Stevens beat P. Morgan 4–2; E. Charlton beat W. King 4–1; David Taylor beat I. Anderson 4–2; J. White beat J. Campbell 4–0; T. Knowles beat Dennis Taylor 4–2.

Quarter-finals: Virgo beat Thorne 5–3; Charlton beat Taylor 5–4; Meo beat Stevens 5–1; Knowles beat White 5–3.

Semi-finals: Virgo beat Meo 6–2; Knowles beat Charlton 6–0.

Final: Knowles beat Virgo 7–3.

1984
LANGS SCOTTISH MASTERS
Sponsor: Langs *Entries*: (invited) 8
Prize money: £28 500
First prize: £10 000

Steve Davis won the event for the third year in succession by easily beating Jimmy White in the final, having been 2–4 down before beating Alex Higgins 6–4 in the semi.

First round: T. Knowles beat T. Griffiths 5–3; J. White beat M. Macleod 5–0; S. Davis beat C. Thorburn 5–2; A. Higgins beat K. Stevens 5–2.

Semi-finals: White beat Knowles 6–5; Davis beat Higgins 6–4.

Final: Davis beat White 9–4.

1984
CARLSBERG TROPHY

Jimmy White's 9–7 victory over Tony Knowles in the final of this new four-man event was of lesser significance than R.T.E's viewing figures. The event attracted an accumulative audience of 2.45 million, a very high figure for a country whose population is only 4 million.

Semi-finals: T. Knowles beat A. Higgins 5–3; J. White beat K. Stevens 5–0.

Final: White beat Knowles 9–7.

1984
COSTA DEL SOL CLASSIC

Dennis Taylor's first prize of £600 was comparatively insignificant but the overall success of the tournament far exceeded the expectations of Snooker Espana, the Stockport-based company which is developing the game in Spain.

Spain's first two snooker centres at Fuengirola and Torremolinos each staged first round matches while the quarter-finals onwards were played, largely to audiences of British holidaymakers and expatriates, in the 380 capacity ballroom of the Las Palmeras Hotel, Fuengirola.

First round: M. Fisher beat E. Hughes 3–2; M. Macleod beat W. King 3–2; E. Sinclair beat T. Drago 3–1; M. Hallett beat B. Oliver 3–0.

Quarter-finals: M. Wildman beat Sinclair 3–2; Dennis Taylor beat Macleod 3–1; J. Johnson beat Fisher 3–1; Hallett beat T. Knowles 3–0.

Semi-finals: Hallett beat Wildman 3–0; Taylor beat Johnson 3–2.

Final: Taylor beat Hallett 5–2.

1984
JAMESON INTERNATIONAL
Sponsor: Irish Distillers *Entries*: 101
Prize money: £150 000
First prize: £30 000

Steve Davis dropped only seven frames in four matches in winning the title for the third time in four years at Eldon Square Recreation Centre, Newcastle.

Both Silvino Francisco and Eugene Hughes reached a major semi-final for the first time, though Francisco did so in tragic circumstances as his scheduled opponent, Dennis Taylor, withdrew owing to the unexpected death of his mother.

Tony Knowles, though making no impact against Davis in the final, was responsible for much of the drama in the early rounds, beating both Steve Newbury and Jimmy White 5–4 before coming from 2–4 to beat Francisco 9–6 in the semi.

Qualifying:

Group A: G. Foulds beat P. Francisco 5–4; I. Williamson beat V. Harris 5–0; Foulds beat Williamson 5–4; Foulds beat J. Donnelly 5–3; J. Campbell beat Foulds 5–3.

Group B: W. Jones beat P. Watchorn 5–0; M. Gibson beat P. Medati 5–3; Jones beat Gibson 5–2; Jones beat G. Scott 5–0; Jones beat M. Wildman 5–0.

Group C: T. Jones beat D. French 5–1; S. Duggan beat Jones 5–2; E. Sinclair beat Duggan 5–0; Sinclair beat P. Mans 5–2.

Group D: B. Bennett beat B. Demarco 5–1; Bennett w.o. P. Morgan scr.; Bennett w.o. J. Wych scr.; N. Foulds beat Bennett 5–0.

Group E: R. Foldvari beat G. Rigitano 5–2; Foldvari beat R. Edmonds 5–1; L. Dodd beat Foldvari 5–3; Dodd beat C. Wilson 5–1.

Group F: B. Mikkelsen beat T. Chappel 5–4; Mikkelsen beat C. Everton 5–0; C. Roscoe beat Mikkelsen 5–1; E. Hughes beat Roscoe 5–1.

Group G: D. O'Kane beat M. Parkin 5–2; O'Kane beat E. McLaughlin 5–1; O'Kane beat J. Fitzmaurice 5–4; O'Kane beat M. Hallett 5–4.

Group H: J. McLaughlin beat D. Greaves 5–3; F. Jonik beat McLaughlin 5–2; M. Gauvreau beat Jonik 5–1; Gauvreau beat J. Parrott 5–0.

Group I: G. Cripsey beat P. Thornley 5–3; J. Dunning beat Cripsey 5–3; F. Davis beat Dunning; J. Virgo beat Davis 5–3.

Group J: J. Hargreaves beat P. Houlihan 5–2; B. Kelly beat Hargreaves 5–2; Kelly beat W. King 5–4; S. Francisco beat Kelly 5–3.

Group K: D. Fowler beat R. Chaperon 5–0; Fowler w.o. P. Mifsud scr.; Fowler beat R. Andrewartha 5–0; Fowler beat D. Martin 5–0.

Group L: M. Bradley beat M. Darrington 5–3; Bradley beat J. Rea 5–2; M. Morra beat Bradley 5–3; J. Johnson beat Morra 5–0.

Group M: D. Chalmers w.o. L. Condo scr.; B. Oliver beat D. Hughes 5–4; Chalmers beat Oliver 5–4; J. Meadowcroft beat Chalmers 5–1; R. Williams beat Meadowcroft 5–4.

Group N: P. Browne beat J. Rea 5–2; I. Black beat Browne 5–4; Black beat M. Watterson 5–3; M. Macleod beat Black 5–3.

Group O: S. Newbury beat S. Longworth 5–4; P. Burke beat T. Kearney 5–4; Newbury beat Burke 5–0; Newbury beat P. Fagan 5–0; Newbury beat G. Miles 5–4.

Group P: R. Bales beat D. Sheehan 5–2; Bales beat T. Murphy 5–4; Bales beat M. Fisher 5–3; D. Reynolds beat Bales 5–4.

First round: David Taylor beat W. Jones 5–4; E. Hughes beat D. Mountjoy 5–1; Newbury beat B. Werbeniuk 5–2; Gauvreau beat K. Stevens 5–1; Johnson beat E. Charlton 5–1; J. White beat Williams 5–3; T. Knowles beat

Reynolds 5–1; S. Francisco beat J. Spencer 5–2; W. Thorne beat O'Kane 5–3; A. Higgins beat Sinclair 5–1; R. Reardon beat Dodd 5–4; Dennis Taylor beat Fowler 5–0; T. Meo beat Macleod 5–1; Virgo beat C. Thorburn 5–0; S. Davis beat Campbell 5–1; T. Griffiths beat N. Foulds 5–3.

Second round: Davis beat David Taylor 5–1; Higgins beat Griffiths 5–4; Hughes beat Reardon 5–1; Thorne beat Gauvreau 5–3; Francisco beat Virgo 5–2; White beat Meo 5–1; Dennis Taylor beat Johnson 5–2; Knowles beat Newbury 5–4.

Quarter-finals: Davis beat Higgins 5–1; Hughes beat Thorne 5–2; Francisco w.o. Dennis Taylor scr.; Knowles beat White 5–4.

Semi-finals: Davis beat Hughes 9–3; Knowles beat Francisco 9–6.

Final: Davis beat Knowles 9–2.

1984
AUSTRALIAN CHAMPIONSHIP

Eddie Charlton retained the Australian Professional Championship by comfortably beating Warren King in the final at Dubbo RSL Club. He first won the title in 1964 and only a defeat by the late Warren Simpson in 1968 spoils his 100 per cent record although it was the first time the championship had been held since 1978.

First round: R. Foldvari beat J. Charlton 6–1; G. Ganim beat I. Anderson 6–5; J. Giannaros beat L. Condo 6–2.

Quarter-finals: E. Charlton beat Foldvari 6–4; P. Morgan beat Ganim 6–4; W. King beat Giannaros 6–5; J. Campbell beat L. Heywood 6–2.

Semi-finals: Charlton beat Morgan 9–2; King beat Campbell 9–6.

Final: Charlton beat King 10–3.

1984
ROTHMANS GRAND PRIX
Sponsor: Rothmans *Entries*: 98
Prize money: £225 000
First prize: £45 000

Dennis Taylor's first major title in his 13 years as a professional gave the snooker world one of its most emotional moments, all the more so as his success came only three weeks after the death of his mother.

Wins over Ray Reardon and Kirk Stevens were followed by a semi-final drubbing of Neal Foulds, who appeared psychologically spent from

the effort of reaching his first major semi-final with wins over Willie Thorne and Tony Knowles.

The match of the tournament was Cliff Thorburn's 9–7 semi-final victory over Steve Davis after the world champion had led 7–6 but the Canadian appeared so exhausted by this performance that he could offer little resistance in the final the following day as Taylor, playing like a man possessed, reeled off the last eight frames in succession for the 10–2 victory which gave him what was then snooker's record first prize of £45 000.

Qualifying:

I. Williamson beat P. Thornley 5–2; J. Donnelly beat J. Hargreaves 5–4; B. Demarco w.o. P. Fagan scr.; V. Harris beat F. Davis 5–1; J. Dunning beat D. Hughes 5–0; D. O'Kane beat B. Kelly 5–4; M. Gauvreau beat R. Foldvari 5–2; E. McLaughlin beat S. Longworth 5–2; M. Morra beat G. Cripsey 5–3; S. Duggan beat P. Browne 5–2; D. Sheehan w.o. L. Condo scr.; Sheehan beat B. Mikkelsen 5–3; P. Burke beat M. Darrington 5–3; D. Chalmers beat R. Andrewartha 5–2; W. King beat D. Greaves 5–0; P. Medati beat L. Dodd 5–4; R. Chaperon beat T. Kearney 5–1; Chaperon beat M. Gibson 5–4; P. Francisco beat I. Black 5–4; G. Rigitano beat R. Edmonds 5–3; M. Bradley beat F. Jonik 5–1; W. Jones beat M. Watterson 5–3; J. Rea beat J. Fitzmaurice 5–2; R. Bales w.o. J. Wych scr.; S. Newbury beat M. Fisher 5–0; B. Oliver beat B. Bennett 5–3; C. Everton beat P. Houlihan 5–3; J. McLaughlin beat J. Meadowcroft 5–1; T. Chappel beat G. Scott 5–1; T. Murphy beat G. Foulds 5–1; T. Jones beat E. Sinclair 5–4; C. Roscoe beat D. French 5–0; P. Watchorn w.o. P. Morgan scr.; D. Fowler w.o. P. Mifsud scr.

First round: T. Knowles beat V. Harris 5–1; Dunning beat P. Mans 5–4; Williamson beat B. Werbeniuk 5–2; Johnson beat Medati 5–1; W. Thorne beat Newbury 5–2; M. Macleod beat King 5–4; N. Foulds beat Demarco 5–2; T. Jones beat T. Griffiths 5–3; R. Reardon beat Roscoe 5–1; C. Wilson beat Donnelly 5–2; Dennis Taylor beat Watchorn 5–1; J. Virgo beat

Bradley 5–0; A. Higgins beat Bales 5–1; M. Hallett beat Sheehan 5–1; R. Williams beat Chalmers 5–0; K. Stevens beat T. Chappel 5–3; C. Thorburn beat Rigitano 5–4; J. Campbell beat W. Jones 5–4; T. Meo beat Burke 5–1; D. Martin beat Chaperon 5–4; D. Mountjoy beat E. McLaughlin 5–4; M. Wildman beat J. McLaughlin 5–3; J. Parrott beat Gauvreau 5–3; E. Charlton beat Everton 5–1; J. White beat Oliver 5–1; S. Francisco beat Duggan 5–3; P. Francisco beat J. Spencer 5–2; D. Reynolds beat Fowler 5–2; David Taylor beat O'Kane 5–1; J. Rea beat E. Hughes 5–4; G. Miles beat Murphy 5–3; S. Davis beat Morra 5–2.

Second round: Knowles beat Dunning 5–1; Williamson beat Johnson 5–4; Thorne beat Macleod 5–3; N. Foulds beat T. Jones 5–0; Reardon beat Wilson 5–4; Dennis Taylor beat Virgo 5–3; Hallett beat Higgins 5–3; Stevens beat Williams 5–3; Thorburn beat Campbell 5–1; Meo beat Martin 5–4; Mountjoy beat Wildman 5–0; Charlton beat Parrott 5–1; S. Francisco beat White 5–1; David Taylor beat Rea 5–1; S. Davis beat Miles 5–0; Reynolds beat P. Francisco 5–4.

Third round: Knowles beat Williamson 5–2; N. Foulds beat Thorne 5–1; Dennis Taylor beat Reardon 5–3; Stevens beat Hallett 5–3; Thorburn beat Meo 5–4; Mountjoy beat Charlton 5–4; Reynolds beat S. Francisco 5–1; S. Davis beat David Taylor 5–1.

Quarter-finals: N. Foulds beat Knowles 5–2; Dennis Taylor beat Stevens 5–2; Thorburn beat Mountjoy 5–3; S. Davis beat Reynolds 5–0.

Semi-finals: Dennis Taylor beat N. Foulds 9–3; Thorburn beat S. Davis 9–7.

Final: Dennis Taylor beat Thorburn 10–2.

1984
CORAL UK OPEN
Sponsor: Coral Racing *Entries*: 94
Prize money: £100 000
First prize: £20 000

Steve Davis won the title for the third time in five years but had to hold off a recovery from Alex Higgins in which the Irishman narrowed the gap in the final from

2–8 to 8–9 before the world champion pulled away to win 16–8.

Davis's closest match was in the second round when Tony Meo led him 7–4 and by 25 points with one red remaining in the twelfth.

Meo refused a long straight red which would have given him a simple chance to clinch 8–4 and from the indifferent safety shot he played instead gave Davis the initiative. Davis won the frame on the black, cleared the table with 134, the highest break of the tournament, in the next, and completed a five frame winning streak to win 9–7.

There was another notable recovery in the quarter-finals when Cliff Thorburn beat Ray Reardon 9–8 after trailing by four frames with five to play but Thorburn's progress was halted by Alex Higgins 9–7 in the semi.

This match turned when Thorburn, having snookered himself, nominated green. The referee did not hear him and called a foul. The Canadian appealed to Higgins for his support but the Irishman said that he had not heard him either.

Thorburn was leading 6–5 at the time but won only one further frame and afterwards admitted that his concentration had been broken by the incident.

Group 1: T. Jones beat R. Chaperon 9–1; Jones beat P. Fagan 9–2; Jones beat M. Wildman 9–2.

Group 2: P. Watchorn beat B. Harris 9–7; Watchorn beat C. Everton 9–6; M. Fisher beat Watchorn 9–5; R. Williams beat Fisher 9–8.

Group 3: R. Foldvari beat D. Greaves 9–5; G. Cripsey beat Foldvari 9–7; J. Fitzmaurice beat Cripsey 9–8; J. Parrott beat Fitzmaurice 9–6.

Group 4: P. Francisco beat D. Sheehan 9–5; P. Francisco beat I. Williamson 9–2; E. Sinclair beat P. Francisco 9–8; S. Francisco beat Sinclair 9–4.

Group 5: D. Fowler beat B. Demarco 9–3; Fowler beat B. Oliver 9–3; Fowler beat F. Davis 9–4; Fowler beat N. Foulds 9–6.

Group 6: D. O'Kane beat W. Jones 9–7; O'Kane beat S. Duggan 9–6; G. Scott beat O'Kane 9–7; M. Macleod beat Scott 9–5.

Group 7: S. Newbury beat G. Rigitano 9–6; Newbury beat

F. Jonik 9–3; L. Dodd beat Newbury 9–6; C. Wilson beat Dodd 9–8.

Group 8: J. McLaughlin beat D. French 9–3; McLaughin w.o. P. Morgan scr.; McLaughlin beat C. Roscoe 9–8; McLaughlin beat G. Miles 9–8.

Group 9: R. Bales beat D. Chalmers 9–2; Bales beat E. McLaughlin 9–4; M. Gauvreau beat Bales 9–8; Gauvreau beat P. Mans 9–6.

Group 10: G. Foulds beat D. Hughes 9–7; P. Browne beat Foulds 9–5; W. King beat Browne 9–5; King beat J. Virgo 9–4.

Group 11: J. Rea beat B. Bennett 9–5; Rea beat J. Dunning 9–3; Rea beat R. Edmonds 9–6; J. Johnson beat Rea 9–6.

Group 12: T. Chappel beat P. Houlihan 9–3; Chappel beat I. Black 9–3; Chappel w.o. R. Andrewartha scr.; Chappel beat D. Reynolds 9–6.

Group 13: J. Hargreaves beat P. Medati 9–6; M. Gibson beat Hargreaves 9–8; J. Donnelly beat Gibson 9–6; J. Campbell beat Donnelly 9–6.

Group 14: M. Bradley beat V. Harris 9–8; Bradley beat B. Kelly 9–6; Bradley beat J. Meadowcroft 9–7; M. Hallett beat Bradley 9–8.

Group 15: S. Longworth beat M. Darrington 9–5; Longworth beat P. Burke 9–4; M. Morra beat Longworth 9–1; E. Hughes beat Morra 9–8.

Group 16: T. Murphy beat A. Kearney 9–2; Murphy beat M. Watterson 9–4; Murphy beat D. Martin 9–8.

First round: A. Higgins beat T. Jones 9–7; S. Davis beat T. Murphy 9–1; J. White beat J. Campbell 9–7; R. Williams beat B. Werbeniuk 9–1; W. Thorne beat J. Parrott 9–7; E. Charlton beat S. Francisco 9–4; D. Mountjoy beat M. Hallett 9–2; T. Meo beat E. Hughes 9–4; R. Reardon beat D. Fowler 9–2; K. Stevens beat T. Chappel 9–7; Dennis Taylor beat W. King 9–5; C. Wilson beat T. Griffiths 9–6; J. Johnson beat J. Spencer 9–6; David Taylor beat M. Macleod 9–6; T. Knowles beat M. Gauvreau 9–5; C. Thorburn beat J. McLaughlin 9–4.

Second round: Thorne beat Charlton 9–7; White beat Mountjoy 9–2; Higgins beat Williams 9–7;

Stevens beat Johnson 9–2; Reardon beat David Taylor 9–4; Knowles beat Dennis Taylor 9–2; Thorburn beat Wilson 9–3; S. Davis beat Meo 9–7.

Quarter-finals: Higgins beat Thorne 9–5; Davis beat White 9–4; Thorburn beat Reardon 9–8; Stevens beat Knowles 9–7.

Semi-finals: Higgins beat Thorburn 9–7; Davis beat Stevens 9–2.

Final: Davis beat Higgins 16–8.

1984
HOFMEISTER WORLD DOUBLES
Sponsor: Courage *Entries*: 45 pairs
Prize money: £150 000
First prize: £34 500

The new partnership of Alex Higgins and Jimmy White broke the Steve Davis/Tony Meo dominance with a 9–6 victory in the semi-finals after the holders had led 6–5. In the last three frames, Higgins made breaks of 75, 84 and 37 in sweeping his team to victory with a 32 break by Davis as the only score by the losers in this period.

Higgins and White comfortably disposed of another new partnership Cliff Thorburn and Willie Thorne in the final.

Qualifying: J. Donnelly and C. Roscoe beat S. Longworth and D. French 5–3; D. Chalmers and J. McLaughlin beat P. Fagan and B. Harris 5–0; M. Morra and M. Bradley beat I. Williamson and M. Darrington 5–1; G. Miles and P. Francisco beat J. Hargreaves and S. Duggan 5–1; T. Chappel and S. Newbury beat G. Rigitano and G. Scott 5–0; M. Gauvreau and D. Fowler beat B. Bennett and P. Houlihan 5–1; R. Bales and B. Oliver beat J. Rea and E. McLaughlin 5–2; J. Meadowcroft and R. Edmonds beat F. Jonik and R. Chaperon 5–4; V. Harris and J. Fitzmaurice beat P. Burke and B. Kelly 5–2; D. Sheehan and P. Watchorn beat M. MacLeod and M. Gibson 5–0; M. Watterson and F. Davis beat C. Everton and R. Foldvari 5–3; P. Medati and P. Browne beat I. Black and E. Sinclair 5–1; D. Hughes and T. Kearney w.o. J. Dunning and B. Demarco scr.

First round: D. Mountjoy and W. Jones beat Chappel and Newbury 5–1; S. Francisco and T. Jones beat J. Campbell and W. King 5–4; A. Higgins and J. White beat D. Martin and

83

G. Cripsey 5–2; David Taylor and M. Hallett beat E. Hughes and L. Dodd 5–3; P. Francisco and Miles beat C. Wilson and J. Johnson 5–4; D. Reynolds and D. O'Kane beat Gauvreau and Fowler 5–4; Dennis Taylor and R. Williams beat Medati and Browne 5–0; Bales and Oliver beat Neal Foulds and Geoff Foulds 5–2; S. Davis and T. Meo beat D. Hughes and Kearney 5–2; R. Reardon and T. Murphy beat Watterson and F. Davis 5–2; M. Wildman and M. Fisher beat Edmonds and Meadowcroft 5–3; E. Charlton and B. Werbeniuk beat Sheehan and Watchorn 5–2; T. Griffiths and J. Parrott beat Chalmers and J. McLaughlin 5–0; J. Virgo and K. Stevens beat Donnelly and Roscoe 5–0; C. Thorburn and W. Thorne beat Morra and Bradley 5–1; T. Knowles and J. Spencer beat V. Harris and Fitzmaurice 5–2.

Second round: Davis and Meo beat Miles and Francisco 5–2; Virgo and Stevens beat Dennis Taylor and Williams 5–3; Higgins and White beat Reynolds and O'Kane 5–4; Thorburn and Thorne beat Mountjoy and Jones 5–3; Reardon and Murphy beat S. Francisco and Jones 5–3; Griffiths and Parrott beat Bales and Oliver 5–4; David Taylor and Hallett beat Charlton and Werbeniuk 5–4; Knowles and Spencer beat Fisher and Wildman 5–4.

Quarter-finals: Knowles and Spencer beat Reardon and Murphy 5–4; Higgins and White beat Griffiths and Parrott 5–2; Thorburn and Thorne beat Virgo and Stevens 5–3; Davis and Meo beat Hallett and David Taylor.

Semi-finals: Thorburn and Thorne beat Knowles and Spencer 9–1; Higgins and White beat Davis and Meo 9–6.

Final: Higgins and White beat Thorburn and Thorne 10–2.

1984
TOLLY COBBOLD ENGLISH CHAMPIONSHIP

Steve Davis retained the title he had won under the sponsorship of John Courage in 1980 when the championship was revived at the Corn Exchange, Ipswich with the aid of a transferred sponsorship and television slot from the Tolly Cobbold Classic.

Davis had to make breaks of 75 and 107 in the last two frames to beat Tony Meo 9–8 in the semi-final before disposing of Tony Knowles 9–2 in the final.

Qualifying: D. Fowler beat B. Oliver 9–7; M. Bradley beat I. Williamson 9–8; T. Jones beat P. Houlihan 9–1; L. Dodd beat R. Bales 9–5; J. Fitzmaurice beat D. Greaves 9–3; M. Fisher beat D. French 9–8; S. Duggan beat B. Harris 9–8; D. Hughes beat M. Watterson 9–5; D. Chalmers beat J. Meadowcroft 9–3; S. Longworth beat R. Edmonds 9–4; P. Medati beat J. Hargreaves 9–8; G. Foulds beat F. Davis 9–2; G. Cripsey beat B. Bennett 9–0; G. Scott beat V. Harris 9–7.

First round: Longworth beat M. Wildman 9–3; J. White beat Chalmers 9–5; Medati beat J. Spencer 9–4; N. Foulds beat Hughes 9–3; David Taylor beat Cripsey 9–5; J. Parrott beat G. Foulds 9–4; D. Martin beat G. Miles 9–7; T. Knowles beat Bradley 9–8; S. Davis beat Fowler 9–3; M. Hallett beat Duggan 9–4; J. Johnson beat Scott 9–1; T. Meo beat Fisher 9–3; J. Virgo beat M. Darrington 9–0; D. Reynolds beat Fitzmaurice 9–2; R. Williams beat Jones 9–6; W. Thorne beat Dodd 9–1.

Second round: Virgo beat Johnson 9–4; Reynolds beat Thorne 9–6; Davis beat Williams 9–2; Meo beat Hallett 9–4; Knowles beat Martin 9–3; David Taylor beat Parrott 9–7; White beat N. Foulds 9–7; Longworth beat Medati 9–7.

Quarter-finals: Meo beat Reynolds 9–4; Longworth beat White 9–5; Knowles beat Taylor 9–2; Davis beat Virgo.

Semi-finals: Knowles beat Longworth 9–6; Davis beat Meo 9–8.

Final: Davis beat Knowles 9–2.

1985
MERCANTILE CREDIT CLASSIC
Sponsor: Mercantile Credit
Entries: 94 *Prize money*: £200 000
First prize: £40 000

This new sponsor, taking over the slot previously occupied by the Lada Classic, provided Willie Thorne with his first major first prize, the key to which was his 9–8 semi-final victory over Steve Davis.

Thorne's 13–8 final victory over Cliff Thorburn was achieved through winning five frames in succession

from 8–8 but it was the middle session which provided one of the very best ever seen on the circuit, producing three centuries, 105 and 118 by Thorne and 100 by Thorburn, two more fine displays of break building and three close finishes in its eight frames, in one of which Thorne snatched an 8–6 lead after needing two snookers.

Preliminary round: P. Watchorn beat D. Hughes 5–0; B. Mikkelsen beat D. Chalmers 5–1.

Qualifying round A: T. Jones beat D. Greaves 5–2; J. Giannaros beat T. Chappel 5–2; S. Newbury beat V. Harris 5–3; G. Foulds beat R. Chaperon 5–3; D. Sheehan beat J. Rea 5–2; R. Bales beat B. Bennett 5–1; R. Foldvari beat P. Houlihan 5–1; P. Medati beat G. Cripsey 5–4; J. McLaughlin beat B. Demarco 5–1; S. Longworth beat P. Francisco 5–4; T. Kearney beat D. French 5–1; P. Browne beat M. Bradley 5–3; W. Jones beat D. O'Kane 5–0; D. Fowler beat G. Rigitano 5–0; J. Hargreaves beat M. Darrington 5–2.

Qualifying round B: T. Jones beat M. Gibson 5–0; Newbury beat P. Burke 5–1; G. Foulds beat F. Jonik 5–2; E. McLaughlin beat Sheehan 5–2; Bales beat B. Kelly 5–3; Foldvari beat Rea 5–4; J. McLaughlin beat I. Black 5–0; Longworth beat B. Oliver 5–1; Watchorn beat Mikkelsen 5–1; I. Williamson beat Kearney 5–3; Browne beat C. Everton 5–0; S. Duggan beat W. Jones 5–0; Fowler beat T. Murphy 5–0; R. Edmonds beat Hargreaves 5–2.

Qualifying round C: T. Jones beat L. Dodd 5–1; M. Gauvreau beat Giannaros 5–3; Newbury beat M. Morra 5–2; G. Foulds beat J. Fitzmaurice 5–1; E. McLaughlin beat F. Davis 5–1; Medati beat C. Roscoe 5–4; G. Scott beat J. McLaughlin 5–4; Longworth beat M. Fisher 5–1; J. Donnelly beat Watchorn 5–1; P. Fagan beat Williamson 5–1; W. King beat Duggan 5–4; Fowler beat J. Meadowcroft 5–2; Edmonds beat M. Watterson 5–2.

Qualifying round D: S. Francisco beat T. Jones 5–1; Fagan beat M. Wildman 5–3; M. Hallett beat F. Goulds 5–4; M. Macleod beat E. McLaughlin 5–4; Medati beat

Willie Thorne with his first major trophy, the Mercantile Credit Classic

J. Parrott 5–3; C. Wilson beat Fowler 5–4; Gauvreau beat E. Sinclair 5–1; J. Johnson beat Edmonds 5–4; Scott beat J. Campbell 5–4; E. Hughes beat Newbury 5–3; King beat D. Reynolds 5–2; R. Williams beat Donnelly 5–3; J. Virgo beat Bales 5–1; Longworth beat N. Foulds 5–3; Foldvari beat D. Martin 5–2; Browne beat G. Miles 5–3.

Round 1: Longworth beat D. Taylor 5–4; Johnson beat T. Knowles 5–1; C. Thorburn beat Scott 5–1; King beat J. Spencer 5–2; T. Griffiths beat Fagan 5–0; J. White beat Browne 5–2; E. Hughes beat T. Meo 5–4; Macleod beat E. Charlton 5–1; A. Higgins beat Gauvreau 5–3; Virgo beat B. Werbeniuk 5–2; Wilson beat D. Mountjoy 5–4; Williams beat Dennis Taylor 5–3; R. Reardon beat Hallett 5–3; S. Davis beat Francisco 5–0; W. Thorne beat Foldvari 5–2; K. Stevens beat Medati 5–4.

Round 2: Reardon beat E. Hughes 5–1; S. Davis beat Higgins 5–2; Virgo beat Macleod 5–0; Thorne beat Stevens 5–1; Thorburn beat Longworth 5–3; Griffiths beat Williams 5–3; Johnson beat Wilson 5–0; King beat White 5–2.

Quarter-finals: S. Davis beat Reardon 5–1; Thorburn beat Griffiths 5–4; Johnson beat King 5–3; Thorne beat Virgo 5–1.

Semi-finals: Thorne beat S. Davis 9–8; Thorburn beat Johnson 9–2.

Final: Thorne beat Thorburn 13–8.

1985
BENSON AND HEDGES MASTERS
Sponsor: Gallaher
Entries: (invited) 16
Prize money: £150 000
First prize: £37 500

Cliff Thorburn won the tournament for the second time in three years by beating Doug Mountjoy 9–6 in the final but it was his 6–4 semi-final win over Jimmy White after the defending title holder had led 3–0 which was the key to his success.

Alex Higgins scored a 5–4 first round win over Steve Davis whose merit was obscured by the behaviour of a section of his supporters but he was unable to recapture the same inspiration in his 5–1 defeat by Terry Griffiths who in turn petered out 6–2 the following day against Mountjoy.

Curiously, the 103 which gave Thorburn the highest break prize was compiled in the very first frame in the tournament.

First round: C. Thorburn beat Dennis Taylor 5–3; D. Mountjoy beat T. Knowles 5–3; R. Reardon beat David Taylor 5–1; J. White beat W. Thorne 5–2; J. Spencer beat E. Charlton 5–3; T. Meo beat K. Stevens 5–2; T. Griffiths beat B. Werbeniuk 5–2; A. Higgins beat S. Davis 5–4.

Quarter-finals: Thorburn beat Reardon 5–0; White beat Spencer 5–2; Mountjoy beat Meo 5–4; Griffiths beat Higgins 5–1.

Semi-finals: Mountjoy beat Griffiths 6–2; Thorburn beat White 6–4.

Final: Thorburn beat Mountjoy 9–6.

1985
DULUX BRITISH OPEN
Sponsor: ICI Paints Division
Entries: 92
Prize money: £250 000
First prize: £50 000

Like Dennis Taylor and Willie Thorne earlier in the season, Silvino Francisco won his first major first prize with a run of successes over Jimmy White, Tony Meo, Alex Higgins and Kirk Stevens.

His 12–9 final victory over Stevens provided the circuit with its first final involving no British player.

Stevens beat Steve Davis 9–7 in a gripping semi-final while the young New Zealander Dene O'Kane, in his first professional season, reached a major professional quarter-final for the first time.

The event carried world ranking points and replaced the Yamaha International Masters, which did not.

Qualifying: T. Chappel beat

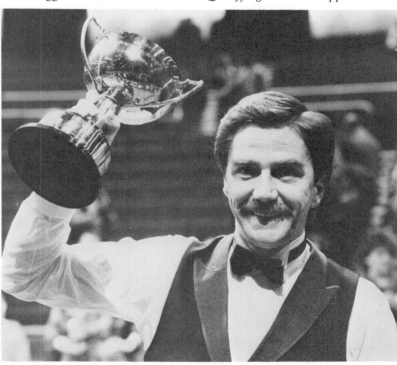

Cliff Thorburn secures the Benson and Hedges Masters trophy for the second time in 1985.

I. Williamson 6–5; D. Chalmers beat P. Burke 6–5; J. Rea beat M. Fisher 6–0; W. King beat P. Medati 6–4; D. Fowler beat C. Everton 6–1; T. Murphy beat D. Sheehan 6–3; R. Foldvari beat S. Duggan 6–4; V. Harris beat L. Dodd 6–1; T. Jones beat G. Foulds 6–0; P. Francisco beat B. Kelly 6–3; D. O'Kane beat G. Cripsey 6–4; S. Newbury beat P. Browne 6–0; M. Bradley beat M. Morra 6–2; T. Kearney beat M. Watterson 8–4; D. French beat E. McLaughlin 6–0; R. Chaperon beat P. Fagan 6–5; B. Harris beat J. Meadowcroft 6–1; S. Longworth beat F. Davis 6–1; B. Mikkelsen beat D. Hughes 6–0; G. Scott beat M. Darrington 6–3; J. Giannaros beat C. Roscoe 6–1; F. Jonik beat J. McLaughlin 6–2; W. Jones beat J. Donnelly 6–1; P. Watchorn beat J. Fitzmaurice 6–1; R. Bales beat I. Black 6–4; M. Gauvreau beat D. Greaves 6–3; M. Gibson beat B. Demarco 6–1; R. Edmonds beat D. Mienie 6–1.

First round: D. Reynolds beat Giannaros 6–3; M. Macleod beat Murphy 6–5; E. Hughes beat Watchorn 6–4; Longworth beat C. Wilson 6–3; W. Jones beat J. Johnson 6–5; M. Hallett w.o. Mikkelsen scr.; C. Thorburn beat G. Rigitano 6–3; A. Higgins beat Bales 6–3; Chaperon beat B. Werbeniuk 6–1; S. Francisco beat Kearney 6–4; T. Meo beat Foldvari 6–0; W. Thorne beat B. Oliver 6–3; B. Harris beat E. Charlton 6–3; J. White beat T. Jones 6–5; T. Knowles beat D. French 6–2; N. Foulds beat J. Hargreaves 6–1; Newbury beat E. Sinclair 6–3; M. Wildman beat Gibson 6–1; J. Spencer beat Jonik 6–0; Harris beat D. Mountjoy 6–5; D. O'Kane beat J. Campbell 6–4; G. Miles beat Edmonds 6–1; T. Griffiths beat Chalmers 6–0; R. Reardon beat King 6–5; J. Parrott beat Rea 6–4; Bradley beat David Taylor 6–3; K. Stevens beat Gauvreau 6–3; J. Virgo beat P. Francisco 6–2; Fowler beat R. Williams 6–4; D. Martin beat B. Bennett 6–0; S. Davis beat T. Chappel 6–5; Dennis Taylor beat G. Scott 6–2.

Second round: Newbury beat Griffiths 5–3; Bradley beat Fowler 5–4; S. Davis beat Virgo 5–2; Knowles beat Longworth 5–2;

O'Kane beat V. Harris 5–3; Thorburn beat Reynolds 5–3; Higgins beat N. Foulds 5–1; Dennis Taylor beat Parrott 5–2; Macleod beat Thorne 5–0; Martin beat Reardon 5–4; Miles beat Spencer 5–3; S. Francisco beat White 5–4; Meo beat Hallett 5–4; E. Hughes beat B. Harris 5–4; Stevens beat Wildman 5–2; Chaperon beat W. Jones 5–2.

Third round: Meo beat Knowles 5–2; S. Davis beat Bradley 5–2; O'Kane beat Martin 5–4; S. Francisco beat Chaperon 5–2; Dennis Taylor beat Newbury 5–3; E. Hughes beat Macleod 5–2; Stevens beat Miles 5–2; Higgins beat Thorburn 5–2.

Quarter-finals: Stevens beat Dennis Taylor 5–2; S. Davis beat O'Kane 5–1; S. Francisco beat Meo 5–4; Higgins beat E. Hughes 5–2.

Semi-finals: Stevens beat S. Davis 9–7; S. Francisco beat Higgins 9–6.

Final: S. Francisco beat Stevens 12–9.

1985
GUINNESS WORLD CUP
Sponsor: Guinness
Entries: 8 teams
Prize money: £125 000
First Prize: £40 000

Ireland, controversially amalgamated as one team in contrast to the established practice of entering separate trios from Northern Ireland and the Republic of Ireland, deposed England, the reigning champions, 9–7, in an exciting final at a new venue, Bournemouth International Centre. Alex Higgins was the hero, winning five of his six frames including the last four of the match, though Dennis Taylor and Eugene Hughes also made timely contributions.

First round: Wales beat Australia 5–4; England beat Scotland 5–4; England B beat Rest of the World 5–2; Ireland beat Canada 5–2.

Semi-finals: Ireland beat Wales 5–3; England A beat England B 5–2.

Final: Ireland beat England A 9–7.

1985
BENSON AND HEDGES IRISH MASTERS
Sponsor: Gallaher
Entries: (invited) 12
Prize money: IR£80 000
First prize: IR£20 000

Jimmy White recovered from 1–4 in the semi-finals to beat Tony Knowles

6–4 and from 4–4 beat Alex Higgins 9–5 to win his only individual first prize of the season. Higgins had scored his fourth win over Steve Davis in the semi-finals, their seventeenth meeting in a major event, after Davis had been taken the full distance in the quarter-finals by Eugene Hughes.

First round: E. Charlton beat Dennis Taylor 5–4; J. White beat T. Meo 5–1; E. Hughes beat R. Reardon 5–0; A. Higgins beat T. Griffiths 5–2.

Quarter-finals: A. Knowles beat Charlton 5–3; White beat C. Thorburn 5–3; S. Davis beat Hughes 5–4; Higgins beat K. Stevens 5–3.

Semi-finals: White beat Knowles 6–4; Higgins beat Davis 6–2.

Final: White beat Higgins 9–5.

1985
STRONGBOW IRISH PROFESSIONAL CHAMPIONSHIP

Dennis Taylor regained the title which he had lost to Alex Higgins in 1983 the last time the event had been staged, by defeating the holder in the final at the Ulster Hall, Belfast. Taylor, who earned £7500, had earlier survived a 6–5 finish against Eugene Hughes in the semi-finals after Hughes, leading 5–3, had needed to pot only a simple yellow to qualify for the final.

Qualifying round: J. McLaughlin beat D. Sheehan 6–3.

First round: J. Rea beat McLaughlin 6–5; B. Kelly beat P. Watchorn 6–2; T. Murphy beat P. Browne 5–3; P. Burke beat A. Kearney 6–4.

Quarter-finals: P. Fagan beat Murphy 6–2; Dennis Taylor beat Rea 6–0; E. Hughes beat Kelly 6–2; A. Higgins beat Burke 6–0.

Semi-finals: Taylor beat Hughes 6–5; Higgins beat Fagan 6–3.

Final: Taylor beat Higgins 10–5.

1985
EMBASSY WORLD PROFESSIONAL SNOOKER CHAMPIONSHIP
Sponsor: W. D. and H. O. Wills
Entries: 103
Prize money: £300 000
First prize: £60 000

Dennis Taylor made an amazing recovery from 0–8 to beat Steve Davis on the final black, 18–17, to win the game's richest ever first price – £60 000.

The final frame alone lasted 68 minutes and the match as a whole provided a bewildering kaleidoscope of skill, fortitude, heart, nerve, fear, will and courage.

Taylor, who had begun his recovery by drawing up to 7–9 by the close of the first day's play, had won all his matches prior to the final by wide margins.

Even so, after Neal Foulds had given him a tough battle in the first round, Davis was a strong favourite to win the title for the fourth time in five years before the quality of Taylor's resistance and the inward pressures he was feeling caused him to falter at the very last.

Bill Werbeniuk's break of 143 in the first round ranked third equal with Willie Thorne's 1982 effort in the list of championship bests, and below only Doug Mountjoy's 145 in 1982 and Cliff Thorburn's 147 in 1983.

Considerable publicity was attracted by the WPBSA decision, in line with Sports Council recommendation, to introduce compulsory drug testing for all competitors.

Qualifying:
Round 1: G. Rigitano beat D. Sheehan 10–9; D. O'Kane w.o. J. McLaughlin scr; S. Longworth beat J. Giannaros 10–1; R. Chaperon beat R. Bales 10–7; D. Hughes beat D. French 10–5; M. Hines beat T. Chappel 10–8; D. Fowler beat J. Hargreaves 10–0.

Round 2: Rigitano beat B. Harris 10–4; O'Kane beat V. Harris 10–5; Longworth beat G. Cripsey 10–8; Chaperon beat L. Heywood 10–1; S. Newbury beat M. Hughes 10–9; Hines beat P. Watchorn 10–4; Fowler w.o. G. Watson scr; D. Chalmers beat D. Greaves 10–3; G. Foulds beat M. Parkin 10–6; P. Medati beat B. Bennett 10–4; I. Anderson beat A. Kearney 10–8; W. Jones beat J. Rea 10–3; M. Bradley beat D. Mienie 10–4; P. Francisco beat B. Demarco 10–4; T. Jones beat M. Darrington 10–2.

Round 3: M. Gibson beat Hines 10–7; Fowler w.o. J. Caggianello scr; R. Foldvari beat B. Oliver 10–3; Chalmers beat E. McLaughlin 10–9; G. Foulds beat C. Everton 10–2; Medati beat I. Williamson 10–8; Rigitano beat B. Kelly 10–6; O'Kane beat F. Jonik 10–5; J. van Rensberg beat Longworth 10–7; Chaperon beat P. Morgan 10–3; Newbury beat P. Burke 10–3; P. Browne beat Anderson 10–5; W. Jones beat J. Dunning 10–6; Bradley beat B. Mikkelsen 10–9; P. Francisco beat T. Murphy 10–4; T. Jones beat S. Duggan 10–8.

Round 4: Rigitano beat M. Fisher 10–2; O'Kane beat L. Dodd 10–7; M. Gauvreau beat van Rensberg 10–9; F. Davis beat Chaperon 10–9; Newbury beat G. Scott 10–2; P. Fagan beat Gibson 10–8; Fowler beat J. Donnelly 10–0; R. Edmonds beat Foldvari 10–3; Chalmers beat I. Black 10–4; G. Foulds beat C. Roscoe 10–7; Medati beat W. King 10–9; M. Morra beat Browne 10–6; W. Jones beat M. Watterson 10–5; J. Wych beat Bradley 10–7; P. Francisco beat J. Meadowcroft 10–5; T. Jones beat J. Fitzmaurice 10–4.

Round 5: N. Foulds beat Rigitano 10–8; O'Kane beat D. Martin 10–8; D. Reynolds beat Gauvreau 10–1; R. Williams beat F. Davis 10–6; E. Hughes beat Newbury 10–6; Fagan beat C. Wilson 10–9; J. Parrot beat Fowler 10–2; Edmonds beat M. Wildman 10–7; M. Hallett beat Chalmers 10–1; J. Johnson beat G. Foulds 10–6; S. Francisco beat Medati 10–7; J. Campbell beat Morra 10–9; W. Jones beat G. Miles 10–8; J. Virgo beat Wych 10–4; M. Macleod beat P. Francisco 10–7; T. Jones beat E. Sinclair 10–2.

Competition proper:
First round: S. Davis beat N. Foulds 10–8; David Taylor beat O'Kane 10–4; A. Higgins beat Reynolds 10–4; T. Griffiths beat Williams 10–3; Reardon beat E. Hughes 10–9; Fagan beat W. Thorne 10–6; Parrott beat J. Spencer 10–3; K. Stevens beat Edmonds 10–8; C. Thorburn beat Hallett 10–8; B. Werbeniuk beat Johnson 10–8; Dennis Taylor beat S. Francisco 10–2; E. Charlton beat Campbell 10–3; J. White beat W. Jones 10–4; T. Meo beat Virgo 10–6; D. Mountjoy beat Macleod 10–5; T. Knowles beat T. Jones 10–8.

Second round: S. Davis beat David Taylor 13–4; Griffiths beat Higgins 13–7; Reardon beat Fagan 13–9; Parrott beat Stevens 13–6; Thorbun beat Werbeniuk 13–3; Dennis Taylor beat Charlton 13–6; White beat Meo 13–11; Knowles beat Mountjoy 13–6.

Quarter-finals: S. Davis beat Griffiths 13–6; Reardon beat Parrott 13–12; Dennis Taylor beat Thorburn 13–5; Knowles beat White 13–10.

Semi-finals: S. Davis beat Reardon 16–5; Dennis Taylor beat Knowles 16–5.

Final: Dennis Taylor beat S. Davis 18–17.

1985
BCE WELSH PROFESSIONAL CHAMPIONSHIP

Terry Griffiths won the title for the first time with three emphatic victories at Abertillery Leisure Centre. He took £6000.

First round: S. Newbury beat W. Jones 6–2; T. Chappel beat M. Owen 6–0.

Quarter-finals: R. Reardon beat C. Everton 6–2; D. Mountjoy beat Newbury 6–5; C. Wilson beat C. Roscoe 6–3; T. Griffiths beat Chappel 6–0.

Semi-finals: Griffiths beat Reardon 9–3; Mountjoy beat Wilson 9–2.

Final: Griffiths beat Mountjoy 9–4.

Next page: The Billiards Tournament at Joseph Bennett's rooms, 315 Oxford Street, London.

BILLIARDS

Elements of the Game

Snooker has achieved its current status through an erratic process of evolution which can be traced back through its parent game, billiards, and, further still, to a recognizable form of billiards which was played, like croquet, on a lawn.

Although the Greeks and Romans played many games with balls and sticks, it was not until the 1340s that a game in which an arch and pin, common features of early table billiards, were placed on a lawn and in which maces, the precursors of cues, were used to propel the wooden balls.

Louis XI of France (1461–83) is believed to have been the first to transfer the game to a table, and billiard tables became quite a common item of furniture among the French and then the English nobility.

Although the lawn version survived into the 1600s, billiards was by this time played almost exclusively on tables.

Mary Queen of Scots, only months before she was beheaded, complained bitterly that her 'table de billiard' had been taken away by her captors who were later to rip the cloth off the table and half cover her decapitated corpse with it.

By the Elizabethan Age tables were common in the taverns of London and the cafes of Paris and billiards had come to be one of those games of skill and chance at which it was the done thing for gentry and aspiring gentry to gamble.

Bartley's famous billiard room at Bath, 1798.

CUE

Around 1670 the thin end of the mace started to be used not merely when the cue-ball was under the cushion rail – originally designed, of course, merely to prevent the balls dropping off the table – but for other shots as a matter of preference. The complete change from mace to cue – the word deriving from the French *queue* meaning 'a tail' – took until about 1800.

Since then the design of the cue has altered very little, though recent years have seen a rapid increase in the number of players using two-piece cues, that is, those with either a wooden or metal joint in the middle. John Spencer was the first player to win the World Professional Championship with such a cue in 1977.

In November 1938, Alec Brown, a London professional, was the central figure in an incident which led the governing body to stipulate that a cue 'must be at least 3ft in length and conform to the accepted shape and design'. With the cue ball marooned in the middle of a pack of reds, Brown produced from his pocket a tiny ebony cue, complete with tip, which his father had made. He duly chalked the tip and played his shot but his opponent protested. Thurston's resident referee, Charlie Chambers, sensing no doubt that the use of this implement was outside the spirit if not the letter of the law, awarded a foul – and the rule was changed.

TIP

Before tips were invented, players tried to strike the cue-ball as centrally as possible to avoid a miscue. Striking low (to bring the cue-ball back from the object-ball) or high (to make it follow through) were two skills current only in a limited way before the invention of

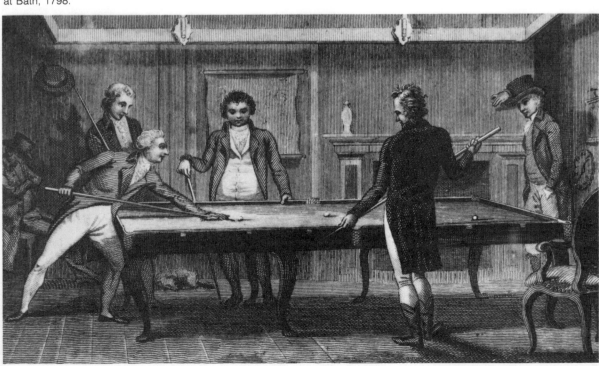

tips by a French infantry captain, Mingaud, in 1807.

Languishing in a Paris prison for debt, Mingaud devoted his ample leisure to a study of billiards, experimenting successfully with a leather tip and astounding all and sundry with his cuemanship on his release.

Mingaud also discovered that by raising the cue almost vertically – in fact into the position in which the mace was used – extraordinary spin effects could be obtained by striking a sharp downwards glancing blow to the left or right across the cue-ball. This type of stroke is called a *massé* – French for mace.

CHALK

In pre-tip days it was common for players to twist the points of their cues in a wall or ceiling so that the chalk-like deposit was at least partial insurance against a miscue. Ordinary chalk also came to be used but the first marketing was done by John Carr, a marker in John Bartley's Billiard Rooms at Bath.

Between 1818 and 1823 either Bartley, who subsequently showed Carr, or Carr himself discovered the positive uses of side spin (or 'side' as it has come to be known). If the cue-ball was struck to the right or left of centre, it was discovered that the spin thus imparted would affect the angle at which it rebounded from the cushion. In some cases, too, side could be used to help the cue-ball into the pocket when playing an in-off.

Carr attributed the strange new effects he was producing to a special brand of 'twisting chalk' which he sold in small boxes though it was, of course, merely ordinary chalk.

Today's leading players use American chalk manufactured in such a way as to give maximum adhesion between tip and cue-ball.

TABLE

The demand for tables and equipment was first met by furniture makers, carpenters and the like, some of whom, like John Thurston (established 1799) went over entirely to this new specialist trade (1814).

Thurston was responsible for many of the improvements which were to bring the manufacture of tables almost to perfection. Table beds were originally of wood but Thurston began experimenting with slate in 1826 and by 1840 slate, naturally found in flat layers which make it ideal for the permanently flat surface necessary for the game, was generally accepted.

Early cushions were layered strips of felt but after trying hair, list, Russian duck, white swan-skin and other substances, rubber was introduced in 1835.

This innovation was not without its problems. Cold weather caused the rubber to lose all its elasticity, a contingency which Thurston's met temporarily with cushion warmers – metal pans or tubes to hold hot water. But the real breakthrough was the development of the vulcanizing process, raising the temperature of the natural rubber and combining it with sulphur to produce a substance more resistant to temperature

changes. In 1845, Queen Victoria received the first set of their new patented vulcanized rubber cushions.

In essence, the modern table was in existence though there were subsequent refinements. Strip rubber was replaced by block rubber and the highest degree of predictability in the angle of rebound from cushions was obtained with the advent of steel blocks, which were used as backing for the rubber.

Pockets changed, not so much in size as in shape. Initially, the cushion rubbers were shaped as squarely at the entrance to the pockets as they were elsewhere but this meant that a ball could not enter a pocket unless it did not touch the sides or at any rate brushed a jaw by the merest fraction.

Easier access was promoted by cutting away the underside of the rectangular shape of the rubber in such a way that the ball was turned towards the pocket rather than allowed to bounce off the cushion at the usual angle.

The extent and angle of this cut-away of the underside of the rubber has a crucial influence on the ease of pocket entry. The greater the undercut, the more it is possible for the rounded surface of the ball to tuck underneath it and thus enter the pocket.

The simple mathematics are that the top of the nose of the cushion is $1\frac{1}{2}$ inches from the bed of the table. A ball is $2\frac{1}{16}$ inches in diameter or, as the Irish would say, $1\frac{1}{32}$ inches at its fattest point. Therefore, if the cushion nose at the pocket entrance starts $1\frac{1}{32}$ inches or less from the bed of the table, the ball cannot tuck underneath the cushion and the pocket will reject it.

The Billiards and Snooker Control Council's (B & SCC), formerly the Billiards Association and Control Council, official templates, adopted in 1892 were of limited value in that they measured only the width of the pockets and took no account of the undercut. Thus, the templates could fit either a pocket which players found very easy or one which they found nearly impossible. The ease or difficulty of pockets on championship tables thus became largely a matter of custom or preference with a general tendency, after snooker superseded billiards as the most popular game, towards ease.

After decades of petty wrangling among the trade firms, who of course had to produce tables incorporating any new official specifications, a sub-committee of the International Billiards and Snooker Federation (IBSF) was entrusted with the design of a new template specifying the degree of undercut and ensuring that the pocket did not narrow beyond the edge of the playing surface. Pockets which had not incorporated the latter stipulation tended to reject even accurately struck balls if played at speed from narrow angles – that is positions in which players could not aim at the full width of the pocket opening.

The new template, designed by Norman Clare, was accepted by the IBSF and B & SCC in 1980 but certain practical difficulties still made uniformity difficult to obtain.

CLOTH

Early tables were covered with green cloth to simulate the grass on which the parent outdoor version of the game was played. Cloth also deadened the noise which the balls would otherwise have made on a polished wooden table and made control a little easier.

Initially, cloths were coarse and heavy but once improving technology had made it possible to mow the previously long nap very short, cloths were developed specifically for billiards.

Some grades sold on cheapness and durability, chiefly to public rooms where tables could expect heavy and prolonged usage, but the very best grades were of the smooth, superfine texture which led to them being adopted for championship play.

Two West of England firms, Strachans and Hunt and Winterbotham's, later amalgamated, led the way with billiard table cloth, though in recent years two Yorkshire companies, Hainsworth's and Booth's, have obtained a substantial share of the market. The Belgium company, Iwan Simonis, who dominate the market in the European pocketless games, have also become increasingly interested in the billiards and snooker scene in recent years.

A Manchester firm, Reddaways, introduced a cotton napless cloth, the Janus, in the 1930s and contracted the leading professionals to play on it. Some large breaks were made but despite rather than because of the quality of the surface. 'Like playing on a shirt', was Joe Davis's succinct description.

The venture ended in bankruptcy and West of England cloth resumed its reign as the championship surface.

The chief selling point of the Janus cloth – that both sides provided an equally good surface – was actually its greatest disadvantage for serious players. Through the elimination of any 'nap', players were not only deprived of an important degree of control but had to cope with 'side' having the opposite effect to that which it had on a woollen cloth.

As on velvet, the nap of a billiard table feels smooth when stroked in one direction – in the case of a table from the baulk end, where the 'D' is situated, towards the top where, in snooker, the black is spotted – and rough in the other.

Even on the best tables, a ball will run more truly with the nap than against it or, sometimes, across it. For example, even on championship tables, a ball played slowly from the pink spot area towards a middle pocket will curl towards the near jaw. Against the nap, too, any right-hand side imparted to the cue-ball will cause it to drift to the left rather than to the right, as it would if played with the nap.

These apparent disadvantages carry numerous compensations in the ways players may use the nap to help them control various spins.

In recent years, some championship cloths have had shorter naps than ever before. Balls tend to run straighter against these naps than they would against the naps of other cloths but a degree of control is often lost because the cue-ball (like a golf ball flighted to a parched glassy green) has nothing to 'bite' on.

Cloths are kept in condition by regular brushing (always with the nap) and ironing. The heat of the room and the frequency and temperature at which the iron is used tends to affect the speed of the table.

BALLS

The earliest and most primitive balls were of wood but even in the early 19th century ivory was the accepted material.

Balls were generally of $1^7/_8$ inches diameter until Thurston began to supply 2-inch balls with all his tables in 1830, one advantage of which was that the cue-ball was easier to strike when it lay against a cushion. Ever since the game's earliest official rules, the standard size has been $2^1/_{16}$ inches.

Apparently, only a female elephant tusk was suitable for billiard ball manufacture and even this had to be of such a size that as little of its exterior as possible had to be pared away. Even the best ivories were somewhat unpredictable and the worst, lacking interior consistency, were unplayable, but the distinctive click they produced was, at least in Britain, considered as vital to the character and tradition of the game as the sound of leather on willow in cricket.

Ivory, which had to be ground regularly in order to keep the balls round, was also extremeley expensive so composition balls were introduced as cheap substitutes before it was recognized that they were also very much more reliable.

In 1868, John Wesley Hyatt, a New York inventor, discovered that collodion (nitro-cellulose, camphor and alcohol), which printers brushed on their fingers to protect them from cuts and grazes, hardened when it was dry and could be made into balls. Hyatt and his brother Isaac patented their process in 1870 under the trade name of celluloid, the world's first commercial synthetic plastic. As it was also used to make piano keys and false teeth it was perhaps appropriate that the new ball should have some teething problems: celluloid was highly flammable and, if struck too hard, a ball could explode! Nevertheless, this initial discovery led directly to the cast resin and cast phenolic balls which are used today.

The Rules and how they changed

Before John Roberts Snr and William Cook met for the championship at St James's Hall in 1870 in front of the Prince of Wales the leading players and trade representatives of the day met to draw up championship rules. In February 1885 the situation was formalized when a similar gathering founded the Billiards Association. Only one further meeting was necessary to approve a universal set of rules. In essence, the rule changes that have taken place since then reflect the need to curb various repetitious scoring methods in the wider interests of the game.

The spot stroke was the first such method to be so limited. Before organized competition, when champions were determined by public opinion on the results of challenge matches for money, Jonathan Kentfield, the first recognised champion, made a break of 196 which included 57 consecutive pot reds off the spot. As cushions were not then made of rubber this was no mean feat as position had to be maintained by screwing straight back (see Diagram 1) or rolling through at just the right angle (see Diagram 2). Their lack of bounce made it extremely difficult to utilize the cushions for position. Even rubber cushions, which dated from 1935, needed many refinements before they could be considered consistent and reliable.

By 1870 the best tables were good enough for the spot stroke to be a formidable weapon. Cook was a spot stroke specialist so Roberts, who had the better all-round game, pressed for the pocket openings to be reduced to 3 inches (as against the usual and present day 3½ inches) and for the red spot to be placed 12½ inches from the top cushion instead of the usual 13¼ inches or the present day 12¾ inches.

Regardless of the disadvantage at which this put him, Cook won anyway but when Roberts's son, John Roberts Jnr, defeated Cook comfortably for the title two months later, Cook belatedly realized how his greatest asset had been negated. He also realized, at a time when leading players were starting to derive income from admission charges as well as side-stakes, that billiards would be more attractive to the public if it could be presented as a varied three ball game rather than a repetitive potting contest. Accordingly, he introduced the 'spot barred' game which stipulated that the red could not be potted twice in succession from its own spot.

It was not until 1898 that this was incorporated, as an amendment, into the Billiards Association rules. It was a move which led to the championship being contested again in 1899 after lapsing since 1885, much of the intervening period having been spent in squabbles between those who preferred spot barred and those who favoured all in.

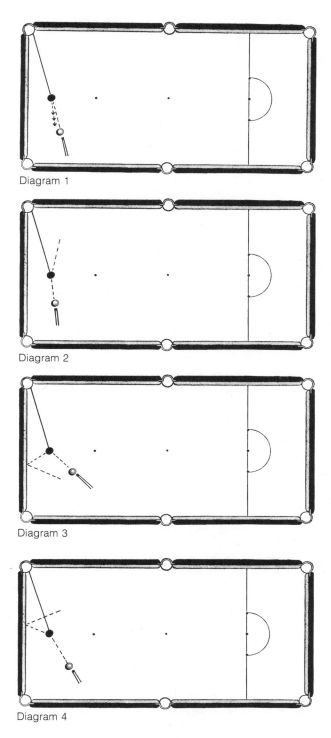

Diagram 1

Diagram 2

Diagram 3

Diagram 4

Two spot stroke manoeuvres made easy through the advent of the rubber cushion. Stunning the cue-ball off the top cushion (3) and bouncing through off the top cushion (4).

Several players could make thousand breaks with the aid of the spot stroke. W. J. Peall, the spot stroke king, made the first recorded two thousand break – 2413 in 1886 – and went on to make a 3304 in 1890. Roberts, who assiduously developed the top of the table game based on cleverly maintained sequences of pot reds and cannons with the object-white near the red spot, made the first public spot barred thousand – 1392 – in 1894. But Peall had no chance with Roberts at spot barred and Roberts, the game's dominant personality and impressario, had no chance with Peall at all in. The Billiards Association unavailingly tried to end the deadlock by awarding cups for both codes.

The revival of the official championship on a spot barred basis in 1899, however, effectively killed the spot stroke, not before time. This key rule remained in force until 1964 when the Billiards Association, in a desperate but not very clearly thought out attempt to halt the decline in the popularity of billiards, permitted 15 consecutive pots and/or in-offs, the reference to consecutive pots off the spot being deleted. This limited restoration of the spot stroke destroyed much of the game's essential character. It meant, in effect, that players who potted the red from its spot the better part of 15 times then played one simple cannon before compiling another sequence of pot reds, had the advantage over players who had to exercise greater skill to control all three balls. The net result of the amendment was that it drove more players out of the game than it brought in.

Recognizing their mistake, if only in part, the Billiards Association amended the rule in 1968 to stipulate that the red must be placed on the middle spot after being potted five times consecutively from its own spot.

This restored a limited degree of genuine top of the table play to the game. Interest started to pick up and standards, which had sunk very low, began to rise. When big breaks started to be made with 'five pot' the tide of opinion began to run in favour of a further reduction.

The International Billiards and Snooker Federation, by now effectively the rule amending authority, although the Billiards Association (now the Billiards and Snooker Control Council) continued to claim copyright on the rules, voted to reduce consecutive pots from five to three, the amendment coming into force on 1 January 1979. Almost simultaneously, the professional governing body, the WPBSA altered the rule from 'five' to 'two', thus restoring it, for professional tournaments, to what it had been from 1898 to 1964. The amateur world changed to 'two' in 1983.

Just as the spot stroke had to be curbed to prevent the spot red specialists from unbalancing the game so legislation became necessary to limit the exploitation of the in-off (or losing hazard) game. In the days of ivory balls, the inconsistency of reaction led to some in-offs being missed through no fault of the player. Ivories, though, were never used in Australia and with

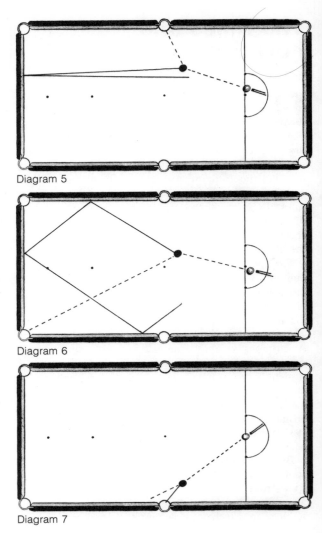

Diagram 5

Diagram 6

Diagram 7

the much more consistent and controllable composition balls, mammoth breaks could be made just as easily with the in-off game as with the spot stroke.

When a 19-year-old Australian, George Gray, came to Britain for the 1910–11 season he made 23 breaks over 1000 including one of 2196. The in-off in the middle pocket – in Cardiff he made 289 in succession – was his basic shot (see Diagram 5). When the red dropped short, position was restored by a top pocket in-off which brought the red back again for middle pocket in-off position (see Diagram 6). If the red drifted towards the side of the table it was a simple matter to pot red in the middle, leave the cue-ball just past the jaws of the middle pocket and play the half ball in-off from the spotted position to restore prime position (see Diagram 7).

All these moves are still very much part of the fabric of the game but with Gray they were, until his formidable concentration flagged, the entire game. Gray's rivals were not slow to suggest various limitations on this method of scoring but his one challenge for the championship in 1914 foundered on the use of ivories with which he was only half the player that he was with composition. He lost in the first round, returned to Australia and was never the same player again.

Although the immediate threat had been dealt with, the wider issues which Gray had posed were not tackled until British professionals visiting Australia were given further doses of red ball play from such players as Walter Lindrum and Clark McConachy, who both became nursery cannon specialists later. Lindrum made 7348 points out of 8000 off the red in beating H. W. Stevenson and a break of 1589 after losing the white at 292 against Claude Falkiner.

Lindrum would not at that stage come to Britain because British professionals were unwilling to surrender the advantage they felt they had in playing with ivories but the 1926 professional championship did nevertheless introduce a limit of 25 consecutive hazards (i.e. posts or in-offs). This limit was also applied to the English Amateur Championship in 1927 after the victory the previous year of Joe Earlam, a red ball specialist, composition balls being used in this event for the first time. In 1927, largely for commercial considerations, the professionals abandoned ivories.

With composition balls, though, even a limit of 25 hazards led to too much repetition. In 1931, the hazard limit was reduced to 15 for the English Championship and remained at that figure until 1960 when it was again increased to 25. It remained at 25 until, along with partial restoration of the spot stroke (see above), it was again reduced to its present 15 in 1964.

Tom Reece

Whereas the curbs on potting and in-offs effectively preserved the balance and character of the game, the lack of effective limitations on cannon play not only killed billiards as a public entertainment but, with the game's apex of professional championships and tournaments removed, had serious repercussions on the amateur side.

The earliest cannon breaks where made with the two object-balls jammed in a corner pocket, none more notably than in a match for £1000 between Roberts Jnr and an American, Frank Ives, at Knightsbridge. Robert's henchman, Tom Taylor, had played into the American's hands by agreeing to play the match on a table with pockets of 3¼ inches (smaller than usual) and with balls of 2¼ inches (larger than usual). Ives jammed the balls on the fourth evening and compiled a break of 2539 before voluntarily breaking up the position, and won by nearly half the game.

They played two return matches. In Chicago, where Ives won, a baulk line 7 inches long was drawn across each corner pocket within which only two consecutive strokes could be made. In New York, Roberts, hoping to make his all-round game tell, had the pockets widened to 3 inches. Roberts won the match but not before Ives had given, decades in advance of the Lindrum years, a classic exhibition of nursery cannons, that is 'nursing' the two object-balls along the cushion an inch or so at a time. Ives, of course, was a master of the 'cannons only' game played on the pocketless tables of Europe and the USA, parts of the world where English tables with pockets are few and far between.

Roberts himself employed runs of nurseries but only within a varied overall pattern. He was also much

Willie Smith, *left*, and Joe Davis, *third from left*, watch the weighing of the balls before one of their challenge matches.

helped by the fact that push strokes were still permitted, at least until 1898, when he withdrew his influential opposition to a move outlawing them.

It was not until Tom Reece of Oldham came on the scene that cannons threatened to dominate billiards to anything like the extent that the respective specialities of Peall and Gray had earlier threatened. J. P. Mannock, a teaching professional, discovered the anchor cannon; W. A. Lovejoy, amateur champion in 1904, first exhibited it to the public; and Reece perfected it. The outcome was a break of 499 135 unfinished by Reece at Burroughes and Watts in 1907. With one object-ball suspended on either jaw of the top left-hand pocket (see Diagram 8) Reece proceeded to score at the rate of some 10 000 a session for five weeks. Not particularly fond of his opponent, Joe Chapman, who sat helplessly by for several sessions until he departed in disgust, Reece indulged his biting sense of humour with such witticisms at his expense as: 'How do you find the table?' or 'What sort of chalk do you use?'

The break ended, still unfinished, when the hall was required for another match. An official record certificate was refused on the grounds that press and public were not present throughout the break although the referee was. The anchor stroke was then barred.

Over the next twenty years, nursery cannons became an increasingly important part of almost every leading player's armoury. Long top of the table sequences interspersed with runs of nurseries became the norm for all the top players except Melbourne Inman and Wille Smith who relied on all-round play and top of the table. The danger signals were out as early as 1925 when, in advance of official legislation, a *News of the World* Test series between Newman and Smith specified a limit of 25 consecutive cannons – Newman being a cannon specialist – and 25 consecutive red hazards.

Again it was Reece who forced the legislator's hand by perfecting the pendulum cannon and introducing it in his match against his arch rival Inman in the 1927 championship. Though not quite a revival of the 'jam' shot, the two object-balls were trapped, one on either jaw of a top pocket, while the cue-ball flicked across them (see Diagram 12). This was physically more arduous than the anchor cannon as the player had to walk round the corner of the table for each shot. Since the anchor cannon had been outlawed by the stipulation that no more than 25 consecutive cannons could be played without the cue-ball striking a cushion, this sequence had to be broken by achieving a cannon cushion first (see Diagram 13).

It was not quite so foolproof as the anchor but Reece nevertheless made 568 consecutive cannons with it in a break of 1151 against Inman during which he once gestured towards his hapless opponent with the words: 'Has that man paid to come in? He's a spectator.'

Reece spent so much time trying to obtain pendulum cannon position, no easy task, that he ended on the losing side. A few weeks later while Joe Davis was contesting the world final against Newman, Reece made a pendulum break of 3964. Davis, who was trailing Newman at the time, decided after a brief morning practice session to employ the pendulum if he could. He duly obtained position and compiled a 2501 but Newman also made a pendulum 1012 and an orthodox 1073 and retained the title. It was clear, moreover, that the pendulum had to be barred.

Although it had required considerable skill to get the balls in position for the pendulum, it did not require exceptional skill or touch to compile breaks once they were there. Nurseries required a great deal more skill but it was the kind of art which concealed art, for Lindrum, Davis, McConachy and Newman could play them so well that it was amazing that spectator interest lasted as long as it did.

Diagram 14 shows the 'rocker' cannon sequence

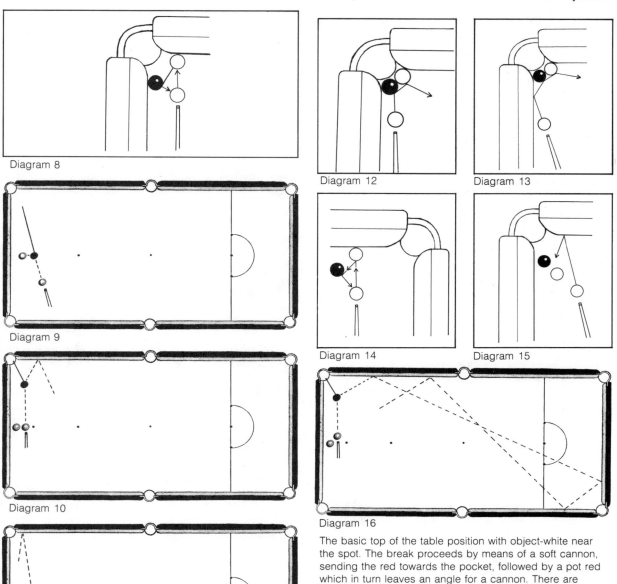

Diagram 8

Diagram 9

Diagram 10

Diagram 11

Diagram 12

Diagram 13

Diagram 14

Diagram 15

Diagram 16

The basic top of the table position with object-white near the spot. The break proceeds by means of a soft cannon, sending the red towards the pocket, followed by a pot red which in turn leaves an angle for a cannon. There are many variables within this basic pattern and the strokes which can be employed to keep the object-white near the spot offer considerable scope for artistry. In contrast to this 'floating white' technique in which the object-white is kept moving within a limited area, the 'postman's knock' sequence (see diag. 11) depends on the object-white being kept pinned on the top cushion by a full contact from the cue-ball.

which was maintained by playing, with a touch of right-hand side, full on the object-white so that the cue-ball made the finest of contacts on the red as it rebounded to its original position. Such was Lindrum's delicacy of touch that the second object-ball was grazed so thinly that it did not move.

In one of his great matches against Smith in Australia in 1929, Lindrum, reached 1000 in 36 minutes by almost exclusive use of nurseries; he made a century in 95 seconds. His fastest ever thousand took only 26 minutes, his fastest century only 29 seconds. In 1932, McConachy made the then record of 297 nurseries, in which, instead of taking the balls 'round the corner' of the top pocket he turned them no less than nine times back and along the top cushion (see Diagram 15).

With the top players scoring between a third and a half of their points with nurseries it was clear that the game had become chronically unbalanced. The Billiards Association, for the 1932–3 season, tried to counteract this by introducing the '100 points baulkline' rule which insisted that the cue-ball should cross the baulkline (in a red spot to baulk direction) in every 100 points in a break of 100 or more.

McConachy made a break of 850 in the first match played under this rule for it was easy enough, for a top player, to cross the baulkline, the most favoured method being to leave a simple thin cue pot red in the top pocket so that the cue-ball could be brought round off three or four cushions to maintain top of the table position (see Diagram 16).

The rule, even if it appeared slightly artificial, did generally achieve its stated objective of breaking up long runs of nurseries but Lindrum, quite unjustifiably, thought it a threat to his supremacy. The promoters of the *News of the World* tournament gave the five entrants (Lindrum, Davis, Newman, McConachy, Smith) the option of playing under this rule or a '75 consecutive cannon' rule (after which a pot or in-off had to be played). Lindrum and Newman opted for the latter, Davis and McConachy said they did not mind and Smith withdrew.

The governing body weakened, modifying the baulk-line rule to 'once every 200 points' which meant, in effect, that if the baulkline was crossed early in the break, the better part of 400 points could be made with nurseries. Lindrum was not keen even on this restriction, though he ridiculed it by taking the balls two-and-a-half times round the table with a run of 529 nurseries negotiating not only the middle pockets but the required line crossings with apparent ease. The rule was then tightened (for professionals only) to stipulate that baulkline crossings had to be made between 180 and 200 in every 200 but this amendment was too artificial and too late. The inhuman skill of the top players, the repetitive nature of the game they played, the incessant internal strife and the coming of snooker combined within a very few years to bury billiards as a public entertainment.

No world professional championship was held

between 1933 and 1951 and there was a further gap from 1951 to 1968. In these 35 years, professional standards declined grievously. The top amateur game held its standards but the overall trend was to rules which made the game easier rather than more difficult. The explosion of snooker's popularity in the seventies, pulling billiards along on its coat tails, stimulated a minor but encouraging revival of interest in billiards and its skills. The baulkline rule was abolished and to encourage the preservation of nursery cannon play, a far cry from the Lindrum era, 75 consecutive cannons, direct or indirect, were in 1970 allowed instead of the limit of 35 direct cannons having then to be broken by an indirect cannon. Professionals also returned to the essence of billiards by limiting, in 1978, consecutive pots from the spot to two – as the amateur world did in 1983 – and the revival continued with an increase in the number of worthwhile tournaments. There was more prize money for the World Professional Billiards Championship and in 1985 the game received television exposure on Channel 4 through the Blue Arrow Masters.

The young Tom Newman (1919).

The Early Championships

In its early days billiards was either a gambling activity, as most games were, or a leisurely relaxation for the gentry. The twin traditions of billiards were epitomized by the country mansion and the tavern or public room. The gentry were often great patrons of the game but the best players invariably came from much lower down the social scale even though their successes were sometimes to establish them securely in the middle class.

The origins of competitive billiards are reminiscent of the prize-ring beginnings of boxing. Long before any official governing body was set there were recognized 'champions' whose titles were current on the strength of public opinion. This opinion was largely determined by a series of challenge matches for money.

Edwin Kentfield of Brighton, known as Jonathan Kentfield, was the first player to be recognized as champion, around 1820. John Carr of 'twisting chalk' fame, like Kentfield a marker, challenged him in 1827 but fell ill before the match and Kentfield remained champion until 1849 when he failed to meet a challenge from John Roberts Snr of Liverpool.

The title 'champion' meant, of course, champion of England and it was perhaps a reflection of the nation's self-confidence that this was simply assumed to be champion of the world. Incredibly, the Billiards Championship was known simply as 'The Championship' until 1933.

Roberts remained number one until he signed to play William Cook for £200 and the title on 11 February 1870. Roberts took what advantages he could from manipulating the rules and conditions (see page 24) but Cook won a battle which lasted from 8.27 p.m. to 1.38 a.m., 1200–1083.

For attractive matches – one of the attractions being heavy betting between spectators – it was not unusual to offer 500 tickets at £1 each, but demand was such on this occasion that the larger arena of St James's Hall had all its 800 seats filled, with many spectators standing. When it leaked out that the Prince of Wales would attend, tickets rose in value with £5 changing hands for front row seats shortly before the off.

The unduly tight pockets of the championship table kept breaks small and prolonged the length of the match in an atmosphere thick with smoke. Though Roberts was only 47, years tended in those days to weigh more heavily, heavily enough for 'Bell's Life in London' to refer to him throughout their exhaustive blow-by-blow report as 'the old 'un'.

Cook, who was barely 21, has remained the youngest champion. Roberts, having trailed throughout, actually got his nose in front in the penultimate hundred but Cook finished the fresher with breaks of 26, 31 and 68 unfinished, the highest of the match, to win by 117.

His Royal Highness retired at midnight praising Cook's skill but stating that he would not watch another match on the 'championship' table but only on the tables ordinarily in use as he wanted to see some of the big breaks which the best exponents were currently recording.

Immediately after the first match, John Roberts Jnr, seeking to avenge family honour, challenged Cook for the title. In the absence of a governing body, *The Sportsman* fulfilled most of its functions, providing a referee, weighing the balls, dealing with other preliminaries . . . and holding the stake-money – £100 a side, the minimum specified in the championship conditions.

The highest breaks were even smaller than in the first match, 55 by Roberts and 46 by Cook, but Roberts won very easily by 478 points in front of another capacity crowd.

The third match, held in the smaller auditorium at St James's Hall, was a dreadful anti-climax not only in standard but in dramatic content. Alfred Bowles of Brighton was not in Roberts's class.

Seeking to enliven a predictable evening, a spectator offered 20/1 against Bowles but Roberts, in a rare display of jocularity, was the only taker! Roberts won by 241.

Roberts then lost his title to Joseph Bennett by a mere 95 points (28 November 1870) but regained it on 30 January 1871 by beating Bennett by 363. On the latter occasion, Bennett did not enjoy the best of fortune. His cue-ball was found to be light, thus causing it to bounce off the other balls at a wider than usual angle, and one of his strokes was spoiled when his cue was knocked out of his hand by a passing waiter.

On 25 May 1871, Cook regained the title, his winning margin of 15 points being likely to remain the closest finish in the history of the championship. The referee, unable to decide whether one shot was a foul or not, referred the issue to a show of hands.

Cook then fought off Bennett by 58 and Roberts twice, by 201 (making the first championship century, 116) and by 216.

On 24 May 1875 Roberts wrested the title from Cook at the Criterion Restaurant by 163 and beat him again at the St James's Hall on 20 December 1875 by 135. When Roberts went off to tour Australia, Cook claimed the title but Roberts challenged him on his return and beat him at the Gaiety Restaurant on 28 May 1877 by 221. Roberts made a break of 118 and 'Oxford Jonathan', reported Bell's, 'marked the game with his usual accuracy'.

Roberts then went off on tour and Cook, announcing himself to be champion, accepted a challenge from Bennett. Cook led 938–864 but Bennett won by 51.

Bennett also beat Tom Taylor at St James's Hall on 12–13 January 1881 by 90 points. Bennett made a new championship record of 125 but Bell's commented acidly on the late start and the slow play. 'Closing time was now rapidly approaching, and it was evident that unless Bennett went right away the match could not be finished before the period arrived at which a paternal Government decrees that licensed premises shall be closed. Both players, however, took their time, and though naturally desirous of finishing, did not abate one atom of their care, Bennett in particular playing as leisurely as if it had been an hour earlier.'

At 12.30 a.m., Bennett led 976–882 with Taylor in play with an additional 26. The match had to be resumed the following afternoon whereupon Taylor added only two more and Bennett ran out with 24.

Shortly afterwards, Bennett broke his arm when he was thrown out of a gig and resigned the title. Roberts billed himself as 'Champion of the World' but stated that he had no intention of ever again playing in the championship under the rules then appertaining and Cook, more or less by default, held the title for the next three years.

Roberts conceded start to all and sundry both at spot barred and spot in and the situation was – as it was to be many times in the future – that the players whom the public knew to be the best devalued the championship by not playing in it. In short, the personality of the top player was stronger than the game's administration.

Interest was centred not on the championship but on matches, often of a week's duration, between the leading players on ordinary tables. Thousand breaks utilizing the spot stroke became common and, on ordinary tables, even the spot barred record rose from Cook's 309 to 322, 327 and 360, all by Roberts, in 1884.

Gradually a collective desire for proper organization and a universally agreed set of rules led to a meeting in February 1885 at which the Billiards Association came into being and an official set of rules, after one further meeting, was agreed.

Roberts, who had been in the chair at this meeting, now decided to play for the championship again. Cook did not reply to Roberts's challenge within the stated time but immediately challenged when the cup went to Roberts. As it was clearly better to have two full houses than one, the match was scheduled for two days at the Billiard Hall, Argyll Street over the extended distance of 3000 up.

Roberts made a championship break record of 129 and won by a mere 92, a much closer margin than that which he usually achieved over Cook on ordinary tables. In fact, he conceded Cook 2000 in 12 000 shortly afterwards and beat him by 2759.

Roberts's next defence against Bennett at the Royal Aquarium, Westminster was extended to four days, 1–4 June 1885. Roberts made breaks of 147 and 155, a new championship record, and won by a resounding 1640.

Roberts had never made more than 16 consecutive spot strokes on the championship table but Peall made 128 in succession in a break of 445 in a match in which, receiving one sixth of the game in 12 000 up, he beat Roberts by 441. Ordinary tables would have given the spot stroke still greater potency so Roberts was under-

standably reluctant to play Peall 'all in' for the title under these conditions. Even with the 3 inch pockets of the archaic championship table the outcome would have been in doubt.

The Billiards Association tried to resolve the difficulty by awarding cups for all in and spot barred and devising a new official template which regulated the pockets to a strict 3⅝ inches at the fall of the slate. Peall claimed the title of 'Champion of Ordinary Billiards', and William Mitchell for 'Spot Barred' but without Roberts it was all meaningless.

Roberts so clearly was billiards that he could override the Billiards Association with impunity. He said that he could not regard 'a letter from the secretary of a moribund association as other than a gross impertinence'. He grandly offered the Association a venue, a table and a trophy for their championship – but declined to play in it.

Thus, the championship lapsed and with it the championship table for which there had never been any logical justification in the first place. The present day's only connection with this dinosaur of the game is the beautifully kept table with 3 inch pockets which is still in regular use at the Victoria Club, London.

It was not until October 1898 that the Billiards Association took action which made it possible to revive the championship, officially declaring the all in game obsolete by stipulating that the red, after being potted twice from its spot, should be placed on the middle spot.

Roberts, of course, considered himself above the championship though, after much jockeying for position, he did agree to play Charles Dawson in a fortnight's match for £100 and the whole of the gate.

By the time this took place, Dawson had overwhelmed Joe North in a week's match of 9000 up – the first time that the championship had been played over such a distance – starting on 9 January 1899 at the Gaiety Restaurant. Regrettably, the profit did not cover the cost of crockery breakages.

As matches had lengthened, sessions had come to be divided in such a way that the score of the player who was leading had to be 750 multiplied by the number of sessions played. If the trailing player rallied, that session tended to be longer than if the leader simply extended his advantage.

For instance, on the penultimate day of the Roberts v Dawson match, Dawson, who had led for most of the first week but had fallen 3078 behind, outpointed Roberts 1275–748 in 2 hours 55 minutes in the afternoon session and 1495–751 in 3 hours 10 minutes in the evening.

It may well have been that Roberts wanted to raise visions of a grandstand finish, thus increasing the gate, for on the final night he scored his last 750 in only 70 minutes to win 18 000–16 186.

This appears to have been the first match in which averages, obtained by dividing a player's total by the number of completed innings he has had, were officially recorded. Roberts averaged 28.04 and Dawson 25.24. More to the point, Roberts took Dawson's £100 and the whole of the then fabulous £2154 from the gate.

In addition, the dubious principle was reinforced of the 'Champion in Exile' standing out of the official championship in order to play a lucrative match with the official champion for what the public regarded as the number one position.

JOHN ROBERTS Jnr (1860–19??)

John Roberts Jnr was to billiards in the late nineteenth century what Joe Davis was to become to snooker in the middle of the twentieth: not only so universally considered the best player that he could ignore the championship as an irrelevance but so securely in control of the game's promotional and trading interests that everyone knew who was boss.

Roberts first became champion in April 1870 by beating William Cook two months after Cook had beaten Roberts Snr in the first championship match. Twice, subsequently, Roberts lost to Cook but three consecutive victories over Cook left him, in 1877, so indisputably the number one that he could concede start to everybody and opt out of the championship. He went East to set up a billiard table factory in Calcutta, transported several tables by elephant to show the Maharajah of Jaipur, a piece of enterprise which led to an annual salary of £500 with full expenses as court billiards player for life for coming to India one month a year. In all, Roberts made 11 visits to India, three to Australia, two to New Zealand, two to America and one to South Africa.

At home, Roberts took the first professional billiards circus round the provinces with short games on handicap and promoted week's matches between himself and various selected opponents at the Royal Aquarium (now the site of the Horticultural Hall, Westminster), the Argyll Street billiard hall (where the London Palladium now stands), the Egyptian Hall, Piccadilly and large provincial venues.

As a promoter he was sensitive to what the public would or would not pay to see. Seeing the spot stroke as boring and repetitive, he developed top of the table technique and an array of recovery shots, not as difficult as they appeared, for when he 'accidentally' lost position. He also developed the 'drag shot' for length of the table strokes, thus minimizing the possibility of the imperfections of balls or tables (or both) causing the shot to be missed. Curiously enough, the public would have paid to see Roberts play Peall 'all in' but Roberts clearly perceived this as too great a risk to his reputation. Peall beat Roberts easily in an extraordinary contest in which at the start of each break the striker could place the balls anywhere he pleased; Peall won again in a match in which he was limited to 100 spot strokes in any one break; and, receiving 2000 in 10 000 won 441 all in on the championship table with 3-inch pockets. Peall, in fact, billed himself as 'Champion of Ordinary Billiards' after Roberts had

refused an all in challenge unless there was also a second match, spot barred, with Peall receiving a third of the game in 12 000 up. Roberts, in short, was a master showman and a master negotiator, much preferring to concede start – thus leaving his reputation intact if he lost – than play level unless he felt he had a significant advantage in playing terms and conditions. His name sold cues, chalk, balls, books, cushions, even cigars and crockery. He offered the Billiards Association a venue, a table and a trophy for their championship but declined to play in it, knowing full well that in the public eye he was Billiards. He played here, there and everywhere: from ivory tables in Indian palaces – from one Indian trip he brought the game of snooker back to England – to makeshift boards in Australian mining towns. He made the first recorded thousand without the aid of specialist strokes when he compiled a 1392 against Diggle, at the time considered number two to Roberts, from whom he generally received 8000 or 9000, in Manchester in 1895, but it was his force of personality rather than statistics which accounted for his status. Once, in the early days of electric light, a bulb exploded. The table was quickly brushed and the show immediately continued with Roberts, despite burns, cuts and lingering minute pieces of glass, compiling a 400-odd break. In old age, he went through with a 1000 up match against Mitchell in Manchester when he was suffering from malarial fever and ague. He could scarcely walk but, with Mitchell within 40 of game, he ran out, with prodigious determination with 600 unfinished.

When Dawson won the championship, dormant since 1885, in 1899, his backers forced Roberts to a fortnight's match on level terms for £100 with the whole of the gate money to go to the winner. Roberts won by 1814. In 1905, a year before he retired, Roberts successfully conceded 2000 in 18 000 to the then champion Stevenson for £500 with Stevenson wagering a further £100 that he won by more than his start. Stevenson won by 1520 and the players shared a gate of £2500 for the fortnight.

The year he retired, 1906, with his eyesight failing, Roberts scored 1486 in a minute under two hours against J. Duncan in Glasgow, 23 509 in 24 hours and a break of 519 in 27 minutes.

MELBOURNE INMAN (1878–1951)

In 1891, a Twickenham marker's challenge to all and sundry was loftily taken up by W. D. Courtney, a leading amateur. 'To encourage rising talent' as he put it he offered to give 2000 start in 8000 to Inman for £25 a side. Inman won by over 4000 points and a return match level and entered the professional mainstream.

Since John Roberts's second and final retirement from championship play, there had been two champions, Charles Dawson of Huddersfield, whose book *Practical Billiards* Joe Davis confessed late in his life had been useful to him in his early days, and H. W. Stevenson of Hull. These two hated each other, none the less so when the Billiards Association declared Stevenson champion in 1901 because Dawson said the dates suggested for the title match were inconvenient. This gave Stevenson the £100 annual stipend which the Billiards Association awarded to the player it recognized as champion. When, in 1903, Dawson beat him for the title at the National Sporting Club, the customary handshake was lacking. 'So much for the Billiards Association champion', snarled Dawson as he made the winning shot.

But as Dawson's eyesight failed and Stevenson failed to endear himself to the Association by appealing in vain that the choice of tables should rest with the players, the championship lapsed from 1903 to 1908 at which point, to get it going again, the Association declared Inman champion. Inman defended successfully against Albert Williams in 1909 but dissatisfaction with the Association's government of the professional game was growing and the Billiards Control Club effectively assumed control of the professional sphere by declaring Stevenson champion in 1909.

The first Stevenson v. Inman championship match in 1910 was abandoned three-quarters of the way through because of the death of Stevenson's wife, but Stevenson won the other two in 1910 and 1911 before he passed up the 1912 championship in favour of a lucrative domestic and overseas tour with George Gray. For three consecutive years Inman beat Reece for the championship and after the war, in 1919, beat Stevenson for what was to prove his last title.

Inman was above all a great competitor. His knack of pulling out brilliant recovery strokes when he had apparently lost position, his aggressive personality and his ability to irritate his opponents made him formidable opposition not only at his peak but long after this had passed.

His legendary rival was Reece, temperamental, artistic with a taste for close, delicate control, Inman's antithesis in almost every respect. Inman's open style tended to produce flukes more often than is usual with top players.

'How did you do that?' Reece asked acidly after one such. 'I believe you know my terms for tuition, Mr Reece', Inman replied.

There were many such verbal exchanges though Reece produced the most memorable on the night Inman clinched the 1919 championship. Lord Alverston, then president of the Billiards Association, who had earlier that week sentenced Dr Crippen to death, was just presenting Inman with the cup when Reece interjected: 'Excuse me, my Lord. But if you knew as much as I do about Inman you would have given Crippen the cup and sentenced Inman to death.'

Inman was a master of safety play and of frustrating, containing tactics. In the 1913 championship match, for instance, Inman scored 196 by misses and coups and Reece 181, the rules then allowing any number of misses or coups without other penalty than one or three away respectively. (In 1920, a player was forbidden to

Melbourne Inman

play two consecutive safety misses without an intervening score on pain of giving his opponent the option of playing from hand with object-white on the middle spot and red on the spot. In 1970 safety play was still further limited by making a miss or coup a foul unless the cue-ball is in hand and no object-ball out of baulk.)

The 1920 limitation on safety play was to Inman's disadvantage but as late as 1927 he was still tactically acute enough to lead the young Joe Davis by over a thousand points in their champioship semi-final before Davis threw all caution to the winds, went for everything and got home by 1105 points.

No one could, of course, have reached Inman's standard without the capacity to make breaks. His 744 in 70 minutes against Reece in the 1914 final was a championship record and he had a 701 against Newman in 1923 but it was most characteristic of him to make his best break when the situation demanded, notably in the 1913 final when Reece wiped out his lead with a break of 535 only for Inman to restore it with one of 522.

WILLIE SMITH (1885–1982)
Willie Smith, alone among the giants of the Golden Age of Billiards, did not employ an endlessly repetitive method of scoring. His contempt for nursery cannon artists – 'cushion crawlers' in his phrase – knew no bounds and George Gray, the Australian red ball specialist, whom he sensationally defeated in 1911 when he was still a Darlington linotype operator, he dismissed as 'not a billiards player at all'.

Smith himself played the all-round game which ordinary players played in clubs and halls. He played it infinitely better and at a very fast tempo but the common man could identify with it in a way he never could with the mysterious art of nurseries. He always regarded 'the working classes' or 'average chap' as his strongest supporters and always preferred to play in large halls where there was room for cheap seats rather than at the select Thurston's which seated only 172.

His own attitude to the Establishments was coloured by being declared a professional at the age of 15 for accepting 10s 6d expenses for playing at Middlesbrough Conservative Club. The older he grew, the less inclined he was to co-operate in any scheme which he himself had not suggested. He won the championship in 1920 at his first attempt and again in 1923 but for one reason or another – terms, dates, rules, equipment to be used – never played in it otherwise.

In part, Smith took his cue from Inman, the 1919 champion, who did not enter in 1920 but who referred to himself on the night of Smith's championship triumph as 'the undefeated champion'.

'Of course you are', said Smith. 'If you don't enter you can't be beaten.' There was an acrimonious exchange which led to a great money match at Thurston's. Inman was 10–11 and Smith allowed him to get 1000 in front. When Smith's supporters had placed all the bets they wanted, Smith sailed past him to win by over 4000.

Now no. 1 in the public eye Smith saw no need to defend his title in the 1921 championship which was to be played at Thurston's and from which he could expect

less financial return than from touring the provinces or arranging weeks matches on his own terms. He also stood out in 1922 when he played Tom Newman, by now the official champion, seven 'Tests' week matches. It was clear that the rewards lay in matches between the official champion and the champion in exile. Reporters commented on the regularity with which a player holding a substantial lead was caught.

Smith *v.* Newman in the 1923 championship was a true test but Smith submitted his entry for the 1924 championship two hours late. He nevertheless remained number one as far as the public was concerned, improving his consistency and breakmaking capacities until the switch from ivory balls to composition in 1928–9 saw him compile 15 breaks over 1000 during the season. His greatest effort was a break of 2743 against Newman at Manchester but he was under no illusions about his chances in Australia against their new scoring phenomenon, Walter Lindrum. Smith was as fast a scorer as any all rounder could be but it still took him between four and five minutes to compile a century. Lindrum, with his nurseries, could do so in less than half this time.

He split his first two matches with Lindrum, replying in the second to a break of 1434 by the Australian with one of 1383 and ensuring victory with a further effort of 1028 in 67 minutes. A break of 2030 against Clark McConachy involved playing through an entire session and he was playing so well that there was heavy betting on his rubber match with Lindrum, so heavy that the Sydney betting fraternity broke the cue Smith had used all his life, his beloved 'pit prop'.

The match was abandoned because of the death of Lindrum's young wife, with Lindrum leading 21 431–

Willie Smith

19 308 and the respective averages 114.6 and 102.7 but when Lindrum returned with Smith to play a British season the gulf between them widened. Neither played in the championship but their matches in Britain were regarded as being for the number one position. Lindrum's superiority was so clearcut that Smith averaged 147 for the fortnight at London's Farrington Hall – an average no one remotely approached in the championship – and still lost by 6011. Smith, who had been instrumental in bringing Lindrum to Britain, complained that he was being used as a punchbag. Lindrum relented for a while until, in their last fortnight's match, he averaged 262 and won by no less than 21 285. Smith averaged 109.

Though Lindrum stood supreme, there were other nursery cannon specialists – Joe Davis, Newman and McConachy – who were not far behind. While these became the Big Four, Smith, cushioned by what was at the time a handsome retainer from Burroughes and Watts, drifted further and further into the wilderness, spending most of his time playing his protégé, Sidney Smith. He grew ever more cantankerous and difficult to deal with, indulging in much verbal sparring but reluctant to commit himself to real contests. One bout of sparring with Davis went on for three years until they finally met in 1933, by which time Smith's absence from the main stream had dulled his competitive edge. Davis beat him easily and that was the end of his serious competitive career.

In a way this proved to be all for the best. He and Davis became friends again and as billiards died as a public entertainment the bickering which it had stimulated died with it. He did not care much for snooker but its rising popularity made it inevitable that he played more of it and he actually reached the world final twice, in 1933 and 1935. Club exhibitions became more and more his way of life and he continued with them until well into his seventies. He accumulated a store of anecdotes, quite the most extraordinary of which was his recollection of touring as a young man with Diggle, who suffered from an obsession that someone was always following him. This caused Diggle to be always constantly looking sharply behind him and even to keep a gun beside him when he slept. One night, Smith, who was sharing a room, was just dozing off when Diggle abruptly sat up in bed. 'They're here, Willie, they're here', he shouted, fired two shots through the bedroom door and went to sleep.

TOM NEWMAN (1894–1943)

Born Tom Pratt, Tom Newman was a boy prodigy who made his first billiards century break when he was eleven and his first 500 when he was fifteen. He was given a three-year contract by the great John Roberts with whom he toured extensively.

From his world title success in 1921 to his last in 1927 – six in all – he lost in the championship only to Willie Smith in 1923. Three losses to Davis at the end of this period made up ten consecutive appearances in

the final. With the elbow of his cue arm awkwardly tucked in, he lacked the cue action to excel at power strokes, at long distance or at difficult opening pots, but in cannon play and close quarter work of all kinds he was exceptionally skilful and consistent.

His match temperament, particularly against such forceful characters as Smith and Davis (once the latter had won his first championship in 1928) was a little suspect, partly perhaps because of his mild and easygoing nature, but his breakmaking feats included the first thousand, 1024, without the aid of push or specialist strokes in 1921, 1370 with ivories (the ivory record) in 1924, 1021, the first championship thousand in 1924 and, another championship record, 1567 in 1930, later superseded.

Newman played some of his finest billiards in the international tournament of 1930–1 held in seven cities ranging from Bradford to Plymouth. Playing level against Davis and McConachy and receiving 7000 from Lindrum, the tournament ended in a triple tie. He beat Davis, for the third time in succession, in a play-off, averaging 122.3 for the fortnight and went on to average 169.3 for the fortnight's final against Lindrum. Even with 7000 start this was not good enough for Lindrum averaged 248.1 and won by 8371.

WALTER LINDRUM (1898–1960)

Walter Lindrum mastered billiards so thoroughly, to so considerably greater a degree than any other practitioner of his chosen sport, that he and his nearest rivals killed it as a public entertainment: they became

Tom Newman, *left*, and Claude Falkiner shake hands before the start of a match.

Walter Lindrum. Note that tables of the period were lit by six conically-shaped shades before the trough-shaped shade was found to shed a more even illumination.

so skilled, so free from error that billiards enthusiasts could no longer identify their own game with the refined, perfected version which Lindrum, Joe Davis, Tom Newman and Clark McConachy presented.

Lindrum was born to billiards. His father, Fred senior, was the 'native born' Australian title holder – an expatriate Englishman Harry Evans was the Australian champion – and his elder brother, Fred junior, became Australian champion.

As soon as he could walk, he would wander into the billiard saloons which his family owned at Donnybrook, Kalgoorlie (Walter's birth place on 29 August 1898) and Broad Arrow. As soon as he was old enough he would field out for hours as his brother practised, unconsciously absorbing the methods and sequences with which it was possible to compile big breaks.

At first, his father thought there were enough billiard players in the family and forbade him to play. When Walter stole the key to the room and crept in unobserved, his father appreciated the depth of his younger son's desire and relented, but he was to prove a hard taskmaster.

Diagram 17
The cue-ball, struck with right-hand side, strikes the red about three-quarter ball. The effect of the right-hand side is to spin the cue-ball back into the cushion and finally into the pocket even as it bounces away from it.

Having made his first century break at the age of 12, young Lindrum was given a daily four-hour practice schedule using only two balls. In this time, he had to practise the spot stroke and the cushion run through shot (see Diagram 17) – nothing else.

When he was allowed the third ball, his practice schedule was increased to two hours every morning, three every afternoon and two every night.

He was on the verge of his first double century when his father told him he was not to leave the room that day until he had made a 250: starting at 2 that afternoon he battled on until 8.30 that evening until he made it.

On and on went the backbreaking practice routine until, at 14, he went on tour with his father, who promptly carried his education a stage further by crushing him unmercifully.

Walter soon overtook his idolized elder brother but would not challenge him for the Australian title, which he was content to have remain in the family. His father backed with £200 a challenge for him to play anyone in the world with bonzoline balls but there were no takers.

In his youth, Lindrum was primarily a red ball player. He beat the former world champion H. W. Stevenson 16 000–6545 in Sydney in 1922 making a break of 1417 almost entirely off the red and at one stage scoring 7348 out of 8000 by this method. Two years later, he beat Claude Falkiner, one of the best British players never to win the championship, in two matches out of three, averaging 108 for the fortnight in the last.

Falkiner could not persuade Lindrum to visit Britain, where the British professionals insisted on playing with ivory balls as an aid to maintaining their superiority over colonial challengers, but did impart much of his knowledge of the nursery cannons which the Australian was later to display with such devastating effect.

Partly through a disinclination to play with ivories – he had played all his billiards with a composition ball

– partly through, as it proved, ill-founded fears that the damp English climate would adversely affect the bronchial condition from which he suffered, Lindrum stayed in Australia for the next few years though both he and McConachy frequently recorded breaks and averages superior to those which were good enough to win the world championship. With 1380 and 1415 at Wellington, Lindrum became the first player ever to make thousand breaks in successive days.

In the 1928–9 season, Crystalate balls were adopted for professional matches in Britain. Willie Smith, who opted out of the offical championship but was still regarded as number one by the public, crushed Fred Lindrum by no less than 19 178 points, averaging 161.6 for the fortnight's match, and accepted an offer to visit Australia where he played three epic matches against Walter.

Walter won the first in Melbourne 24 234–23 147 and Smith the second in Sydney 23 446–22 317, Smith replying to a break of 1434 with one of 1383 and clinching the match with a 1028 in 67 minutes on the last day, Lindrum being in play with 701 at the close. In this match, Lindrum compiled breaks of 965 and 1090, reaching four figures in only 36 minutes and scoring exclusively with nurseries after 350.

As a prelude to the decider in Sydney, the local betting fraternity broke Smith's cue but the match was left uncompleted in tragic circumstances. Lindrum's pregnant 20-year-old wife had been knocked over by a bus and was convalescing when the match started but complications set in after a few days. Under the strain, Lindrum faltered and from 3000 in front had fallen behind by the second Thursday.

By Thursday teatime his wife had rallied. She had set her heart on the silver tea service which a Sydney newspaper had offered for the winner of the match and Lindrum was determined to win it for her. 'You've got to make a 2000 break for me', she said.

He resumed with 144 unfinished and played through all but ten minutes of the evening session to reach 2002 but returned to the dressing room to discover that his wife had suffered a relapse. She died within a few hours and the match was abandoned with Lindrum leading 21 431–19 308.

Made as it was under such severe emotional pressure, Lindrum always regarded that break as his greatest, but the whole traumatic experience created an emotionally tender area which made him more and more obsessive about billiards, harder to deal with in contracts and personal arrangements and, except when he was actually playing before the public, prone to depression and lethargy.

The immediate step he took towards recovering from his grief was to sign a contract with Burroughes and Watts and return to Britain with Smith. One of the many interminable trade and contractual wrangles of the day led to neither Lindrum nor Smith competing in the official championship but the public was shrewd enough to recognize where the number one position was truly being contested.

With the promise of unlimited backing from John Wren, a Melbourne sporting patron, Lindrum intended to coast for a while but without going flat out he quickly demonstrated who was boss. Ill-pleased with their first venue, a cellar in Glasgow, Lindrum nevertheless made a 910 break in his first session and a 1083 in his second. He won their first week's matches by comparatively modest margins but cut loose with six thousands in the third week, when he won by nearly 8000. With his first triple thousand, 3262, and five other thousands, Lindrum won 28 003–21 962 at the Farringdon Hall, London where Smith, who made a 1490 and averaged 147, was beaten out of sight.

Smith began to express resentment that he was being used as a punchbag and, as if by magic, won two matches by narrow margins, but Lindrum, after beating Joe Davis 29 056–26 172 in a match which eclipsed the record aggregate for a fortnight by 5500, hammered Smith 30 817–19 334. Finally, to avenge in full the drubbing Smith had given his elder brother, Lindrum averaged 262 and made eleven thousands and a 998 in beating him 36 256–14 971. Incredibly, Smith averaged 109 and lost by 21 285.

The 1930–1 British season was dominated by an international round robin tournament in which Lindrum conceded 7000 to Davis, Newman and McConachy. Against McConachy, Lindrum averaged 313 for the second week and made a new record of 3905 which spanned the whole of the afternoon session and 80 minutes of the evening. In the deciding match against Newman, Lindrum averaged 248 and made breaks of 2835 and 2583.

Against Davis in January 1932, at Thurston's, Lindrum played through most of a Tuesday afternoon and all evening to reach the close with 3151 unfinished. On Wednesday afternoon he carried this to a new record of 4137 to which Davis replied with 1247. He toured the United States and Canada rather than compete in the championship but returned for the *News of the World* tournament in the autumn by which time the BA & CC had introduced an experimental 100 point baulkline rule, a device to curb long runs of nursery cannons by making it obligatory for the cue-ball to cross the baulkline once every 100 points.

The BA & CC bowed to pressure in extending this limit to 200, which meant that if the line was crossed early in a break nearly 400 could be scored before crossing it again, but Lindrum thought this rule a threat to his superiority, an empty fear since he had compiled a run of 529 nurseries which had included the appropriate baulkline crossings.

Conceding 6000 to each opponent, Lindrum failed to win a match in the *News of the World* tournament. His scoring power was affected but, proportionately, so was that of his chief rivals and he was still, beyond dispute, the best player.

Nevertheless, his victory in the 1933 championship at the Dorland Hall, London was anything but one-sided. Lindrum made three thousands to Davis's best of 792 but won only by a mere 694, averaging 92 to the loser's 89.

There was uproar when Lindrum declared his intention of defending the title only in Australia but the governing body could do nothing practical about it. In July 1934, Lindrum beat first McConachy and then Davis to retain the title which then remained dormant until he relinquished it in 1950.

The rule changes had come far too late to halt the decline in attendances and were in any case too trifling fundamentally to affect the all too predictable pattern

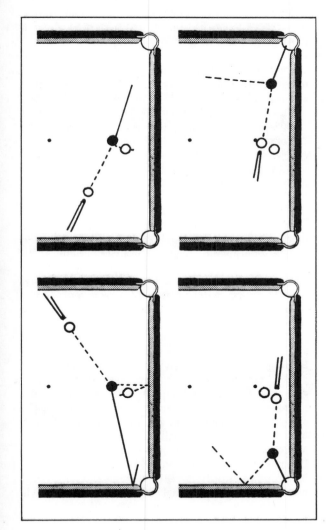

Diagram 18
(a) A soft cannon (2) leaves a pot red and moves the object-white away from the spot. (b) The red is potted (5) to leave the cue-ball at an angle to play the cannon via the top cushion. (c) The cannon (7) leaves the red over the top pocket and nudges the object-white back to its original position shown in (a). (d) The pot red (10) restores the position as it was in (a), thus completing the 'movement of ten'.

of play. No doubt the championship would have been kept alive had Lindrum agreed to visit England again or to play McConachy for the title somewhere in Australia in the late forties but he was disinclined to do either. He was, everyone knew, the best player but total invulnerability was his irrational objective, hence his eccentric refusal, in his latter years, to have any kind of opponent in his exhibitions.

Tom Cleary, later world amateur champion, Lindrum's opponent in many exhibition matches, testified to a most likeable side of Lindrum's character but was never able, he revealed, to persuade him to pass on any of his knowledge of the game. Isolated to some extent by his genius but even more by an inner self buried so deep that no one could reach it, Lindrum surrounded himself with an emotional wall which accounted at least in part for his pathological reluctance to involve himself in matches that really mattered.

Free of this pressure, he scored like a machine. In 1940, he made a break of 3301 under baulkline rules against Fred Lindrum (conceding 7000 and counting only breaks over 700!) and in 1944 breaks of 3737 and 3752 in succession. His efforts for charity during the war earned him the OBE.

He died suddenly while holidaying at Surfers Paradise on 30 July 1960, aged 62. His career had included one quadruple thousand, 17 over 3000, 29 over 2000 and 711 over 1000.

CLARK McCONACHY (1895–1980)

Clark McConachy, son of a Timaru billiard hall proprietor, watched George Gray, the Australian red ball specialist, when he toured New Zealand, and set himself to practise red ball play six hours a day. When he was 17, he made a red ball break of 1983.

In 1914, he beat Bill Stevenson for the New Zealand Professional Championship and held it unchallenged for the rest of his career. He toured New Zealand, Australia, India and South Africa before coming to Britain for the 1922 championship. Playing with ivories, which 'threw' some 1½ inches narrower then the composition balls with which he had played all his life, he was well beaten by Tom Reece but later that year made a break of 985 with ivories which was then a world record.

He changed his game from red ball to top of the table, initially postman's knock but later a 'movement of ten' (see Diagram 18) which, in essence, was already in existence but which he refined into a repetitive method. By means of the latter, he made a break of 500 in 20 minutes in 1926, fast scoring for a player whom his rivals often found disconcertingly slow. Even nurseries, which he mastered comprehensively, did not yield points at quite the rate of Lindrum, Davis or Newman. In 1932, in a then record run of 466 consecutive cannons, he revealed a new way (see page 97) of turning the balls back and along the top cushion instead of taking them round the corner.

He beat all the other membes of the Big Four at one

time or another in week's matches. He averaged 98 – but still lost by 5902 to Davis in the title match in 1932 and came within 1108 of beating Lindrum in the 1934 semi-final but it was something of an anti-climax when he became champion in 1951. He was past his peak but with Lindrum having relinquished the title, Davis not interested in it and Newman dead, he was still far too good for John Barrie. Even Barrie had his shot at the title only because Fred Davis, then UK champion, declined to play on the grounds that the first week in September was too early in the season.

McConachy returned to New Zealand with the title and held it unchallenged until, at the age of 73 and – incredibly – suffering from Parkinson's disease in his cue arm, he was beaten by a mere 265 points by Rex Williams. Even in his eighties he was still practising and coaching in his own private billiard room in Auckland.

Prodigious determination and self-discipline, both hallmarks of his play, led him to maintain a lifelong regimen of running and exercises. His delight in his physical fitness sometimes carried him away. Once, he picked up a chair one-handed and then responded innocently to a challenge to pick up a chair in which Lindrum, due to be his opponent, was sitting. Veins throbbing, he managed this lift as well – but was hardly in an appropriate condition for the delicacies of billiards until the session was well under way!

He was the first player ever to make two breaks over a thousand in consecutive visits to the table. His highest breaks were 1943 against Davis in 1932, and 1927, a then record under baulkline rules, in 1934. At his peak he used a 21–22oz cue, much heavier than his contemporaries, and late in his career a monster of 30oz.

He was awarded the MBE in 1964 and in an age when principle very frequently ran a poor second to profit, his integrity was a byword. Snooker was very much his second game though he was nevertheless good enough, with the close control his billiards mastery gave him, to record a 147 maximum at the Beaufort Club, London in 1951.

JOE DAVIS (1901–78)

Joe Davis, born in Whitwell, Derbyshire on 15 April 1901, learnt to play in his family's pub, The Queens Hotel, in Whittington Moor. Coached by a local man, Ernest Rudge, at whose house he used to practise, he also furthered his knowledge through study of Charles Dawson's *Practical Billiards* and made his first century break at the age of 12.

When he won the Chesterfield and District Championship at the age of 13 it was clear that he had a fine future in the game and Rudge, an entrepreneur, staged exhibitions in the town featuring George Gray, Claude Falkiner, Tom Reece and Willie Smith to give the young Joe an opportunity to study these giants at first hand.

After his first professional match, in which he beat Albert Raynor by 145, receiving 1000 in 7000, at Brampton on the outskirts of Chesterfield, Davis was invited to play in the St Dunstans Christmas Handicap at Thurston's, the home of professional billiards, in Leicester Square. He made a 147 break at his first visit to the table, reached the semi-final and made a good enough impression to be introduced to the then standard grind of week's matches beating Arthur Peall, son of W. J., by 588 receiving 1500 in 8000.

He was beaten by Fred Lawrence for the Midlands professional title in 1921 but won it the following year together with the Second Division Championship, beating Peall in the final, a success which entitled him to compete in the World Championship.

Well beaten by Tom Newman, he did not enter again until 1926, by which time he was enjoying a fair degree of success though he still needed a start of about a third of the game to beat Willie Smith.

Davis's first 500 break – 599 – came in the 1924 Second Division Championship. Later in that event he made a 980 at a time when the highest break under existing rules was only 1274 by Newman. His start against Newman or Smith dwindled to 1500 or 2000 in 18 000 but when it came to a second venture in the championship in 1926 Newman beat him out of sight once again.

Davis increased his best break to 992 but was again beaten, though more narrowly, by Newman in the 1927 championship final despite a break of 2501 by means of Reece's newly-invented pendulum cannon.

By this time, Davis had long since become a master of every phase of billiards: red ball, top of the table and nursery cannons. He made his first thousand, 1070, early in 1928 and took the world title from Newman later that year, retaining it with a new championship record average of 100 by the narrow margin of 781 the following year. He increased his personal best break (by orthodox methods) to 1280.

After their epic matches in Australia in 1929, Smith and Lindrum returned to Britain under contract to Burroughes and Watts, who wanted the championship played on 'nameless' tables. Thurston's were willing to give away the championship which the BA & CC had awarded to them, but John Bisset, the BA & CC's autocratic chairman, would not have its authority questioned. Consequently, neither Lindrum, Smith nor McConachy, who was also under contract to Burroughes and Watts, competed in the 1930 championship in which Davis, averaging 113.1, beat Newman by 801 in the final. During this match, Davis made the highest break of his career, 2052.

For most of this British season, Lindrum played Smith but the one fortnight's match he played against Davis produced a record aggregate of 55 288 in which Lindrum made 23 breaks over 500 and Davis twelve. Lindrum, who made four 1000 breaks, won by 2884.

The following season, when Lindrum returned as a freelance, he (conceding 7000) Davis and Newman each won four matches in the nationwide international tournament. Davis lost a close finish to Newman when victory would have given him the first prize outright and lost to Newman again in a play-off.

No championship was organized in 1931 because of yet another wrangle among the leading players but Davis successfully defended against McConachy in 1932 when he scored over 11 000 of his winning total by nursery cannons. In January of that year, Davis had immediately replied with a break of 1247 to Lindrum's record of 4137.

In the 1932–3 season, the *News of the World* tournament, played under the new baulkline rule, saw Lindrum unsuccessfully conceding a reduced start of 6000 to other members of the Big Four but it was not until the 1933 championship that it came to a test on level terms.

Davis beat McConachy comfortably – in fact he usually, though not invariably, beat both McConachy and Newman in week's or fortnight's matches – and led Lindrum for most of the final until the Australian drew away in the last two days to win by 694. When Lindrum insisted that he would defend the title only in Australia, Davis sailed out . . . only to discover that Lindrum had made no arrangements whatsoever. After a tour in which he struggled desperately to earn enough money to get home again, Davis lost the championship match to Lindrum by 875. He never beat Lindrum level. Many times, Davis was offered contracts to return to Australia but always on condition that Lindrum could be persuaded to play him for the title. He never could.

Back in London, Davis made a break of 2002 in the *Daily Mail* sealed handicap tournament, a world record under the 200 baulkline rule, and beat Newman for the new United Kingdom Professional Championship which, with Lindrum remaining in Australia and the world title thus out of circulation, became the premier event of the British season, albeit with snooker pushing billiards ever further towards the sidelines.

Davis still played billiards of high quality when there was any call for it, scoring wins in the UK final over Newman every year until the outbreak of war. His break of 1784 under the again revised baulkline rule, the crossing having to be accomplished between the 180 and 200 mark in each 200 points of a break, stood as a record from 1936 until the rules were changed, though even today, under easier rules, it has not been bettered.

After the war, Davis's billiards was limited to half-hours in exhibitions as a curtain raiser to the snooker except for an annual week's match of billiards and snooker at Leicester Square Hall with Willie Smith in which, in one session, he achieved the amazingly all-round feat of a 639 break at billiards and two centuries and a 64 in three frames of snooker. Undoubtedly, he could have regained his pre-war standard or even exceeded it but with little public demand for billiards and thus no commercial end product he devoted himself almost exclusively to snooker.

Willie Smith (*left*) and Joe Davis prepare to string for break in their long awaited match at the Dorland Hall, London in January 1933. 'Stringing' is the traditional method of determining which player has choice of ball and/or playing the first shot. Both players play simultaneously from the baulk line: the player whose ball finishes nearest the baulk cushion has the choice.

World Professional Billiards Championship (1870–1920)

1870	(Feb)	W. Cook	J. Roberts Snr	1200–1083
	(Apr)	J. Roberts Jnr	W. Cook	1000– 522
	(Jun)	J. Roberts Jnr	A. Bowles	1000– 759
	(Nov)	J. Bennett	J. Roberts Jnr	1000– 905
1871	(Jan)	J. Roberts Jnr	J. Bennett	1000– 637
	(May)	W. Cook	J. Roberts Jnr	1000– 985
	(Nov)	W. Cook	J. Bennett	1000– 942
1872	(Mar)	W. Cook	J. Roberts Jnr	1000– 799
1874	(Feb)	W. Cook	J. Roberts Jnr	1000– 784
1875	(May)	J. Roberts Jnr	W. Cook	1000– 837
	(Dec)	J. Roberts Jnr	W. Cook	1000– 865
1877	(May)	J. Roberts Jnr	W. Cook	1000– 779
1880	(Nov)	J. Bennett	W. Cook	1000– 949
1881	(Jan)	J. Bennett	T. Taylor	1000– 910
1885	(Apr)	J. Roberts Jnr	W. Cook	3000–2908
	(Jun)	J. Roberts Jnr	J. Bennett	3000–1360
1899		C. Dawson	J. North	9000–4715
1900		C. Dawson	H. W. Stevenson	9000–6775
1901		H. W. Stevenson	C. Dawson	9000–6406
		C. Dawson	H. W. Stevenson	9000–5796
		H. W. Stevenson*		
1903		C. Dawson	H. W. Stevenson	9000–8700
1908		M. Inman*		
1909		M. Inman	A. Williams	9000–7662

Under Billiards Control Club Rules

1909	H. W. Stevenson*		
1910	H. W. Stevenson	M. Inman (match abandoned)	13370–13212
	H. W. Stevenson	M. Inman	18000–16907
1911	H. W. Stevenson	M. Inman	18000–16914
1912	M. Inman	T. Reece	18000– 9675
1913	M. Inman	T. Reece	18000–16627
1914	M. Inman	T. Reece	18000–12826
1919	M. Inman	H. W. Stevenson	16000– 9468
1920	W. Smith	C. Falkiner	16000–14500

*Declared champion – no contest

111

World Professional Billiards Championship (1921–1951)

	Winner (breaks)	Score (average)	Loser (breaks)	Score (average)
1921				
First round	C. Falkiner 560	7 334 (35·3)	H. W. Stevenson	5 084 (24·3)
	T. Newman 467	8 000 (54·0)	T. Tothill	3 267 (22·0)
Semi-finals	Newman 627, 531	8 000 (56·7)	Falkiner 587	6 627 (47·3)
	T. Reece		F. Lawrence	
Final	Newman	16 000 (n.r.)	Reece	10 744 (n.r.)
1922				
First round	T. Reece	8 000 (35·2)	C. McConachy	6 767 (29·9)
Semi-finals	T. Newman 561, 512	8 000 (52·6)	J. Davis	5 181 (34·1)
	C. Falkiner 391	8 000 (41·9)	Reece 455	7 289 (38·2)
Final	Newman	16 000 (56·4)	Falkiner	15 167 (52·7)
1923				
First round	M. Inman	16 000 (n.r.)	A. Peall	11 758 (n.r.)
	C. Falkiner	16 000 (n.r.)	T. Reece	14 952 (n.r.)
Semi-final	T. Newman 850, 705, 500 × 4	16 000 (56·3)	Inman 701	14 506 (51·1)
	W. Smith 688	16 000 (71·7)	Falkiner 782 620	8 695 (29·2)
Final	Smith 451, 446	16 000 (46·4)	Newman 638, 629, 575	15 180 (44·0)
1924				
First round	T. Newman 875	16 000 (71·4)	C. McConachy 349	8 703 (38·9)
Final	Newman 1021	16 000 (43·5)	T. Reece	14 845 (40·3)
1925	T. Newman 957, 672	16 000 (68·4)	T. Reece 512	10 092 (43·1)
1926	T. Newman 637, 574, 588	16 000 (82·0)	J. Davis 414	9 505 (49·0)
1927				
First round	M. Inman 459	8 000 (n.r.)	T. Reece 1151	5 527 (n.r.)
Second round	J. Davis 504, 588	8 000 (n.r.)	Inman	6 895
Challenge round	T. Newman 787, 1073, 1012, 891	16 000 (73·0)	Davis 2501, 727	14 763 (68·0)
1928				
First round	T. Carpenter	8 000 (22·4)	T. Reece	7 283 (20·5)
Second round	J. Davis	8 000 (66·4)	Carpenter	5 602 (41·8)
Challenge round	Davis 529, 525, 501, 425, 408, 404, 403, 400	16 000 (74·4)	T. Newman 564, 489, 467, 455, 451, 427	14 874 (69·5)
1929				
First round	T. Newman 553	8 000 (74·1)	T. Carpenter 453	5 984 (55·4)
Final	J. Davis 838, 609, 599	18 000 (100·0)	Newman 723, 691, 672, 647, 576	17 219 (96·2)
1930				
First round	T. Newman 1567, 1047	24 001 (85·1)	M. Inman	10 104 (35·8)
	J. Davis	21 975 (82·0)	C. Falkiner	19 815 (74·0)
Final	Davis 2052, 500 × 9	20 918 (113·1)	Newman 500 × 12	20 117 (109·9)
1932	J. Davis 1058, 844, 774	25 161 (112·0)	C. McConachy 1432, 916, 889	19 259 (98·0)
1933				
First round	W. Lindrum 1578, 984	21 470 (n.r.)	T. Newman 877, 805	20 252 (n.r.)
	J. Davis 995	20 136 (n.r.)	C. McConachy 675	16 110 (n.r.)
Final	Lindrum 1492, 1272, 1013	21 815 (92·0)	Davis 792	21 121 (89·0)
1934				
First round	W. Lindrum 1065, 807	21 903 (n.r.)	C. McConachy 892, 829	20 795 (n.r.)
Final	Lindrum 1474, 1353	23 533 (n.r.)	J. Davis 824, 728	22 678 (n.r.)
1951	C. McConachy 481, 438, 425, 397, 376	6 681 (60·0)	J. Barrie 367, 336	5 057 (44·8)

United Kingdom Professional Championship (1934–1951)

	Winner (breaks)	Score (average)	Loser (breaks)	Score (average)
1934	J. Davis 537, 504	18 745	T. Newman 809, 693, 603, 547	18 301
1935	J. Davis 609, 1264, 548, 564, 638, 1002, 545	21 733	T. Newman 848, 677, 749, 732, 598	19 919
1936				
First round	W. Smith	10 373 (60·0)	S. Lee	7 212 (42·0)
Semi-finals	T. Newman	9 561 (75·0)	S. Smith	7 792 (60·0)
	J. Davis	10 965 (93·0)	W. Smith	9 566 (80·0)
Final	J. Davis	21 710 (125·0)	T. Newman	19 790 (114·0)
1937				
First round	S. Smith	8 135	S. Lee	4 209
	(match abandoned after nine sessions)			
Semi-finals	T. Newman	w.o.	W. Smith	scr.
	J. Davis	12 046	S. Smith	8 516
Final	J. Davis 1191, 1179, 1000, 997, 793, 592, 587, 580, 556, 550, 500	22 601 (146·0)	T. Newman 782, 774, 720, 671, 670, 603, 593, 588, 547	18 321 (118·0)
1938				
Semi-finals	T. Newman 556, 771, 602, 599	8 959	S. Smith 740	7 227
	J. Davis 1013, 840, 988, 666	15 238	S. Lee	6 048
Final	J. Davis	20 933	T. Newman	19 542
1939–45 No contests				
1946	J. Barrie	8 972	W. Leigh	6 782
1947	S. Smith	7 002	J. Barrie	6 428
1948–9 No contests				
1950				
First round	J. Barrie	7 645 (34·8)	S. Lee	5 593 (25·4)
Semi-finals	J. Barrie	7 009 (46·7)	W. Smith	5 941 (39·6)
	K. Kennerley	w.o.		
Final	J. Barrie	9 046 (48·9)	K. Kennerley	5 069 (27·4)
1951	F. Davis	8 120	K. Kennerley	6 011

Modern Billiards

From 1951, when Clark McConachy won the World Professional Billiards Championship and returned to New Zealand with the trophy, until 1968, when Rex Williams travelled to Auckland to challenge him for the title, professional billiards was dormant. Williams's capture of the title and four successful defences in his 12 year reign as champion revived it fitfully but it was not until the late seventies, notably with the revival of the United Kingdom Championship in 1979, that the professional game could look beyond mere survival. To some extent, though, the explosion of interest in snooker carried the fall-out effect of stimulating new interest in the parent game. Sponsors began to be attracted to it and real hopes are in the air of television bringing the game to a new public.

REX WILLIAMS (1933–)

It was ironic that Rex Williams should become world professional champion at billiards, his 'second' game, which he did not play seriously for some 15 years while failing to fulfil the expectation of those who saw in him, as English amateur snooker champion at the age of 17, a future world professional snooker champion.

He was an outstanding junior at both games, winning the Boys (under 16) Billiards and Snooker Championships twice each and the Junior (under 19) Championships twice each before turning professional when he was 17. At this point, he virtually abandoned billiards

– apart from 20 minutes or so as a curtain raiser to an evening of exhibition snooker it had no place in the professional scene – in favour of working on his snooker.

In 1965, in Capetown, Williams equalled Joe Davis's official break record of 147 but it was his misfortune, at an important stage of his development, to have so few tournaments to get his teeth into. Sound as his technique was, he did not develop into a great winner of matches.

Away from the table, it was entirely through his efforts that the World Professional Snooker Championship which fell into abeyance from 1957 to 1964 through want of public support, was revived on a challenge basis and the Professional Billiards Players Association was resurrected. Williams himself twice challenged the title holder, John Pulman, unsuccessfully.

He did though, on a predominantly snooker trip to Australia, decide, in 1968, to call at Auckland to play Clark McConachy, the 73-year-old New Zealander who had held the world professional billiards title unopposed since 1951. With McConachy suffering from Parkinson's disease in his cue arm and Williams having played little recent billiards, the standard of play was a travesty of what it had been in the heyday of the championship but it did at least bring the event back to life.

Unfortunately, it was also to prove the straw which broke the always fragile bridge between the PBPA and the BA & CC. Williams, not unreasonably, said that he would require a £250 guarantee to defend the title. The BA & CC characteristically hardly appearing to appreciate the financial aspect which loomed so large for professionals, ordered him to defend within six months. No proposal was placed before him by the expiry of this period but he then accepted an offer to defend against Albert Johnson, an Australian. The BA & CC then insisted that he should defend against Leslie Driffield, newly-turned professional who still sat on the BA & CC council. Williams declined and was stripped of the title.

Rex Williams

Ray Edmonds, World Professional Billiards champion 1985.

Karnehm, by now accepted as a WPBSA member, was beaten by almost half the game when he challenged Williams at the Marconi Athletic Club, Chelmsford in September 1973. Two defences in Australia against Eddie Charlton, in 1974 and 1976, yielded two more comfortable wins.

Williams took the leading role in persuading the WPBSA to revert from 'five' to 'two' pots in late 1978. This ruled out the British Open Championship which Jim Williamson intended to run at the Northern Snooker Centre, Leeds. With amateurs now committed to 'three' pots the B & SCC withdrew its support and sanction on behalf of the amateur world.

Williamson then decided to revive the United Kingdom Professional Championship which had lain dormant since 1951. Williams won this event but sustained a surprise defeat at the hands of Karnehm in the 1980 final. His reign as world champion was ended by Fred Davis in a Williamson promotion, sponsored by Yorkshire Bank, in May 1980.

Even during his reign, Williams's energies were generally devoted to snooker, his chairmanship of the WPBSA and his trade interests, notably Power Glide Cues, which he founded, and later Rex Williams Leisure, which specialized in the manufacture and hire of pool tables.

His best snooker championship performance was in 1972 when he beat Ray Reardon 25–23 in the quarter-finals before losing by only the odd frame, 31–30, to Alex Higgins in the semi-final though in 1974 he again reached the semi-final with wins over John Pulman and Perrie Mans. He slipped down the snooker rankings thereafter but had some notable one-off wins at various times over Terry Griffiths, Doug Mountjoy, David Taylor, Jimmy White, Ray Reardon, Bill Werbeniuk and Dennis Taylor.

Later that year, when the event was restored to a tournament format at the Brownsover Hotel, Rugby, he was beaten in the quarter-finals by Mark Wildman but regained the title when it was next staged, in 1982, at the Astra La Reserve Club, Sutton Coldfield after a desperate semi-final finish in which he beat Davis by a mere 6 points. He was beaten by Wildman in the 1983 UK semi-final but retained the world title at Peterborough later that year. Nevertheless, incidents in which he was involved on semi-finals day caused him to be fined £500 by the WPBSA for misbehaviour and he relinquished the chairmanship of that body until he was restored to the chair three months later. He also said that he would not play competitive billiards again and did not in fact compete in the 1984 and 1985 World Championships although he won the sprint style billiards event staged for Channel 4 in 1985.

The PBPA feeling that there was a hidden intention for Driffield to play Jack Karnehm, the BA & CC's chairman for the title, dissociated themselves from the BA & CC renaming themselves the World Professional Billiards and Snooker Association and claimed autonomy for the professional game in December 1970. Driffield and Karnehm, the only professionals not to challenge the authority of the BA & CC did subsequently meet for the BA & CC version of the title and Driffield defended it against Johnson.

Williams, meanwhile, continued to be recognized by everyone except the BA & CC (who no longer had any authority in professional matters) as champion though it hardly enhanced the status of the event that his first challenger was Bernard Bennett, who provided the venue and the required financial guarantee but hardly the appropriate quality of opposition in 1971 at his own Castle Club in Southampton.

World Professional Billiards Championships (1968–85)

	Winner (breaks)	Score (average)	Loser (breaks)	Score (average)
1968	R. Williams 293	5499 (n.r.)	C. McConachy 236, 200	5234 (n.r.)
1971	R. Williams 480, 372, 353, 325, 302	9250 (n.r.)	B. Bennett 132	4058 (n.r.)
1973	R. Williams 528, 363, 309	8360 (50·7)	J. Karnehm 215	4336 (26·1)
1974	R. Williams 506, 365, 308, 307	7017 (43·6)	E. Charlton 488, 401	4916 (30·4)
1976	R. Williams 532, 349, 382, 306	9105 (42·1)	E. Charlton 333	5149 (23·9)
1980 (May) *Challenge*	F. Davis 403, 225, 234, 239, 239, 275, 583	5978 (30·9)	R. Williams 226, 202, 439, 229	4452 (29·9)

With Ivan Cawood, a Rugby auctioneer and billiards enthusiast underwriting the event, the World Professional Championship was restored to a tournament format and played at the Brownsover Hall Hotel, Rugby. Fred Davis took the £4000 first prize, Mark Wildman £2000 second prize and Ray Edmonds and John Barrie £1000 each as losing semi-finalists. The match of the tournament was the quarter-final in which Rex Williams led Wildman by 614 only to fade badly in the closing stages to lose by 61.

	Winner (breaks)	Score (average)	Loser (breaks)	Score (average)
1980 (Nov) *Qualifying*	P. Morgan	1655 (21·5)	J. Dunning	1107 (12·9)
	M. Wildman 580	1968 (26·2)	B. Bennett	678 (9·0)
	S. Davis	1809 (16·9)	K. Kennerley	965 (9·1)
Quarter-finals	J. Barrie 252, 212, 335	2186 (53·3)	S. Davis	870 (21·8)
	F. Davis (309)	1907 (43·3)	Morgan	978 (22·2)
	R. Edmonds	1513 (19·4)	J. Karnehm	1306 (17·0)
	Wildman	1476 (25·9)	R. Williams 517	1415 (24·8)
Semi-finals	F. Davis 501	1253 (34·8)	Barrie 246	1153 (32·0)
	Wildman 204	1629 (21·4)	Edmonds	955 (12·6)
Final	F. Davis 200, 361	3037 (30·4)	Wildman	2064 (20·6)

	Winner (breaks)	Score (average)	Loser (breaks)	Score (average)
1982 *First round*	C. Everton	1500 (23·4)	B. Bennett	556 (8·6)
Quarter-finals	F. Davis	1500 (30·6)	Everton	652 (13·6)
	R. Williams	1500 (31·9)	J. Karnehm	569 (11·9)
	R. Edmonds	1500 (16·5)	K. Kennerley	753 (8·2)
	M. Wildman	1500 (21·7)	J. Fitzmaurice	721 (10·5)
Semi-finals	Williams	1500 (20·3)	Davis	1494 (19·9)
	Wildman 203	1500 (24·2)	Edmonds	765 (12·1)
Final	Williams 207, 259, 217	3000 (26·1)	Wildman	1785 (15·5)

	Winner (breaks)	Score (average)	Loser (breaks)	Score (average)
1983				
Qualifying	I. Williamson	1000 (12.5)	D. Martin	710 (8.8)
	B. Bennett	1000 (11.2)	G. Cripsey	683 (6.3)
First round	J. Karnehm	1500 (13.4)	M. Darrington	1199 (10.6)
	Bennett	1500 (10.1)	J. Fitzmaurice	1396 (9.4)
	C. Everton	1500 (16.3)	Williamson	108 5(11.8)
	E. Charlton	1500 (14.3)	T. Murphy	1105 (10.5)
Quarter-finals	R. Williams 228	1500 (31.3)	Bennett	443 (9.0)
	F. Davis 427	1500 (38.5)	Everton	477 (11.9)
	R. Edmonds 358	1500 (20.0)	Karnehm	1075 (14.1)
	Charlton	1500 (15.3)	M. Wildman	778 (8.0)
Semi-finals	Davis 214,228	1500(27.8)	Charlton	956(17.7)
	Williams	1500(60.0)	Edmonds	671(26.8)
Final	Williams 235, 212	1500(38.4)	Davis	605(15.1)

Rex Williams retained the title in 1983 at the Court Snooker Centre, Peterborough but the event was marred by an incident on semi-finals day which caused his match with Ray Edmonds to start 48 minutes late. Williams was subsequently fined £500 by the WPBSA.

	Winner (breaks)	Score (average)	Loser (breaks)	Score (average)
1984				
Qualifying	T. Murphy	1021 (15)	M. Darrington	861 (12.9)
First round	P. Morgan	1021 (15)	b. Bennett	639 (9.5)
	I. Williamson	746 (13.3)	C. Everton	496 (8.9)
	J. Karnehm	1270 (23.1)	G. Ganim Jr.	733 (13.3)
	Murphy	1050 (14.2)	J. Fitzmaurice	868 (11.6)
Quarter-finals	F. Davis	1242 (23.9)	Murphy	852 (16.7)
	E. Charlton 319	944 (24.8)	Karnehm	931 (24.5)
	Williamson	918 (24.8)	R. Edmonds	805 (23.0)
	M. Wildman	1347 (28.7)	Morgan	759 (15.8)
Semi-finals	Charlton	1436 (28.7)	Davis	829 (16.6)
	Wildman 205	1501 (29.4)	Williamson	849 (16.4)
Final	Wildman 241	1045 (19.7)	Charlton	1012 (19.1)

The WPBSA formally supported the event for the first time in 1984 with a contribution of £2500 to the £8000 prize fund. Strachans were the main sponsors with a contribution of £3000 and the Majestic Snooker Centre, Portsmouth, who promoted the event contributed £2500.

With Rex Williams choosing not to defend the title there was a new champion, Mark Wildman, who overcame Eddie Charlton by a mere 33 points in the five hour final. Charlton had come to the table for his last visit 87 behind with 8 minutes to play but had scored only 54 by the time the bell went. In the quarter-finals, Charlton had prevailed in a similarly close finish playing out time with 92 to beat Jack Karnehm by only 13.

1985

The WPBSA introduced for the 1985 Championship a revolutionary new format, playing all matches over the best of five games of 400 up.

First round: P. Francisco beat M. Darrington 3–0; I. Williamson beat B. Bennett 3–0; J. Karnehm beat E. Charlton 3–0; R. Edmonds beat A. Higgins 3–0; M. Wildman beat T. Jones 3–0; N. Dagley beat J. Fitzmaurice (253)–0; F. Davis beat C. Everton 3–1.

Quarter-finals: Dagley beat Karnehm 3(270)–0; R. Foldvari beat Davis 3–0; Wildman beat P. Francisco 3(245)–0; Edmonds beat Williamson 3(252)–1.

Semi-finals: Edmonds beat Wildman 3–0(227); Dagley beat Foldvari 3–0.

Final: Edmonds beat Dagley 3–1(201).

Super Crystalate UK Professional Billiards Championships (1979–83)

	Winner (breaks)	Score (average)	Loser (breaks)	Score (average)
1979				
Quarter finals	J. Karnehm 281, 286	2041 (35.8)	J. Dunning	760 (13.1)
	R. Williams 259, 309	1557 (31.8)	R. Edmonds	1350 (27.0)
	J. Barrie 238, 404, 206 (unf.)	2292 (46.8)	S. Davis	629 (12.6)
	F. Davis	1953 (34.9)	B. Bennett	679 (12.1)
Semi-finals	Williams 224, 372	1539 (32.7)	Karnehm	1182·(24.6)
	Barrie 227, 444	1548 (43.0)	F. Davis 245	1031 (28.6)
Final	Williams 228, 388, 253	2952 (44.4)	Barrie 379	2116 (32.0)
1980				
First round	S. Davis	1670 (21.7)	S. Hood	1029 (13.4)
	B. Bennett	1093 (12.0)	C. Ross	933 (10.1)
Quarter-finals	J. Barrie	2001 (32.8)	M. Wildman	815 (13.1)
	J. Karnehm 322	1990 (28.0)	K. Kennerley	842 (11.9)
	R. Edmonds	1380 (17.7)	Bennett	914 (11.6)
	R. Williams 205	1871 (33.4)	S. Davis	862 (15.4)
Semi-finals	Karnehm 225, 230	1755 (35.1)	Barrie 229	1085 (21.3)
	Williams 230, 234 (unf.)	2159 (41.5)	Edmonds	789 (15.2)
Final	Karnehm 205, 208	2518 (28.0)	Williams 256, 423	2423 (26.6)
1981				
Qualifying	S. Davis	980	B. Bennett	770
	R. Edmonds 206	1881	G. Miles	473
	J. Pulman	1078	K. Kennerley	879
Quarter-finals	J. Karnehm 207	1307 (22.2	Edmonds	935 (15.8)
	J. Barrie 381	1743 (41.5)	Pulman	509 (12.1)
	R. Williams, 265, 385, 290	1575 (50.8)	S. Davis	579 (18.1)
	F. Davis 217	1304 (29.0)	M. Wildman	805 (17.9)
Semi-finals	Karnehm 390	1338 (23.1)	Barrie	1074 (18.5)
	Williams 217, 505, 231	2003 (74.2)	F. Davis	999 (37.0)
Final	Williams 393, 385	1592 (45.5)	Karnehm	1112 (31.8)
1983				
First round	B. Bennett	750 (10·4)	D. Greaves	280 (3·7)
	C. Everton	750 (28·9)	M. Darrington	177 (6·5)
	I. Williamson	750 (14·4)	T. Murphy	625 (11·8)
	R. Edmonds	750 (19·7)	J. Fitzmaurice	505 (13·3)
Quarter-finals	Edmonds	1500 (30·0)	J. Karnehm	1194 (23·4)
	M. Wildman 285, 217	1500 (41·7)	Everton 393	1170 (33·4)
	F. Davis 283, 292	1500 (42·9)	Williamson·	604 (17·3)
	R. Williams 246	1500 (46·9)	Bennett	230 (7·0)
Semi-finals	Wildman 495	1500 (45·5)	Williams 208, 225	1272 (38·5)
	Davis 201	1500 (36·6)	Edmonds	936 (22·8)
Final	Wildman	1500 (21·4)	Davis	1032 (14·5)

Right: Joe Johnson in play during his world amateur record break of 140 against Graham Miles at Middlesbrough in 1978.

ROUND
THE WORLD

ENGLAND

Late in the nineteenth century – indeed for at least the first 30 years of the twentieth – it was assumed by all loyal Englishmen that England was the centre of the universe. Britain had an Empire which was sustained by acceptance of the class divisions within it and an understanding not only that England knew best but that its governing class knew best of all. It seemed entirely natural that the sports world should be run by paternalistic amateurs rather than professionals.

Against this trend, the Billiards Association was founded in 1885 by professional and trade figures but before long amateur enthusiasts were in control. Amateur and professional interests coexisted uneasily and there were several partial and temporary ruptures until the final split between the amateur and professional sides of the game in 1971 when the professionals dissociated themselves from the Billiards and Snooker Control Council (then the Billiards Association and Control Council) and reconstituted the Professional Billiard Players Association as the World Professional Billiards and Snooker Association, thus declaring its autonomy.

Also in 1971, representatives of overseas national associations, increasingly conscious of the anomaly of the same body governing both the English domestic and international amateur games and dissatisfied, moreover, at the BA & CC's conduct of international amateur issues brought into being the World Billiards and Snooker Council.

To placate England's wrath this name was changed to the International Billiards and Snooker Federation in 1973. The IBSF, a one nation, one vote body, took over the conduct of World Amateur Championships and effectively became the rule amending body. The IBSF did not challenge the copyright on the rules which the B & SCC claimed (together with the income therefrom) but persuaded the B & SCC to make no alteration without consulting them.

The B & SCC still described itself as the world governing body but its functions in reality were largely those of an English national amateur association with a senior standing among equals in the international amateur sphere. The IBSF formally became the world amateur governing body in 1984.

The word 'English' was superfluous to the amateur billiards championship, founded in 1888. If the event took place in England it followed that it was the leading event of its kind just as the World Professional Billiards Championship was known simply as 'The Championship' until 1933.

It was in 1920 that Arthur Walker, a South African millionaire, first suggested a British Empire Amateur Billiards Championship but the BA & CC resisted this on the grounds that the amateur championship was sufficient. The Australian champion J. R. Hooper, visited London for the Amateur Championship of 1921 and was beaten by Sidney Fry in the semi-final.

In 1922 an Empire championship was approved in principle but there were various delays before the inaugural event was held at Thurston's, Leicester Square in 1926. At this point Scotland opted out of the Amateur Championship in order to run its own national championship while the BA & CC decided that it could no longer accept entries from Scottish, Irish or colonial players, though it continued to do so from Wales. The present position is that entries are accepted from Scottish, Welsh and Irish players (though not if they are resident in Ireland) so the event retains some of its original open character. This is also true of the English Amateur Snooker Championship, founded in 1916.

A rigid definition of amateurism survived until the 1960s when, in common with other sports, under the table payments for amateurs became so widespread that after a period of turning a blind eye it was tacitly agreed that the time had come for a new formula. An international agreement in 1972 provided that an amateur would be defined as a player who was not a member of the WPBSA, had not declared himself a professional or who did not lend his name to advertising or endorsing goods in connection with the playing of the game. In effect, this made the distinction between amateurs and professionals not one of cash but of which governing body a player chose to acknowledge.

The first championship was a fiasco. S. S. Christey beat W. D. Courtney to win the Southern division (the 44 competitors from England, Scotland and Ireland being divided into four areas) but was then objected to on the grounds that he was a professional. Christey had played against professionals in a tournament the previous year which had been advertised as 'open to amateurs and markers' but nevertheless the objection was upheld. All the players whom Christey had beaten claimed the right to play again and H. A. O. Lonsdale eventually emerged as the first champion.

Christey, who was subsequently reinstated, won the title three times though this total was exceeded in the early days of the championship by A. P. Gaskell (six) and A. R. Wisdom (four). Many of the early championships were conducted on a challenge basis with the winner of a challengers tournament earning the right to play the holder for the title. In 1893, indeed, S. H. Fry had to play Wisdom, the holder, two games of 1000 up. Having won both, Fry then had to play a further 1500 up for the first of the eight titles he won before his last success in 1925. The championship was not played on what is now recognised as an orthodox knock-out basis until 1913.

The standard of play now seems modest. Christey made a break of 146 in the first championship but it was not until the sixth that there was another century, 114 by Gaskell, a useful spot stroke-exponent. A. W. T. Good, a red ball player, who won the title four times between 1902 and 1915, made a championship record of 155 (153 off the red) in 1902. This was broken in 1905 by G. Heginbottom (174), in 1913 by

Billiards Championship

Year	Players	Score		Year	Players	Score
1888	H. A. O. Lonsdale–J. Tither	500– 356	*	1931	S. Lee–M. A. Boggin	3793–3134
	A. P. Gaskell–H. A. O. Lonsdale	1500–1349		1932	S. Lee–F. Edwards	4674–3508
1889	A. P. Gaskell declared champion			1933	S. Lee–H. F. E. Coles	4458–3237
	A. P. Gaskell–E. W. Alabone	1500–1278		1934	S. Lee–F. Edwards	3829–3509
1890	A. P. Gaskell–S. H. Fry	1500–1395		1935	H. F. E. Coles–M. A. Boggin	3707–3272
	A. P. Gaskell–N. Defries	1500–1395		1936	J. Thompson–j. H. Beetham	3179–3149
	W. D. Courtney–A. P. Gaskell	1500–1141		1937	K. Kennerley–J. Thompson	4703–3633
1891	W. D. Courtney–A. P. Gaskell	1500– 971		1938	K. Kennerley–J. Thompson	4714–3925
	A. P. Gaskell–W. D. Courtney	1500–1188		1939	K. Kennerley–A. Spencer	4423–3264
1892	A. R. Wisdom–'Osbourne'	1500–1094		1940	K. Kennerley–A. Spencer	3931–3749
	S. S. Christey–S. H. Fry	1500– 928		1941–45	No contests	
1893	A. R. Wisdom–Mr Buxton	1500– 852		1946	M. Showman–J. H. Beetham	3077–2539
	S. H. Fry–A. R. Wisdom	1500–1239		1947	J. Thompson–A. Hibbert	4104–3185
	A. H. Vahid–S. S. Christey	1500–1395		1948	J. Thompson–H. G. Terry	5202–2816
1894	H. Mitchell–A. Vinson	1500–1464		1949	F. Edwards–J. Tregoning	4813–3297
	W. T. Maughan–H. Mitchell	1500–1202		1950	F. Edwards–J. Tregoning	4968–3385
1896	S. H. Fry–W. T. Maughan	1500–1439		1952	A. L. Driffield–J. H. Beetham	2894–2793
1899	A. R. Wisdom–S. H. Fry	1500–1297		1953	A. L. Driffield–F. Edwards	4136–3016
1900	S. H. Fry–A. R. Wisdom	1500–1428		1954	A. L. Driffield–F. Edwards	4165–3030
1901	S. S. Christey–W. S. Jones	1500–1305		1955	F. Edwards–A. Nolan	4194–3206
1902	A. W. T. Good–S. S. Christey	2000–1669		1956	F. Edwards–A. L. Driffield	3395–3327
	A. W. T. Good–A. J. Browne	2000–1689		1957	A. L. Driffield–F. Edwards	4464–2894
1903	A. R. Wisdom–A. W. T. Good	2000–1783		1958	A. L. Driffield–J. T. Wright	4483–2587
	S. S. Christey–C. V. Diehl	2000–1314		1959	A. L. Driffield–J. H. Beetham	4968–3385
1904	W. A. Lovejoy–A. W. T. Good	2000–1733		1960	J. H. Beetham–R. C. Wright	3426–2289
1905	A. W. T. Good–G. A. Heginbottom	2000–1739		1961	J. H. Beetham–R. C. Wright	4060–2043
1906	E. C. Breed–A. W. T. Good	2000–1620		1962	A. L. Driffield–J. H. Beetham	4312–2993
1907	H. C. Virr–J: Nugent	2000–1896		1962	A. L. Driffield–J. H. Beetham	4312–2993
1908	H. C. Virr–G. A. Heginbottom	2000–1841		1963	J. H. Beetham–N. Dagley	4052–2759
1909	Major Fleming–H. C. Virr	2000–1501		1964	A. Nolan–A. L. Driffield	3455–2188
1910	H. A. O. Lonsdale–Major Fleming	2000–1882		1965	N. Dagley–A. Nolan	2983–2757
1911	H. C. Virr–Major Fleming	3000–2716		1966	N. Dagley–A. Nolan	3018–2555
1912	H. C. Virr–Major Fleming	3000–2993		1967	A. L. Driffield–C. Everton	3395–2328
1913	H. C. Virr–J. Nugent	3000–1956		1968	M. Wildman–C. Everton	2652–2540
1914	H. C. Virr–J. Nugent	3000–1962		1969	J. Karnehm–M. Wildman	3722–2881
1915	A. W. T. Good–G. A. Heginbottom	2000–1444	†	1970	N. Dagley–A. Nolan	4467–2372
1916	S. H. Fry–G. A. Heginbottom	2000–1417		1971	N. Dagley–W. J. Dennison	3672–2019
1917	J. Graham-Symes–S. H. Fry	2000–1540		1972	N. Dagley–A. Nolan	3115–2469
1918	J. Graham-Symes–'Osbourne'	2000–1121		1973	N. Dagley–C. Everton	2804–1976
1919	S. H. Fry–J. Graham-Symes	2000–1729		1974	N. Dagley–A. Nolan	2961–2677
1920	S. H. Fry–W. B. Marshall	3000–2488		1975	N. Dagley–R. Close	2917–2693
1921	S. H. Fry–J. Graham-Symes	3000–2591		1976	R. Close–C. Everton	2412–2194
1922	J. Graham-Symes–W. P. McLeod	3000–2661		1977	R. Close–J. H. Beetham	2951–2031
1923	W. P. McLeod–J. Graham–Symes	3000–2867		1978	N. Dagley–R. Close	4611–2309
1924	W. P. McLeod–J. Graham–Symes	3000–2862		1979	N. Dagley–K. Shirley	3311–1549
1925	S. H. Fry–W. B. Marshall	3000–2778		1980	N. Dagley–C. Everton	2825–2172
1926	J. Earlam–C. M. Helyer	3000–1751		1981	N. Dagley–R. Close	3805–2190
1927	L. Steeples–H. F. E. Coles	3000–2449		1982	N. Dagley–R. Close	4208–2169
1928	A. Wardle–A. W. T. Good	3000–2189		1983	N. Dagley–R. Close	3530–1586
1929	H. F. E. Coles–S. ee	3000–2215		1984	N. Dagley–R. Close	3412–1757
1930	L. Steeples–H. F. E. Coles	3000–2462		1985	R. Close–K. Shirley	2493–2060

*twelve hour finals †ten hour finals

J. G. Taylor (210) and in the same year by Fry (236).

H. C. Virr, a very consistent red ball player, won the title six times between 1907 and 1914 and the immediate post-war years were dominated by Fry, also a championship class golfer, and J. Graham-Symes, three times champion, both of whom were products of London's gentlemen's clubs and thus exuded either privilege or the Corinthian spirit depending on your point of view.

In 1926, composition balls, which were not only cheaper but more consistent, replaced ivories as the approved championship ball. This, together with a reduction in the entry fee from two guineas to half a guinea made the championship socially less exclusive.

Snooker Championship

1916	C. N. Jacques–n.r.	
1917	C. N. Jacques–n.r.	
1918	T. N. Palmer–n.r.	
1919	S. H. Fry–n.r.	
1920	A. R. Wisdom–n.r.	
1921	M. J. Vaughan–S. H. Fry	384–378
1922	J. McGlynn–C. Cox Jnr	423–301
1923	W. Coupe–E. Forshall	432–337
1924	W. Coupe–H. G. Olden	413–333
1925	J. McGlynn–W. L. Crompton	392–308
1926	W. Nash–F. T. W. Leaphard	383–356
1927	O. T. Jackson–A. W. Casey	4–2
1928	P. H. Matthews–F. Whittall	5–4
1929	L. Steeples–F. Whittall	5–4
1930	L. Steeples–F. Whittall	5–1
1931	P. H. Matthews–H. Kingsley	5–4
1932	W. E. Bach–O. T. Jackson	5–3
1933	E. Bedford–A. Kershaw	5–1
1934	C. H. Beavis–P. H. Matthews	5–2
1935	C. H. Beavis–D. Hindmarch	5–3
1936	P. H. Matthews–C. H. Beavis	5–3
1937	K. Kennerley–W. H. Dennis	6–3
1938	P. H. Matthews–K. Kennerley	6–5
1939	P. Bendon–K. Kennerley	6–4
1940	K. Kennerley–A. Brown	8–7
1941–45	No contests	
1946	H. J. Pulman–A. Brown	5–3
1947	H. Morris–C. A. Kent	5–1
1948	S. Battye–T. Postlethwaite	6–3
1949	T. C. Gordon–S. Kilbank	6–4
1950	A. Nolan–G. Owen	6–5
1951	R. Williams–P. Bendon	6–1
1952	C. Downey–J. Allen	6–1
1953	T. C. Gordon–G. Humphries	6–5
1954	G. Thompson–C. Wilson	11–9
1955	M. Parkin–A. Nolan	11–7
1956	T. C. Gordon–R. Reardon	11–9
1957	R. Gross–S. Haslam	11–6
1958	M. Owen–J. T. Fitzmaurice	11–8
1959	M. Owen–A. Barnett	11–5
1960	R. Gross–J. Price	11–4
1961	A. Barnett–R. Edmonds	11–9
1962	R. Gross–J. Barron	11–9
1963	G. Owen–R. Gross	11–3
1964	R. Reardon–J. Spencer	11–8
1965	P. Houlihan–J. Spencer	11–5
1966	J. Spencer–M. Owen	11–5
1967	M. Owen–S. Hood	11–5
1968	D. Taylor–C. Ross	11–6
1969	R. Edmonds–J. Barron	11–9
1970	J. Barron–S. Hood	11–10
1971	J. Barron–D. French	11–9
1972	J. Barron–R. Edmonds	11–9
1973	M. Owen–R. Edmonds	11–6
1974	R. Edmonds–P. Fagan	11–7
1975	S. Hood–W. Thorne	11–6
1976	C. Ross–R. Andrewartha	11–7
1977	T. Griffiths–S. Hood	13–3
1978	T. Griffiths–J. Johnson	13–5
1979	J. White–D. Martin	13–10
1980	J. O'Boye–D. Martin	13–9
1981	V. Harris–G. Wood	13–9
1982	D. Chalmers–M. Bradley	13–9
1983	T. Jones–J. Parrott	13–9
1984	S. Longworth–W. Jones	13–8
1985	T. Whitthread–J. McNellan	13–4

The beginnings of this trend had already been apparent when W. P. Macleod, a Middlesbrough man with a small plumbing business, had won both in 1923 and 1924, following which he had to fight off a challenge to his amateur status after touring more widely than was felt appropriate to his supposed income.

With composition balls and a wider spectrum of entries, the standard rose spectacularly. Joe Earlam, 20, made a new championship record of 278 (165 off the red) in the Liverpool area; Laurie Steeples made a 377 in the Sheffield area, albeit on a table which did not pass championship specifications.

Earlam, so good a red ball player that the 25 hazard limit was imposed after he won the title, also ran away with the inaugural Empire Championship but did not make the grade as a professional. Steeples, whose game was more polished, more balanced, more professional in approach, won two English and two Empire titles before ill-health forced him into premature retirement.

Maurice Boggin increased the championship record to 349 in 1929, Steeples to 354 in 1930 and Horace Coles to 363 in 1933 but it was Sydney Lee, who in 1931 won the first of his four consecutive titles,

supplemented by the Empire title in 1933, who dominated the early thirties. In 1931, acknowledging rising amateur standards, the hazard limit was reduced to fifteen and matches were played on a time limit basis rather than to a points target.

It was Lee's misfortune that he turned professional just as billiards was fading fast as a public entertainment. His long, flowing, in some respects rather flowery cue action was not suited to snooker but with a great deal of hard work he carved a comfortable niche in the game with club exhibitions, coaching and, with the advent of *Pot Black*, refereeing.

Kingsley Kennerley, who won four consecutive titles from 1937–40, was also a victim of the same syndrome although his snooker, which had been good enough to win two English amateur titles – only Wisdom, Fry and Steeples in times when snooker standards were much lower having previously performed the double – stood up better than Lee's did to the demands of the professional game.

Kennerley was a fine top of the table player, a fast, consistent scorer who set championship records which survived 40 years and several changes to easier rules.

His break of 549 in 1937 stood as a championship record until 1978. He made five centuries in a session in 1938; 4234 points in four sessions in 1939; 1218 in a session in the same year though this was just exceeded by Arthur Spencer, his opponent in the final that year, with 1266.

In statistical terms, Kennerley was the finest English amateur champion there had yet been but he was well beaten by the Australian, Bob Marshall, in the 1938 Empire Championship in Melbourne, an event which confirmed that it could no longer be assumed that whoever led English billiards led the world.

After the war, Frank Edwards, (five wins), Leslie Driffield (eight), Herbert Beetham (three) and pre-eminently Norman Dagley (fifteen) dominated English billiards. They were players of contrasting styles.

Edwards, a first time striker who played at headlong pace, had a flair for recovery shots and improvisation. He was very entertaining to watch, but with rare exceptions his statistics were much less impressive than those of the two great Australians, Marshall and Tom Cleary. After his English championship hat trick in 1949–51, Edwards also found Driffield, whom he beat only once in championship play, too consistent. In 1949, though, he did exceed Spencer's 1266 session aggregate record by two in equalling Kennerley's record of five centuries in a session. He broke the latter with six in 1953 and in 1956 set a new four hour aggregate record of 2339. He finished behind Marshall and Cleary in his two world amateur championship appearances in 1951 and 1954.

Driffield's game was greatly influenced by Willie Smith, with whom he played a great deal in his home town of Leeds. He rarely lingered long at the top of the table but his all-round game, based largely on in-offs, was played with relentless efficiency and concentration. His finest hour was his defeat of Marshall in the key match of the 1952 World Championship, his most disappointing defeat to the Indian Wilson Jones in the 1958 championship after leading by 660 with 90 minutes to play.

Resembling his fellow Yorkshireman, Geoffrey Boycott, the England batsman, in the personal importance he attached to averages and statistics, Driffield had an insatiable appetite for points whatever the state of the game. He was a great accumulator of breaks and of high averages and he fought grittily in adversity. His highest championship break was 499 and his best session average one of 102·1, both during the 1958 World Amateur, but his career was studded with averages and breaks not far short of these figures.

Beetham backed an outstanding in-off game with sound all round play and a fine temperament. Beaten four times in the final, once by a mere 30, Beetham won the English title three times in four years in 1960–65 with the 1960 World Amateur title for good measure. All his championship wins came within the period in which the hazard limit was increased from 15 to 25.

Dagley, like Driffield, won two world amateur titles and reached in addition one final and one semi-final. Jack Karnehm had one memorable year, 1969, in which he won both the English and world amateur titles but this was a rare interruption of the dominance which Dagley enjoyed. After his only losing appearance in the final, in 1963, Dagley won 15 titles in 21 attempts, securing in the process every break and average record. In the 1978 semi-final, he compiled a new World and English championship record break of 862 in a session

Norman Dagley

which led to an English record session average of 116·6. In the final, he set further records of 98·9 (highest 2½ hour session average), highest final average (67·8), highest 5 hour aggregate (2381) and highest 10 hour aggregate (4611). The very last session he played in this event, the 1984 final, saw him average 147·7 under the two pot rule.

A top of the table artist of the first order, a well nigh faultless in-off player, a master in fact of all phases of the game except nursery cannons – which no amateur has ever mastered – Dagley's greatest strength is a temperament which enables him to respond to pressure or impose it at the crucial moment.

The Amateur Snooker Championship was founded in 1916 as a charity effort for the British Sportsmen's Motor Ambulance Fund. An American, H. H. Lukens, with only a few weeks' practice at the Palmerston Restaurant, won the 1918 event under the pseudonym T. N. Palmer and the standard remained low until players from London's gentlemen's clubs were overtaken by provincials with an upbringing in money games.

The final was decided on an aggregate score of seven frames until F. T. W. Morley won four of the seven against W. Nash in the 1926 final only to lose the match 383–356. Since 1927, in this as in every championship of stature, matches have been decided on frames.

Cagey, tactical players like Jack McGlynn (two wins), Walter Coupe (two), Pat Matthews (four) and Charles Beavis (two), or billiards players who turned to snooker like Laurie Steeples (two wins) and Kingsley Kennerley (two) dominated the inter-war period. Kennerley, who reached four consecutive finals, displayed the most professional breakbuilding technique and in 1939 set a new amateur championship record with 69, W. L. Crompton's 62 having stood since 1925.

Kennerley was the first amateur champion to make even a marginal impact on professional snooker but several subsequent winners and not a few who failed to become champion did so afterwards. John Pulman (1946), Ray Reardon (1964), John Spencer (1966) and Terry Griffiths (1977, 1978) went on to win the world professional title. Gary Owen (1963), David Taylor (1968), Ray Edmonds (1969, 1974) and Jonathan Barron, who in 1970, 1971 and 1972 recorded the only hat-trick of championship wins, went on to win the World Amateur Championship which was instituted in 1963.

Rex Williams, later world professional billiards champion, was an outstanding winner in 1951, making a break of 74 and demonstrating a technique which was professional in all departments of the game in taking the title, at the age of 17 for the loss of only five frames in the whole event. Geoffrey Thompson, who dramatically made the championship's first century, 115, in 1962, won the first two day final in 1954.

Consistency, steadiness and competitiveness were the hallmarks of the success of Tommy Gordon and Ron Gross, both of whom won the title three times. Marcus Owen, younger brother of Gary, who won four titles, had all these qualities and flair besides. Had he been able to organise his life more clearly he might well have become world professional champion.

Barron, a quiet, competitive Cornishman, who visibly expressed, while his opponent was at the table, the intense nervous strain of championship play, retired when he felt the pressure of travelling and competing was getting too much for him. He was the first champion since 1961 who did not turn professional and indeed never considered doing so.

The 1979 champion, Jimmy White, was at 16 years 11 months the youngest ever. His 130 break in beating Dave Martin, in the final at the Godolphin Club, Helston, was disallowed for record purposes since the pockets were found to be considerably oversize.

Through its senior status and because it is the only national association large enough to maintain a permanent paid staff, the B & SCC also organises a number of British championships at pairs, team and junior level.

Leslie Driffield

British Junior (under 16) Championships

Billiards

1922	W. Donaldson	1952	M. Wildman
1923	W. Leigh	1953	C. Everton
1924	L. Steeples	1954	H. Burns
1925	S. Lee	1955	D. Deakes
1926	R. Gartland	1956	C. Dean
1927	R. Gartland	1957	P. Shelley
1928	R. L. Bennett	1958	P. Morgan
1929	F. Davis	1959	n.r.
1930	H. J. Bennett	1960	A. Matthews
1931	C. Desbottes	1961	B. Whitehead
1932	D. Hawkes	1962–67	No contests
1933	n.r.	1968	C. Williamson
1934	W. Swinhoe	1969	P. Bardsley
1935	D. Cruikshank	1970	W. Thorne
1936	D. Cruikshank	1971	P. Bardsley
1937	D. Curson	1972	P. Bardsley
1938	J. Hamilton	1973	T. Wells
1939	R. Smith	1974	P. Allan
1940	B. Smith	1975	S. McNamara
1941–47	No contests	1976	D. Bonney
1948	R. Williams	1977	D. Bonney
1949	R. Williams	1978	K. Walsh
1950	M. Owen	1979	A. Pyle
1951	E. Parry	1980	K. Walsh
		1981	D. Presgrave
		1982	S. Naisby
		1983	P. Gilchrist
		1984	C. Rowntree
		1985	M Russell

Snooker

1944	G. Owen	1962	J. Virgo
1945	R. Baker	1963	J. Hollis
1946	D. Thomas	1964	D. Clinton
1947	M. Knapp	1965	No contest
1948	R. Williams	1966	J. Terry
1949	R. Williams	1967	No contest
	D. Lewis	1968	E. Stone
1950	M. Owen	1969	P. Hughes
1951	M. Owen	1970	W. Thorne
1952	M. Wildman	1971	J. Mills
1953	J. Board	1972	J. Mills
1954	D. Bond	1973	P. Bardsley
1955	P. Shelley	1974	S. Holroyd
1956	A. Hart	1975	M. Hallett
1957	P. Shelley	1976	W. Jones
1958	D. Bond	1977	J. White
1959	J. Doyle	1978	D. Adds
1960	N. Cripps	1979	A. Pyle
1961	No contest	1980	T. Whitthread
		1981	C. Hamson
		1982	S. Ventham
		1983	S. Hendry
		1984	B. Morgan
		1985	B. Bunn

British Junior (under 19) Championships

Billards

1949	G. Toner	1970	J. Terry
1950	R. Williams	1971	W. Thorne
1951	R. Williams	1972	W. Thorne
1952	J. Sinclair	1973	W. Thorne
1953	M. Wildman	1974	T. Wells
1954	M. Wildman	1975	E. Hughes
1955	D. Scott	1976	S. Davis
1956	C. Everton	1977	I. Williamson
1957	C. Myers	1978	I. Williamson
1958	C. Marks	1979	M. Garvey
1959	P. Morgan	1980	G. Charville
1960	D. Bend	1981	S. Hawkins
1961	P. Morgan	1982	R. Marshall
1962	A. Matthews	1983	S. Naisby
1963	A. Matthews	1984	S. Naisby
1964–67	No contests	1985	S. Naisby
1968	D. Taylor		
1969	D. Burgess		

Snooker

1949	A. Kemp	1967	No contest
1950	J. Carney	1968	J. Maughan
1951	R. Williams	1969	J. Terry
1952	C. Wilson	1970	J. Terry
1953	C. Wilson	1971	J. Johnson
1954	M. Wildman	1972	A. Knowles
1955	W. McGivern	1973	W. Thorne
1956	E. Sinclair	1974	A. Knowles
1957	H. Burns	1975	E. Hughes
1958	W. West	1976	I. Williamson
1959	D. Root	1977	I. Williamson
1960	D. Bend	1978	T. Meo
1961	I. Rees	1979	J. O'Boye
1962	A. Matthews	1980	T. Murphy
1963	A. Matthews	1981	D. Reynolds
1964	J. Fisher	1982	N. Foulds
1965	J. Virgo	1983	M. Thompson
1966	J. Hollis	1984	M. Clark
		1985	W. Rendle

NORTHERN IRELAND

The Northern Ireland BA & CC was founded in May 1924 and first ran a billiards championship the following year. Its billiards standards have remained modest and Jack Bates, who was also qualified at various times to represent both the Republic of Ireland and Scotland, has been its best exponent of the three ball game. His break of 370 in 1963 is still the All-Ireland billiards record. Bobby Taylor's 278 in 1952 is the Northern Ireland championship record.

Northern Ireland's snooker standards have been much higher, particularly in recent years with Alex Higgins and Dennis Taylor both winning the World Professional title. Jack Rea held the Irish Professional title from 1952 until deposed by Higgins in 1972.

A remarkable if isolated success was that of Belfast YMCA, with Higgins playing the starring role, in capturing the British Amateur Team Championship in 1968.

Billiards Championship

1925	T. McCluney–B. Craig
1926	T. McCluney–J. Sloan
1927	J. Sloan–R. Mulholland
1928	A. Davison–S. Stranaghen
1929	J. Blackburn–W. Morrison
1930	J. Blackburn–n.r.
1931	J. Blackburn–W. Mills
1932	W. Lowe–R. Mulholland
1933	W. Mills–J. Dubois
1934	W. Lowe–J. Presley
1935	W. Morrison–W. Lowe
1936	J. Blackburn–G. Hutton
1937	J. Blackburn–E. Haslem
1938	W. Lowe–W. Mills
1939	W. Lowe–E. Haslem
1940	No contest
1941	E. Haslem–R. Scleater
1942–44	No contests
1945	E. Haslem–W. Webb
1946	J. Holness–C. McErlean
1947	J. Bates–J. Sloan
1948	J. Bates–E. Haslem
1949	J. Bates–E. Haslem
1950	J. Bates–E. Haslem
1951	E. Haslem–J. Bates
1952	R. Taylor–D. Turley
1953	W. Scanlon–C. McErlean
1954	W. Scanlon–W. Dennison
1955	D. Turley–J. Stevenson
1956	J. Stevenson–R. Lough
1957	W. Scanlon–R. Taylor
1958	W. Hanna–R. Hanna
1959	W. Hanna–W. Dennison
1960	W. Dennison–R. Taylor
1961	R. Hanna–D. Anderson
1962	N. McQuay–D. Turley
1963	W. Hanna–W. Ashe
1964	D. Anderson
	D. Turley
1965	W. Ashe–E. Loughran
1966	D. Anderson–P. Morgan
1967	W. Loughran–D. Anderson
1968	D. Anderson–W. Loughran
1969	W. Loughran–D. Anderson
1970	S. Crothers–P. Donnelly
1971	J. Bates–n.r.
1972–73	No contests
1974	P. Donnelly–M. Osborne
1975	P. Donnelly–D. Anderson
1976	P. Donnelly–J. Bates
1977	T. Taylor–G. Connell
1978	W. Loughan–P. Donnelly
1979	J. Bates–E. Sharkey
1980	S. Clarke–W. Loughan
1981	W. Loughan–S. Clarke
1982	P. Donnelly–D. Elliott

Snooker Championship

1927	G. Barron–G. R. Duff
1928	J. Perry–n.r.
1929	W. Lyttle–Capt. J. Ross
1930	J. Luney–n.r.
1931	J. McNally–W. R. Mills
1932	Capt. J. Ross–W. R. Mills
1933	J. French–J. Chambers
1934	Capt. J. Ross–W. Price
1935	W. Agnew–Capt. J. Ross
1936	W. Lowe–S. Brooks
1937	J. Chambers–J. Blackburn
1938	J. McNally–W. Sankon
1939	J. McNally–S. Brooks
1941	J. McNally–A. Heron
1945	J. McNally–C. Downey
1946	J. McNally–J. Rea
1947	J. Rea–J. Bates
1948	J. Bates–E. Haslem
1949	J. Bates–J. Stevenson
1950	J. Bates–J. Dickson
1951	J. Stevenson–E. Haslem
1952	J. Stevenson–D. Turley
1953	J. Stevenson–J. Thompson
1954	W. Seeds–J. Stevenson
1955	J. Stevenson–M. Gill
1956	S. Brooks–G. Lyttle
1957	M. Gill–D. Anderson
1958	W. Agnew–W. Hanna
1959	W. Hanna–W. Seeds
1960	M. Gill–D. Anderson
1961	D. Anderson–M. Gill
1962	S. McMahon–D. Anderson
1963	D. Anderson–J. Clint
1964	P. Morgan–M. Gill
1965	M. Gill–S. Crothers
1966	S. Crothers–W. Caughey
1967	D. Anderson–S. Crothers
1968	A. Higgins–M. Gill
1969	D. Anderson–A. Higgins
1970	J. Clint–N. McCann
1971	S. Crothers–n.r.
1972	P. Donnelly–S. Pavis
1973	J. Clint–S. McMahon
1974	P. Donnelly–S. Pavis
1975	J. Clint–S. McMahon
1976	E. Swaffield–D. McVeigh
1977	D. McVeigh–G. Maxwell
1978	D. McVeigh–L. McCann
1979	R. Burke–J. Begley
1980	S. Clarke–D. McVeigh
1981	T. Murphy–W. Mills
1982	S. Davis–K. Erwin
1983	J. McLaughlin Jnr–J. McIntyre
1984	J. McLaughlin Jnr–H. Morgan

REPUBLIC OF IRELAND

In 1905, when the Amateur Championship, hitherto confined to Londoners and wealthy provincials, was thrown open to the whole of the UK, qualifying rounds were staged in London, Manchester and Dublin. In 1911, Dublin staged the final and in the early years of the century, the Irishman, Joe Nugent, was three times the Championship runner-up. Seamus Fenning dominated the early Eire Championships at both games and

its 1947 snooker champion, Charles Downey, won the 1952 English Amateur Championship in style after moving to London.

Overall, snooker standards have risen sharply in recent years with Patsy Fagan and Eugene Hughes making their mark in the professional game and Paddy Browne, his country's amateur champion at the age of 17, threatening to do so.

All-Ireland Billiards Championship

1935	S. Fenning (E)–W. Lowe (NI) joint holders
1936	S. Fenning (E)–n.r.
1937	J. Blackburn (NI)–n.r.
1938	S. Fenning (E)–n.r.
1939	W. Lowe (NI)–n.r.
1940	T. O'Brien (E)–n.r.
1941	T. O'Brien (E)–n.r.
1942–44	No contests
1945	E. Haslem (NI)–n.r.
1946	P. Merrigan (E)–n.r.
1947	J. Bates (NI)–n.r.
1948	J. Bates (NI)–n.r.
1949	J. Bates (NI)–n.r.
1950	S. Fenning (E)–J. Bates (NI)
1951	E. Haslem (NI)–C. McErlean (E)
1952	M. Nolan (E)–R. Taylor (NI)
1953	D. Turley (E)–W. Sanlon (NI)
1954	W. Sanlon (NI)–M. Nolan (E)
1955	D. Turley (NI)–M. Nolan (E)
1956	M. Nolan (E)–J. Stevenson (NI)
1957	W. Sanlon (NI)–M. Nolan (E)
1958	W. Dennison (E)–W. Hanna (NI)
1959–61	No contests
1962	J. N. McQuay (NI)–K. Smith (E)
1963	J. Bates (E)–W. Hanna (NI)
1964	J. Bates (E)–D. Anderson (NI)

1965	W. Ashe (NI)–L. Codd (E)
1966	D. Anderson (NI)–L. Codd (E)
1967	P. Morgan (E)–W. Loughan (NI)
1968	P. Morgan (E)–D. Anderson (NI)
1969	W. Loughan (NI)–J. Rogers (E)
1970	S. Crothers (NI)–L. Drennan (E)
1971	J. Bates (NI)–L. Codd (E)
1972–73	No contests
1974	P. Donnelly (NI)–T. Moore (E)
1975–78	No contests
1979	J. Bates (NI)–L. Codd (E)
1980	S. Clarke (NI) P. Burke (E)

All-Ireland Snooker Championship

1935	S. Fenning (E)–W. Agnew (NI)
1936	S. Fenning (E)–W. Lowe (NI)
1937	P. O'Connor (E)– J. Chambers (NI)
1938	J. McNally (NI)–n.r.
1939	S. Fenning (E)–J. McNally (NI)
1940	P. Merrigan (E)–J. McNally (NI)
1941	P. Merrigan (E)–J. McNally (NI)
1942–44	No contests
1945	J. McNally (NI)–n.r.
1946	J. McNally (NI)–n.r.
1947	J. J. Rea (NI)–C. Downey (E)
1948	J. Bates (NI)–n.r.

1949	J. Bates (NI)–W. Brown (E)
1950	J. Bates (NI)–J. Redmond (E)
1951	J. Stevenson (NI)– P. O'Connor (E)
1952	J. Stevenson (NI)–W. Brown (E)
1953	J. Stevenson (NI)–n.r.
1954	S. Fenning (E)–W. Seeds (NI)
1955	J. Stevenson (NI)– S. Fenning (E)
1956	W. Brown (E)–S. Brooke (NI)
1957	M. Gill (NI)–J. Connolly (E)
1958	J. Gibson (E)–W. Agnew (NI)
1959–61	No contests
1962	J. Weber (E)–S. McMahon (NI)
1963	D. Anderson (NI)–J. Rogers (E)
1964	P. Morgan (NI)–J. Rogers (E)
1965	M. Gill (NI)–n.r.
1966	G. Hanway (E)–S. Crothers (NI)
1967	P. Morgan (E)–D. Anderson (NI)
1968	A. Higgins (NI)–G. Hanway (E)
1969	D. Anderson (NI)–D. Daley (NI)
1970	J. Clint (NI)–D. Sheehan (E)
1971	D. Sheehan (E)–S. Crothers (NI)
1972–73	No contests
1974	P. Donnelly (NI)–P. Burke (E)
1975–78	No contests
1979	E. Hughes (E)–R. Burke (NI)
1980	D. Sheehan (E)–S. Clarke (NI)

Billiards Championship

1933	J. Ayres–S. Fenning
1934	S. Fenning–n.r.
1935	S. Fenning–n.r.
1936	S. Fenning–n.r.
1937	T. O'Brien–n.r.
1938–47	No contests
1948	W. Brown–n.r.
1949	S. Fenning–n.r.
1950–51	No contests
1952	M. Nolan–T. McCucker
1953	D. Turley–M. Nolan
1954	M. Nolan–D. Barry
1955	M. Nolan–D. Barry
1956	M. Nolan–S. Fenning
1957	M. Nolan–E. Morrissey
1958	W. Dennison–K. Smith
1959–60	No contests
1961	K. Smyth–J. Hanlon
1962	K. Smyth–F. Murphy
1963	J. Bates–P. Fenelon
1964	J. Bates–L. Codd
1965	L. Codd–J. Shortt
1966	L. Codd–G. Connell
1967	P. Morgan–L. Codd
1968	P. Morgan–T. Doyle
1969	J. Rogers–L. Codd
1970	L. Drennan–T. Doyle

1971	L. Codd–P. Fenelon
1972	L. Codd–n.r.
1973	T. Martin–n.r.
1974	T. Doyle–A. Roche
1975	P. Fenelon–T. Martin
1976	J. Rogers–P. Fenelon
1977	E. Hughes–T. Martin
1978	E. Hughes–R. Brennan
1979	n.r.
1980	P. Burke–n.r.
1981	P. Burke–n.r.
1982	D. Elliot–T. Reilly
1983	
1984	A. Murphy–L. Codd

Snooker Championship

1933	S. Fenning–J. Ayres
1935	S. Fenning–n.r.
1937	P. J. O'Connor–n.r.
1940	P. Merrigan–S. Fenning
1947	C. Downey–P. Merrigan
1948	P. Merrigan–n.r.
1949	S. Fenning–n.r.
1952	W. Brown–S. Fenning
1953	S. Brooks–W. Brown
1954	S. Fenning–J. Redmond
1955	S. Fenning–W. Brown
1956	W. Brown–S. Fenning

1957	J. Connolly–G. Gibson
1958	G. Gibson–F. Murphy
1959–60	No official contests
1961	W. Brown–F. Murphy
1962	J. Weber–G. Buffini
1963	J. Rogers–G. Hanway
1964	J. Rogers–G. Buffini
1965	W. Fields–J. Grace
1966	G. Hanway–J. Rogers
1967	P. Morgan–J. Rogers
1968	G. Hanway–T. G. Hearty
1969	D. Dally–J. Rogers
1970	D. Sheehan–P. Thornton
1971	D. Sheehan–J. Weber
1972	J. Rogers–D. Sheehan
1973	F. Murphy–J. Bannister
1974	P. Burke–P. Miley
1975	F. Nathan–J. Weber
1976	P. Burke–L. Watson
1977	J. Clusker–F. Murphy
1978	E. Hughes–N. Lowth
1979	E. Hughes–D. Sheehan
1980	D. Sheehan–E. Hughes
1981	A. Kearney–P. Miley
1982	P. Browne–R. Brennan
1983	J. Long–P. Ennis
1984	P. Ennis–J. Long
1985	G. Burns–R. Brennan

Home International Snooker Championship

1969
England beat Wales
Port Talbot 10–8

1970–71
England beat Wales
Harringay 14–4
England beat Ireland
Dublin 14–4
Wales beat Ireland
Port Talbot 17–1

	W	D	L	For	Agst	Pts
England	2	0	0	28	8	4
Wales	1	0	1	21	15	2
Ireland	0	0	2	5	31	0

1971–72
England beat Scotland
Newcastle 10–8
England beat Ireland
Harringay 14–4
England drew with Wales
Neath 9–9
Scotland drew with Wales
Edinburgh 9–9
Scotland beat Ireland
Dublin 12–6
Wales beat Ireland
Dublin 13–5

	W	D	L	For	Agst	Pts
England	2	1	0	33	21	5
Wales	1	2	0	31	23	4
Scotland	1	1	1	29	25	3
Ireland	0	0	3	15	39	0

1972–73
England beat Scotland
Edinburgh 16–2
England beat Ireland
Dublin 13–5
England drew with Wales
Hull 9–9
Wales beat Ireland
Pontygwaith 15–3
Wales beat Scotland
Llay 10–8
Scotland beat Ireland
Dublin 13–5

	W	D	L	For	Agst	Pts
England	2	1	0	38	16	5
Wales	2	1	0	32	22	5
Scotland	1	0	2	23	31	2
Ireland	0	0	3	15	41	0

1973–74
England beat Wales
Garnant 14–4
England beat Scotland
Carlisle 11–7

England drew with Ireland
Bolton 9–9
Wales beat Ireland
Dublin 11–7
Wales beat Scotland
Edinburgh 14–4
Ireland drew with Scotland
Dublin 9–9

	W	D	L	For	Agst	Pts
England	2	1	0	34	20	5
Wales	2	0	1	29	25	4
Ireland	0	2	1	25	29	2
Scotland	0	1	2	20	34	1

1974–75
Wales beat Ireland
Neath 12–6
Wales beat Scotland
Maerdy 14–4
Wales beat England
Exeter 10–8
England beat Scotland
Edinburgh 12–6
England beat Ireland
Glasnevin 11–7
Scotland beat Ireland
Dundee 12–6

	W	D	L	For	Agst	Pts
Wales	3	0	0	36	18	6
England	2	0	1	31	23	4
Scotland	1	0	2	22	32	2
Ireland	0	0	3	19	35	0

1975–76
Wales beat Ireland
Dublin 13–5
Wales beat Scotland
Edinburgh 11–7
Wales beat England
Merthyr 11–7
England beat Ireland
Grimsby 13–5
England beat Scotland
Southport 12–6
Scotland beat Ireland
Dun Laoghaire 12–6

	W	D	L	For	Agst	Pts
Wales	3	0	0	35	19	6
England	2	0	1	32	22	4
Scotland	1	0	2	25	29	2
Ireland	0	0	3	16	38	0

1976–77
England beat Ireland
Dublin 13–5
England beat Wales
Doncaster 12–6

England beat Scotland
Glasgow 11–7
Wales beat Scotland
Trealaw 14–4
Wales beat Ireland
Cardiff 13–5
Scotland beat Ireland
Edinburgh 12–6

	W	D	L	For	Agst	Pts
England	3	0	0	36	18	6
Wales	2	0	1	33	21	4
Scotland	1	0	2	23	31	2
Ireland	0	0	3	16	38	0

1977–78
Wales beat England
Caerphilly 10–8
Wales beat Scotland
Dublin 12–6
Wales beat Ireland
Dublin 15–3
England beat Scotland
Doncaster 10–8
England beat Ireland
Portsmouth 11–7
Scotland beat Ireland
Dublin 12–6

	W	D	L	For	Agst	Pts
Wales	3	0	0	37	17	6
England	2	0	1	29	25	4
Scotland	1	0	2	26	28	2
Ireland	0	0	3	16	38	0

1978–79
England beat Isle of Man
Prestatyn 15–3
England beat Ireland 14–4
England beat Scotland 16–2
England beat Wales 10–7
Wales beat Isle of Man 16–2
Wales beat Ireland 11–7
Wales drew with Scotland 9–9
Scotland beat Isle of Man 15–3
Scotland drew with Ireland 9–9
Ireland beat Isle of Man 15–3

	W	D	L	For	Agst	Pts
England	4	0	0	55	16	8
Wales	2	1	1	43	28	5
Scotland	1	2	1	35	37	4
Rep. of Ireland	1	1	2	34	38	3
Isle of Man	0	0	4	11	61	0

1979–80
England beat Northern Ireland
Prestatyn 16–2
England beat Isle of Man 16–2
England beat Republic of Ireland 11–7

England beat Scotland 10–8
England beat Wales 10–7
Wales beat Northern Ireland 12–6
Wales beat Isle of Man 16–2
Wales beat Scotland 11–7
Wales drew with Republic of
  Ireland 9–9
Republic of Ireland beat Isle of
  Man 12–6
Scotland beat Isle of Man 13–5
Scotland beat Northern Ireland 10–8
Northern Ireland beat Isle of Man 14–4

	W	D	L	For	Agst	Pts
England	5	0	0	63	26	10
Wales	3	1	1	55	34	7
Rep. of Ireland	2	2	1	47	43	6
Scotland	2	0	3	46	44	4
Northern Ireland	1	1	3	39	51	3
Isle of Man	0	0	5	19	71	0

1980–81

England beat Northern Ireland
  Prestatyn 15–3
Scotland beat Isle of Man 14–4
Wales beat Northern Ireland 10–8
England beat Isle of Man 15–3
Wales beat Scotland 12–6
Republic of Ireland beat Northern
  Ireland 11–7
Northern Ireland beat Isle of Man 12–6
Wales beat Republic of Ireland 14–4
Republic of Ireland drew with
  Scotland 9–9
Wales beat Isle of Man 15–3
England beat Republic of Ireland 12–6
Scotland drew with Northern
  Ireland 9–9
Republic of Ireland beat Isle of
  Man 13–5
England beat Scotland 14–4
Wales beat England 10–7

	W	D	L	For	Agst	Pts
Wales	5	0	0	61	28	10
England	4	0	1	63	26	8
Rep. of Ireland	2	1	2	43	47	5
Scotland	1	2	2	42	48	4
Northern Ireland	1	1	3	39	51	3
Isle of Man	0	0	5	21	69	0

1981-82

Northern Ireland drew with Republic of
  Ireland 9–9

Scotland beat Isle of Man 13–5
England beat Isle of Man 17–1
Wales beat Northern Ireland 11–7
England beat Republic of Ireland 11–7
Wales beat Scotland 13–5
Wales beat Republic of Ireland 12–6
England beat Northern Ireland 10–8
Republic of Ireland drew with Isle of
  Man 9–9
Scotland beat Northern Ireland 10–8
Wales best Isle of Man 15–3
Republic of Ireland beat Scotland 10–8
Scotland beat England 10–8
Northern Ireland beat Isle of Man 10–8
*England beat Wales 8–7

*The Wales *v* England match was abandoned
at the point where Wales were assured of
retaining the championship

	W	D	L	For	Agst	Pts
Wales	4	–	–	58	29	8
England	3	–	1	54	33	6
Scotland	3	–	2	46	44	6
Rep. Ireland	1	2	2	41	49	4
Northern Ireland	1	1	3	42	48	3
Isle of Man	–	1	4	26	64	1

1982–83

Wales beat Isle of Man 16–2
England beat Isle of Man 12–6
England drew with Scotland 9–9
Wales beat Northern Ireland 10–8
Republic of Ireland drew with Northern
  Ireland 9–9
Wales beat Scotland 12–6
Isle of Man drew with Scotland 9–9
England beat Republic of Ireland 11–7
Republic of Ireland beat Isle of
  Man 15–3
England beat Northern Ireland 14–4
Northern Ireland beat Scotland 12–6
Wales beat Republic of Ireland 11–7
Scotland beat Republic of Ireland 11–7
*Wales beat England 9–8
Northern Ireland beat Isle of Man 15–3

	W	D	L	For	Agst	Pts
†Wales	4	0	0	49	23	8
†England	3	1	0	46	26	7
Northern Ireland	2	1	2	53	37	5
Scotland	1	2	2	41	49	4
Rep. of Ireland	1	1	3	44	46	3
Isle of Man	0	1	4	26	66	1

†Not including Wales *v* England match which
was curtailed when Wales led 9–8, at which
point they could not be overtaken

1983–84

Wales beat Scotland 13–5
Isle of Man beat Republic of
  Ireland 11–7
England beat Republic of Ireland 13–5
Scotland drew with Northern
  Ireland 9–9
Wales beat Northern Ireland 13–5
Republic of Ireland beat Northern
  Ireland 10–8
Scotland beat Isle of Man 11–7
England beat Isle of Man 14–4
England beat Northern Ireland 13–5
Wales beat Republic of Ireland 14–4
Wales beat Isle of Man 10–8
England beat Scotland 11–7
Northern Ireland beat Isle of Man 13–5
Wales beat England 10–7
Scotland beat Republic of Ireland 10–8

	W	D	L	For	Agst	Pts
Wales	5	0	0	60	29	10
England	4	0	1	58	31	8
Scotland	2	1	2	42	48	5
Northern Ireland	1	1	3	40	50	3
Isle of Man	1	0	4	35	55	2
Rep. of Ireland	1	0	4	34	56	2

1984–85

Republic of Ireland drew with
  Scotland 9–9
England beat Northern Ireland 13–5
Wales beat Isle of Man 15–3
England drew with Scotland 9–9
Northern Ireland beat Republic of
  Ireland 12–6
Scotland drew with Wales 9–9
Northern Ireland beat Isle of Man 11–7
England beat Isle of Man 12–6
England beat Republic of Ireland 11–7
Scotland beat Isle of Man 15–3
Wales beat Northern Ireland 11–7
Wales beat England 10–8
Republic of Ireland beat Isle of
  Man 12–6
Scotland beat Northern Ireland 10–8
Wales beat Republic of Ireland 14–4

	W	D	L	For	Agst	Pts
Wales	4	1	0	59	31	9
England	3	1	1	53	37	7
Scotland	2	3	0	52	38	7
Northern Ireland	2	0	3	43	47	4
Rep. of Ireland	1	1	3	38	52	3
Isle of Man	0	0	5	25	65	0

SCOTLAND

W.M. Green is the earliest recorded professional champion though he is described as having won it from a Glaswegian J. Meaney. J.G.Sala deprived Green of the title in 1888 and retained it unchallenged until his death in 1901.

Tom Aiken beat Tom Rae for the vacant title in 1902 and remained undefeated champion until 1904 during which period he scored many wins on both sides of the border against top English professionals, most of whom forced unwanted starts upon him to guard their reputations.

The redoubtable Major Fleming – no one seemed to have the temerity to accord him either an initial or a first name – won the Amateur Championship in 1909 and was runner-up in the next three before Scotland opted out of the BA & CC organised amateur championship in favour or organising their own national championship in 1925.

Walter Ramage who won 14 Scottish amateur billiards titles between 1948 and 1967, must be regarded as the best billiards player Scotland has ever produced. A master of the red ball game, if limited in other departments, he made his highest championship break, 283, in the World Amateur Championship in Edinburgh in 1960.

Walter Donaldson (see page 53) has been Scotland's only snooker professional to reach world class but the Scottish professional game now possesses fair strength in depth.

Eddie Sinclair beat Chris Ross for the revived Scottish Professional Championship in 1979 and has since won it once more. The title has also been won by Ian Black and Murdo Macleod (twice).

WALES

Wales has always possessed world class players but only in the seventies did it begin to play its rightful part in the world game. In the days before Sports Council grants were even dreamt of, finance was usually an insuperable problem. It required an immense effort to compete in the English Amateur Championship in London and competing further afield, with rare exceptions, was out of the question.

As long as the BA & CC (later B & SCC) remained, simultaneously and incompatibly, the English and world amateur governing bodies, its near neighbours, like Wales, inevitably remained poor relations. England, through the BA & CC, exerted a dictatorial control over the game and monopolised status, influence and resources while associations like that of Wales, who reckoned their assets only in petty cash, struggled to stay afloat.

What has made South Wales and the valleys in particular such fruitful nurseries of snooker talent has been the way in which their closely knit communities,

Billiards Championship

1933	A. Ramage–n.r.	1968	A. Kennedy–L. U. Demarco	1958	J. Phillips–J. Ferguson
1934	N. Canney–n.r.	1969	A. Kennedy–R. Eprile	1959	J. Phillips–E. Sinclair
1935	H. King–n.r.	1970	D. Sneddon–L. U. Demarco	1960	E. Sinclair–A. Kennedy
1936	N. Canney–R. Pollock	1971	D. Sneddon–R. Eprile	1961	J. Phillips–L. U. Demarco
1937	J. McGhee–J. S. Patterson	1972	L. U. Demarco–D. Sneddon	1962	A. Kennedy–L. U. Demarco
1938	J. McGhee–n.r.	1973	D. Sneddon–L. U. Demarco	1963	E. Sinclair–D. Miller
1939–45	No contests	1974	D. Sneddon–M. McCurley	1964	J. Phillips–E. Sinclair
1946	J. Levey–R. McKendrick	1975	D. Sneddon–A. Sutherland	1965	L. U. Demarco–P. Spence
1947	A. Ramage–G. Aitken	1976	D. Sneddon–J. Craig	1966	L. U. Demarco–P. Spence
1948	W. Ramage–A. Ramage	1977	J. Nugent–L. U. Demarco	1967	E. Sinclair–L. U. Demarco
1949	W. Ramage–A. Ramage	1978	n.r.	1968	E. Sinclair–J. Zonfrillo
1950	A. Ramage–W. Ramage	1979	H. Nimmo–A. Sutherland	1969	A. Kennedy–L. U. Demarco
1951	W. Ramage–G. Jardine	1980	D. Sneddon–H. Nimmo	1970	D. Sneddon–M. McLeod
1952	J. Murray–R. Gillon	1981	D. Sneddon–J. Nugent	1971	J. Phillips–D. Miller
1953	J. Bates–W. Ramage	1982	W. Kelly–D. Pratt	1972	D. Sneddon–L. U. Demarco
1954	J. Bates–J. Murray	1983	H. Nimmo–T. Paul	1973	E. Sinclair–J. Zonfrillo
1955	W. Ramage–A. Ramage			1974	D. Sneddon–E. Sinclair
1956	W. Ramage–A. Ramage	**Snooker Championship**		1975	E. Sinclair–J. Phillips
1957	W. Ramage–M. Morrin	1946	J. Levey–N. McGowan	1976	E. Sinclair–D. Sneddon
1958	W. Ramage–P. Spence	1947	J. Levey–T. Gray	1977	R. Miller–E. McLaughlin
1959	W. Ramage–W. Taylor	1948	I. Wexelstein–R. Walls	1978	J. Donnelly–E. McLaughlin
1960	A. Ramage–C. Spence	1949	W. Ramage–P. Spence	1979	S. Nivison–I. Wallace
1961	P. Spence–W. Ramage	1950	W. Ramage–R. McKendrick	1980	M. Gibson–R. Miller
1962	W. Ramage–A. Kennedy	1951	A. Wilson–A. Wishart	1981	R. Lane–J. Rea
1963	W. Ramage–A. Kennedy	1952	D. Emerson–P. Spence	1982	P. Kippie–K. Baird
1964	W. Ramage–A. Kennedy	1953	P. Spence–H. Thompson	1983	G. Carnegie–J. Rea
1965	W. Ramage–A. Kennedy	1954	D. Edmond–P. Spence	1984	S. Hendry–D. Sneddon
1966	W. Ramage–L. U. Demarco	1955	L. U. Demarco–P. Spence	1985	S. Hendry–J. McNellan
1967	W. Ramage–A. Kennedy	1956	W. Barrie–R. McKendrick		
		1957	T. Paul–H. D. Thompson		

Right, Terry Parsons

Billiards Championship

1920	H. F. E. Coles–n.r.
1921	H. F. E. Coles–n.r.
1922	H. F. E. Coles–n.r.
1923	H. F. E. Coles–n.r.
1924	H. F. E. Coles–n.r.
1925	n.r.
1926	n.r.
1927	n.r.
1928	G. Moore–n.r.
1929	J. Tregoning–n.r.
1930	n.r.
1931	L. Prosser–n.r.
1932	T. Jones–n.r.
1933	T. Jones–n.r.
1934	n.r.
1935	I. Edwards–n.r.
1936	J. Tregoning–n.r.
1937	R. Gravenor–n.r.
1938	J. Tregoning–n.r.
1939–45	No contests
1946	T. G. Rees–n.r.
1947	T. C. Morse–R. Smith
1948	J. Tregoning–I. Edwards
1949	I. Edwards–T. Jones
1950	W. Pierce–W. T. Jones
1951	W. Pierce–n.r.
1952	J. Tregoning–L. Davis
1953	B. Sainsbury–W. Pierce
1954	R. Smith–R. Keats
1955	J. Tregoning–R. W. Oriel
1956	A. J. Ford–A. Davies
1957	R. Smith–A. J. Ford

1958	R. W. Oriel–A. J. Ford
1959	A. J. Ford–E. Marks
1960	C. Everton–P. J. Morris
1961	R. W. Oriel–P. J. Morris
1962	R. W. Oriel–E. Marks
1963	R. W. Oriel–P. J. Morris
1964	R. W. Oriel–D. E. Edwards
1965	R. W. Oriel–N. Jaynes
1966	R. W. Oriel–A. Davies
1967	R. W. Oriel–C. Jenkins
1968	D. E. Edwards–R. W. Oriel
1969	R. W. Oriel–T. J. Entwistle
1970	R. W. Oriel–D. E. Edwards
1971	R. W. Oriel–C. Everton
1972	C. Everton–R. W. Oriel
1973	C. Everton–J. Terry
1974	R. W. Oriel–C. Everton
1975	R. W. Oriel–C. Everton
1976	C. Everton–R. W. Oriel
1977	C. Everton–R. W. Oriel
1978	R. W. Oriel–C. Everton
1979	R. W. Oriel–D. E. Edwards
1980	Discontinued

Snooker Championship

1947	T. Jones–R. Smith
1948	R. Smith–A. J. Ford
1949	A. J. Ford–C. Coles
1950	R. Reardon–A. J. Ford
1951	R. Reardon–n.r.
1952	R. Reardon–A. J. Ford
1953	R. Reardon–A. Kemp

1954	R. Reardon–A. J. Ford
1955	R. Reardon–A. J. Ford
1956	C. Wilson–V. Wilkins
1957	R. D. Meredith–N. Williams
1958	A. Kemp–R. D. Meredith
1959	J. R. Price–M. L. Berni
1960	L. Luker–A. Kemp
1961	T. Parsons–J. R. Price
1962	A. J. Ford–M. L. Berni
1963	R. D. Meredith–J. R. Price
1964	M. L. Berni–A. J. Ford
1965	T. Parsons–A. J. Ford
1966	L. L. O'Neill–D. Mountjoy
1967	L. L. O'Neill–K. Weed
1968	D. Mountjoy–J. Terry
1969	T. Parsons–J. T. Prosser
1970	D. T. May–G. Thomas
1971	D. T. May–R. W. Oriel
1972	G. Thomas–T. Griffiths
1973	A. Lloyd–G. Thomas
1974	A. Lloyd–G. Thomas
1975	T. Griffiths–G. Thomas
1976	D. Mountjoy–A. Lloyd
1977	C. Wilson–D. Thomas
1978	A. Lloyd–S. Newbury
1979	C. Wilson–G. Thomas
1980	S. Newbury–A. Lloyd
1981	C. Roscoe–E. Richards
1982	T. Parsons–M. Berni
1983	W. Jones–T. Parsons
1984	T. Parsons–W. Jones
1985	M. Bennett–D. John

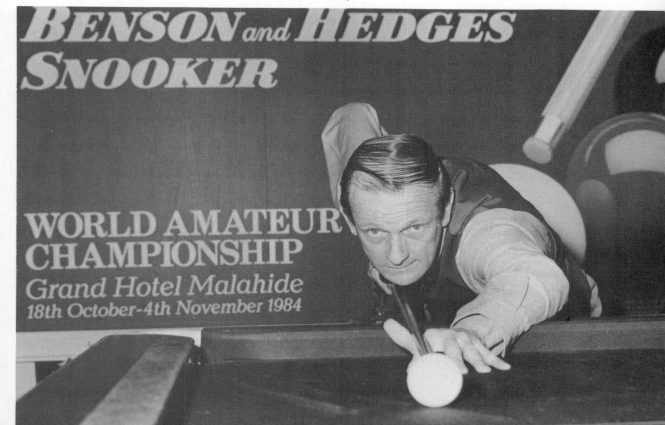

often revolving round a local club or billiard hall, have transmitted from generation to generation the skills and tactical know-how of their local heroes.

The origins of the national association and the national championships have defied research. It appears that the earliest billiards championship was that of 1920 which, like the next four, was won by Horace Coles, who subsequently represented both Wales and (because of his performances in the English Amateur Championship) England in the Empire Championship, the forerunner of the World Amateur Championship. It was in England's colours that Coles won that title in 1935.

Joe Tregoning, whose first and last titles were separated by 36 years, was another outstanding billiards exponent whose finest feat was reaching three consecutive English finals between 1949 and 1951.

Tom Jones, who with John Ford shares the distinction of having won the Welsh title at both games, took Wales into second place in the 1933 Empire Championship, the principality's best Empire/world amateur billiards placing.

In the last two decades Welsh billiards has been dominated by Roy Oriel (14 times champion) and Clive Everton (five). Oriel, an extremely fast scorer for a player specialising in the in-off game, set the Welsh championship break record of 345 in the 1971 quarterfinal.

Although there was a match for the Welsh Professional Snooker Championship in 1922–J.S. Nicholls beating W. Davies 1032–777 over the aggregate score of 18 frames—the best Welsh players tended to flourish in the atmosphere of money matches rather than tournament play. George Hargest, manager of the local billiard hall at Blackwood, Monmouthshire, made a total clearance of 112 in 1915 but appears never to have played competitively.

Snooker flourished in South Wales as it did in any area where unemployment was high and where the local billiard hall or institute became not only a refuge from the weather but a focus for activity which provided diversion and the hope of a few extra shillings. Bill Withers was one of the few Welshmen to gain even a precarious foothold in the professional tournament world, beating Fred Davis 17–14 on his world championship debut in 1937 before Fred's elder brother Joe, full of wrath at this blot on the family escutcheon, hammered him 30–1 in the next round.

Times were still hard when Ray Reardon and Cliff Wilson fought their great battles in the early fifties. Reardon won six consecutive Welsh titles, the first when he was only 17, between 1950 and 1955 but Wilson enjoyed his share of success when they met in the English Championship and in the money matches in which the whole town seem to have an interest. Wilson, three times Welsh amateur champion, also won the World Amateur title in 1978, keeping in Welsh hands the trophy Doug Mountjoy had won in 1976.

Reardon and Wilson, though very much part of the current scene, were essentially products of snooker's hungry fifties. Mountjoy and Terry Griffiths, world professional champion at his first attempt in 1979 after a very successful amateur career, are products of the seventies when government grants helped make it possible for leading Welsh amateurs to enjoy the experience of amateur internationals and overseas competition.

Terry Parsons, a Trealow postman who won four Welsh amateur titles, won the 1982 world amateur title and was runner-up in 1984. The highest break in the Welsh Amateur Championship is 123 by Tony Chappel, now a professional, in 1980.

AUSTRALIA

The father of billiards in Australia was Henry Upton Alcock, a Dubliner who learnt the billiard table trade in London and emigrated to Australia in 1852. Soon, he was manufacturing some 150 tables a year, not only for clubs and private homes but for out of the way places like gold diggings for which the slates were made in eight or ten pieces so that they could be transported by packhorse.

Alcock brought British professionals over to tour, notably John Roberts Snr in 1864 and later William Cook and John Roberts Jnr. It was almost certainly Roberts Jnr, who had been introduced to snooker on a tour of India in 1885, who brought snooker to the attention of Frank Smith Snr who is generally credited with introducing the game to Australia in 1887.

Early billiards championships were run on a challenge basis. Joseph Byrne (Victoria) beat J. James (New South Wales) 1000–878 to win the first contest for the Australian Championship on 8 September 1881 at Perkin's Exchange Hotel, Sydney. Byrne made a 66 break by all round play and a 59 which included 18 spots as he took the £100 side stake in front of a crowd of about 200 who had paid ten shillings each.

Harry Evans, an expatriate Englishman, dominated the championship from 1882 to 1892, keeping at bay, among others, Fred Lindrum, father of Walter, and Harry Gray, father of George. Lindrum beat Gray for the 'native born' Australian Championship in 1887.

Charles Memmott beat Evans to become champion in 1892, making a break of 1238, largely through the spot stroke. As occurred in Britain, the game then diverged into two codes with Memmott supreme at all in and Fred Weiss at spot barred.

From 1900–10 the top Australians were Fred Lindrum Jnr (born 1888), who took the title from Memmott, and George Gray (born 1892), who was only 14 when he made a 513 break entirely by in-off reds. Lindrum, an excellent top of the table player, certainly had the better all-round game but himself concentrated much more on the red ball after Gray had once beaten him with the aid of an 836 break which included 831 off the red.

Fred Lindrum Jnr, who had beaten Memmott in 1908 for the Australian title, was never challenged for it either by Gray or his younger brother Walter but eventually lost it in 1934 to his nephew, Horace Lindrum (neé Morell). Walter Lindrum's career is profiled on page 104.

Horace, a player of outstanding natural gifts, first came to Britain for the World Professional Snooker Championship in 1936, leading Joe Davis 27–24 in the final before losing 31–27. With his fluent, attractive style he was much in demand as an exhibition player but his relish for the cut and thrust of matchplay, never great, diminished with the years. He reached the world professional final of 1946 but the world championship which he won in 1950 was a travesty, recognised as such by the public since only he and Clark McConachy, who was not a front rank snooker player, remained loyal to the event conducted by the Billiards Association and Control Council while all the other professionals supported the rival championship organised by the professionals' own association.

Although he never beat Joe Davis on level terms, Horace was several times successful in weeks matches when receiving 7 points start in each frame. In one of these encounters, he made breaks of 141 and 135 which were not ratified as records and in another, at Thurston's, one of 135 which was.

Urged on, particularly early in his career, by his aggressive, domineering mother, he found 'the

Lindrum name' an increasingly heavy burden in his mature years.

He retained unchallenged until his retirement from competition in 1957 both the Australian professional snooker title he won from Frank Smith Jnr in 1931 and the Australian professional billiards title he won with the aid of a break of 1431 from his uncle Fred in 1933. He made a 147 snooker maximum in an exhibition at Penrith School of Arts, New South Wales in 1941. He died in 1974.

Norman Squire, who was New Zealand-born, and Warren Simpson were the two other outstanding snooker players on the Australian scene until the emergence of Eddie Charlton, who won the Australian professional title every year except one since 1964. Charlton's career is profiled on page 00.

Squire, who made over 2000 centuries, including one maximum, was no one's inferior in touch and close positional control. His long game was not of comparable standard and limited his success against players of similar ability to his own and he was at his best conceding huge starts for money to poor players, mostly in City Tattersalls Club, Sydney where Simpson was also a regular.

Simpson, also a great money player played the game of his life to beat Charlton 27–22 in the 1970 World

Billiards Championship				Snooker Championship	
1913	G. B. Shailer	1955	R. Marshall	1954	W. Simpson
1914–19	No contests	1956	J. Long	1955	E. Pickett
1920	J. R. Hooper	1957	R. Marshall	1956	R. Marshall
1921	G. B. Shailer	1958	T. Cleary	1957	W. Simpson
1922	G. B. Shailer	1959	R. Marshall	1958	F. Harris
1923	G. B. Shailer	1960	J. Long	1959	K. Burles
1924	E. Eccles	1961	R. Marshall	1960	K. Burles
1925	G. B. Shailer	1962	R. Marshall	1961	M. Williams
1926	L. W. Hayes	1963	R. Marshall	1962	W. Barrie
1927	L. W. Hayes	1964	J. Long	1963	F. Harris
1928	L. W. Hayes	1965	T. Cleary	1964	W. Barrie
1929	A. H. Hearndon	1966	T. Cleary	1965	W. Barrie
1930	S. Ruan	1967	J. Long	1966	M. Williams
1931	H. L. Goldsmith	1968	J. Long	1967	M. Williams
1932	A. Sakzewski	1969	R. Marshall	1968	M. Williams
1933	L. W. Hayes	1970	R. Marshall	1969	W. Barrie
1934	L. W. Hayes	1971	M. Williams	1970	M. Williams
1935	L. W. Hayes	1972	P. Tarrant	1971	M. Williams
1936	R. Marshall	1973	P. Tarrant	1972	M. Williams
1937	R. Marshall	1974	J. Reece	1973	M. Williams
1938	R. Marshall	1975	J. Long	1974	L. Condo
1939	R. Marshall	1976	G. Ganim Jnr	1975	R. Atkins
1940–45	No contests	1977	G. Ganim Jnr	1976	R. Atkins
1946	R. Marshall	1978	G. Ganim Jnr	1977	R. Atkins
1947	T. Cleary	1979	G. Ganim Jnr	1978	K. Burles
1948	R. Marshall	1980	G. Ganim Jnr	1979	J. Campbell
1949	R. Marshall	1981	G. Ganim Jnr	1980	W. King
1950	T. Cleary	1982	R. Foldvari	1981	W. King
1951	R. Marshall	1983	R. Foldvari	1982	J. Giannaros
1952	R. Marshall	1984	F. Humphreys	1983	G. Lackenby
1953	R. Marshall	1985	R. Marshall	1984	G. Wilkinson
1954	R. Marshall	**Snooker Championship**		1985	J. Bonner
		1953	W. Simpson		

Professional Championship semi-final but, partly through the diabetes which he suffered, partly through his easy-going nature, rarely recaptured this standard in match play.

Apart from Simpson, Charlton's toughest opposition came from two expatriates, Gary Owen, born in Llanelli but twice winner of the World Amateur Championship in England's colours when he was a Birmingham fireman, and Paddy Morgan, born in Belfast, who reached the semi-final of the 1968 World Amateur Championship in Sydney.

Australia produced surprisingly few amateur snooker players of top quality. Their most consistent performer was Max Williams, who won eight national titles and came within one frame of beating England's David Taylor in the 1968 World Amateur final, and Ron Atkins made good the handicap of having his right leg amputated above the knee after a teenage shooting accident to the extent of winning three national titles and reaching the final of the 1980 World Amateur in his native Launceston.

Australia did, though, produce two of the finest amateur billiards players of all time, Bob Marshall and Tom Cleary. Between 1936 and 1970, Marshall won 19 titles, Cleary five and, as they passed their peak, Jim Long the other five. Coming out of retirement at the age of 75, Marshall also won the 1985 title.

Marshall, who first won his national title in 1936 went on to win four world amateur titles (two when the event was known as the Empire Championship) while Cleary, who first became Australian champion in 1950, won the world amateur title in 1954. Their rivalry inspired record upon record, Marshall, the harder man, relentlessly piling up points with deadly repetitive sequences of 'postman's knock', Cleary only marginally less prolific with the more varied and artistic version of top of the table, 'floating white'.

After his first world amateur title in Johannesburg in 1936 Marshall successfully defended in Melbourne in 1938 when, averaging 49, he hammered Kingsley Kennerley, an outstanding English champion 6639–4705 in the deciding match, Kennerley's match average of 35 being nearly six points higher than the English record he had just set.

In the second of the six sessions of the match Marshall made two triple centuries and three doubles in setting a new amateur session average record of 115. Twice during the event he made seven centuries in a session and set a two hour session aggregate record of 1864 which stood until he himself broke it with 1876 in the 1959 Australian amateur.

Cleary held the Australian break record with 435 in 1947 but Marshall beat it with 500 and 540 in 1948. Cleary set a four hour aggregate record of 3185 in 1950.

Marshall retained the World Amateur Championship, held for the first time since 1938, at Burroughes and Watts, London in 1951. The superfine super fast cloth was foreign to his style and the usual run of Australian tables but he was still much too good both

for Cleary and Frank Edwards, the English champion, who was then at the peak of his form.

Shortly before coming to London, Marshall made a 589 unfinished in the Australian Championship plus 498, 418 and nine more over 300. Unexpectedly, he lost to the Indian no. 2, Chandra Hirjee in the 1952 World Amateur in Calcutta and failed to beat England's Leslie Driffield in the last match to force a play off.

He trailed Cleary by 400 with less than an hour to go in the 1953 Australian final, but, starting with a fluke from a double baulk, all but played out time with a new world amateur record break of 702 to win the title.

Cleary's compensation was a victory over Marshall in the 1954 World Amateur in Sydney. With this vital success behind him, Cleary made a new championship record of 682 and went on to win the title.

Marshall's supremacy was only briefly interrupted. In the 1957 Australian Championship he set a new world four hour aggregate record of 3364 and in the course of the event made a 596, three 400s and eight 300s. He did not defend in 1958 when Cleary equalled his record of seven centuries in a session and made two breaks of 446 but won again in 1959 with a new world session aggregate record of 1876, a new four hour record of 3391, a new session average record of 115 which he increased to 118·7 on a tour of India in 1961.

In 1962, in his home city of Perth, Marshall was a strong favourite for the World Amateur but seemed to have lost his chance when he was beaten by 168 points by the Indian Wilson Jones. Cleary lost to the other Indian, Samir Banerjee, but then beat Jones to take the championship into a play-off between Marshall and Jones.

Jones made a 489 break in the first session but in a fabulous third session Marshall outpointed him by 1200 in setting a new session average record of 128·4.

Robbie Foldvari won two titles and turned professional after losing in the 1983 World Amateur semi-final.

The official Australian break records are – Billiards: R. Marshall 702 (1953) (two pots); J. Long 472 (1967) (15 pots); P. Tarrant 388 (1973) (five pots); G. Ganim Jnr 423 (1979) (three pots). Snooker: M. Williams (1973), J. Campbell (1980) 101 (national championships); M. Williams (1965) 118 (state championship).

CANADA

Until the late seventies, when the game began to acquire a genuine tournament structure, snooker in Canada was sustained almost exclusively as a gambling and leisure activity. A number of clubs did possess tables but essentially the game was based in public saloons.

Championships were promoted from time to time but with no national governing body or affiliation to world governing bodies to lend them any kind of official status, such events were subject to the whims of

George Chenier (*left*) and Joe Davis at Leicester Square Hall, 1950.

promoters and a maelstrom of personal squabbles.

Though the billiard players of old toured Canada as they toured all countries where there was substantial British influence, billiards never became popular enough to produce a first class Canadian player. Snooker, with its wider scope for gambling, struck a much more responsive chord.

In January 1923, Con Stanbury potted the last 14 reds, 14 blacks, yellow and green in a break of 125 at the Palace Billiard Hall, Winnipeg. When he became Canada's first World Professional Snooker Championship entrant in 1935, his style was greeted with amazement. Unlike the British players, who, having received their grounding in the gentler game of billiards tended to avoid power shots for aesthetic reasons, Stanbury revelled in them.

Despite many near misses he could never quite achieve a major breakthrough although he spent the last 40 years of his life in London, chiefly as a coach, until his death in 1975.

Clare O'Donnell, who hit even harder than Stanbury

and eccentrically kept his chalk under his bridge hand when striking, entered the championship in 1936.

The first Canadian of genuine world class was George Chenier, who lost honourably to Joe Davis 41–30 in a week's match in Bermuda and was thence invited to Britain for the 1949–50 season. During this visit Chenier brought home to British professionals the possibilities of plants and sets, these combination shots being much used in pool, snooker's American sister game played on smaller tables with larger pockets, at which Chenier was a player of high standard.

Disappointingly, Chenier finished last in the *News of the World* tournament but beat the South African champion Peter Mans 37–34 in the world quarter-final before losing 43–28 to Fred Davis in the semi. He also made a world record break of 144 at Leicester Square Hall though this stood for only five weeks before Joe Davis eclipsed it with 146.

Back in Canada, Chenier retained his Canadian and North American titles against a variety of opponents though he was beaten by Fred Davis in Vancouver in 1957 in a match enthusiastically billed by the promoter as being for the World Championship.

In 1963, Chenier trounced the former world cham-

Billiards Championship		Snooker Championship	
1979	E. Fisher	1979	J. Wych
1980	S. Holden	1980	Jim Bear
1981	R. Chaperon	1981	R. Chaperon
1982	R. Chaperon	1982	
		1983	A. Robidoux
		1984	T. Finstad

pion Irving Crane 150–0 in the World 14·1 Pool Championship. He was still recognised as Canadian snooker champion when he died in 1970.

As snooker in Canada was played on tables with generous pockets and with Vitalite balls which were much livelier than Crystalate or even the later Super Crystalate, century breaks were common-place. In these flattering conditions, there was even a sprinkling of 147s, the first by Leo Levitt at Windsor Billiards and Bowling Club, Montreal on 24 November 1948.

The visits of Fred Davis and Rex Williams and John Spencer, then reigning world champion, in 1971 were a vague general stimulus but more crucially introduced Thorburn to the authentic international circuit. The tournament performances of Thorburn (who first entered the World Professional Championship in 1973) and Werbeniuk (who first did so in 1974) stimulated interest in Canada and kindled a demand that Canada itself should stage international tournaments.

The Canadian Open Championship, first staged during the annual Canadian National Exhibition in Tornoto in August 1974 brought to the country a whiff of international competition but was discontinued in 1981 because the leading British players could no longer be attracted to it by the limited prize money available.

Kirk Stevens, who first attracted international attention as an 18-year-old in this event was only 19 when he reached the 1978 world amateur semi-finals in Malta and went on to the distinguished professional career profiled on page 24.

Several other Canadians have joined the professional circuit, amongst them Jim Bear, who was runner-up for the world amateur title in Calgary in 1982.

INDIA

When the Indian Billiards and Snooker Association (later Indian Billiards and Snooker Federation) was founded in 1930, M. M. Begg was one of its joint honorary secretaries. Begg won the inaugural billiards championship but it was as an administrator that he made his outstanding contribution. It was, for instance, due to his persistence that the World Amateur Snooker Championship came into being. The BA & CC had delayed from 1952 until Begg donated a cup and concluded arrangements for a tournament in Calcutta in 1963 to which the BA & CC and other interested nations agreed.

It was not until after the war that India produced a player of genuine world class in Wilson Jones, whose

wealthy patron R. K. Vissanji arranged a not too onerous job for him which allowed him to practise several hours a day in Vissanji's own beautifully appointed billiard room.

Visits by leading overseas amateurs also provided a stimulus for the game and several were invited to compete in the Indian championships, thus explaining why there are several non-Indians in the championship rolls.

Jones started as a snooker player, winning the Indian title in 1948, but a tour that year by Kingsley Kennerley interested him in top of the table play. Bob Marshall's 1949 tour, in which he made an Indian all comers record break of 405 and an aggregate of 1379 in two hours, aluo furthered his billiards education.

Beaten by T. A. Selvaraj a redoubtable red ball player, Jones won his national title in 1950 by beating another tourist, Frank Edwards, by 67 in the semi-final before beating Selvaraj to earn a trip to the 1951 World Amateur Championship in London.

Partly through inexperience, Jones could not settle to the conditions and won only one of his six matches, a dismal showing he repeated in the 1952 World Amateur in Calcutta where his great domestic rival Chandra Hirjee gave India something to shout about by beating Marshall by 105 in the Australian's second match. Hirjee also led Leslie Driffield, who was to go on to win the title, by 43 with 20 minutes to go before the Yorkshireman got home with a late spurt. Hirjee then ran out of steam and finished third.

Jones restored some of his confidence by beating Hirjee by 61 in 1954 for the fourth of the 12 Indian billiards titles he was to win—Hirjee winning four—but again cut no ice in the 1954 World Amateur in Sydney.

It was four years before the event was held again and Jones, by now at his peak, won it in Calcutta in 1958 in spectacular fashion.

Aided by a 501 break, Jones beat Tom Cleary, the holder, by 1069 and was undefeated when he tackled Driffield, his penultimate opponent. Driffield led by 660 with only 90 minutes to play before Jones came to life with 170 and 232 to narrow the gap to 262. Driffield made 124 but Jones, with 113 and 117, got to within 170 and, with 147 and 106 went 68 in front. He held on to win by 136 and, starting with three double centuries and three single centuries in the first session, overwhelmed his last opponent, Hirjee, by 1768 to become champion.

Hirjee retired shortly afterwards with a mysterious skin complaint to leave Jones in a class of his own domestically. He compiled a world record eight centuries in a session in the Bombay State Champion-

Right O. B. Agrawal, the first Indian to win the title, receives the 1984 World Amateur Snooker Championship trophy from Lord Killanin.

Billards Championship

1931	M. M. Begg
1932	P. K. Deb
1933	Major Meade
1934	Mg Ba Sin
1935	P. K. Deb
1936	P. K. Deb
1937	M. M. Begg
1938	P. K. Deb
1939	P. K. Deb
1940	S. H. Lyth
1941	V. R. Freer
1942	V. R. Freer
1943–45	No contests
1946	C. Hirjee
1947	C. Hirjee
1948	V. R. Freer
1949	T. A. Selvaraj
1950	W. Jones
1951	W. Jones
1952	W. Jones
1953	L. Driffield (Eng)
1954	W. Jones
1955	W. Jones
1956	C. Hirjee
1957	W. Jones
1958	C. Hirjee
1959	T. Cleary (Aus)
1960	W. Jones
1961	W. Jones
1962	R. Marshall (Aus)
1963	W. Jones
1964	W. Jones
1965	W. Jones
1966	W. Jones
1967	A. Savur
1968	S. Mohan
1969	M. Ferreira
1970	S. Mohan
1971	S. Mohan
1972	S. Mohan
1973	S. Mohan
1974	M. Ferreira
1975	G. C. Parikh
1976	M. Ferreira
1977	M. J. M. Lafir (Sri)
1978	M. Ferreira
1979	M. Ferreira
1980	M. Ferreira
1981	G. Sethi

Snooker Championship

1939	P. K. Deb
1940	P. K. Deb
1941	V. R. Freer
1942	P. K. Deb
1943–45	No contests
1946	T. A. Selvaraj
1947	T. Sadler
1948	W. Jones
1949	T. A. Selvaraj
1950	F. Edwards (Eng)
1951	T. A. Selvaraj
1952	W. Jones
1953	A. L. Driffield (Eng)
1954	W. Jones
1955	T. A. Selvaraj
1956	M. J. M. Lafir (Sri)
1957	M. J. M. Lafir (Sri)
1958	W. Jones
1959	M. J. M. Lafir (Sri)
1960	W. Jones*
1961	M. J. M. Lafir (Sri)
1962	R. Marshall (Aus)
1963	M. J. M. Lafir (Sri)
1964	S. Shroff
1965	S. Shroff
1966	T. Monteiro
1967	S. Shroff
1968	S. Mohan
1969	S. Shroff
1970	S. Shroff
1971	T. Monteiro
1972	S. Shroff
1973	S. Shroff
1974	M. J. M. Lafir (Sri)
1975	M. J. M. Lafir (Sri)
1976	A. Savur
1977	M. J. M. Lafir (Sri)
1978	A. Savur
1979	A. Savur
1980	J. White (Eng)
1981	G. Pariklh
1982	
1983	
1984	M. G. Jayaram
1985	G. Sethi

ship in 1959 but Collins Music Hall, Edinburgh, was not the most promising of settings for Jones to defend his world title in 1960.

Accustomed to warmth and large, excited crowds, Jones could not reproduce his best and the English red ball specialist Herbert Beetham defeated him by 138. A second defeat by the Australian Jim Long put him down to third place.

A win over Marshall by 168 gave Jones a flying start in the 1962 World Amateur in Perth but Jones then lost to Cleary, who had previously lost to India's no. 2, Samir Banerjee. Marshall also beat Cleary to force a play-off with Jones and beat him by 732 for the title.

Jones, determined to add a world title on foreign soil to the one he had won in Calcutta, achieved his ambition in the small New Zealand country town of Pukekohe in 1964 when he went through the ten man round robin undefeated.

His closest match—a winning margin of 144—was against his young compatriot, Michael Ferreira, who in due course was to take over his position as India's no. 1. This, though, did not become undisputed until Satish Mohan had won five of the six domestic championships between 1968 and 1973. Ferreira, meanwhile, achieved third place in the World Amateur of London in 1969, a tournament in which his break of 629 set a world amateur record under the five pot rule.

Mohan, who had finished third in the 1971 World Amateur, was favourite for the 1973 championship in Bombay but pressure of home expectation took its toll. In finishing second, he displayed disturbing signs of the instability of temperament which led him into heavy drinking and a swift disappearance from the competitive scene, a tragic fate for one of the quickest and most exciting players in modern billiards.

Ferreira, who finished third, amassed four world records against the Scot Bert Demarco: a four hour aggregate of 3202, a two hour aggregate of 1688, ten centuries in a session and 16 in a four hour match. Further world records fell to his skill and fluency in his 1975 national championship: a 128·4 average for a two hour session and 69·7 for a four hour match but, in his early career, his best tended to elude him when it was most urgently required.

This was certainly the case in the 1975 World Amateur final against Norman Dagley and it was to be the case in the 1979 World Amateur semi-final against Paul Mifsud. In the interim, he won the 1977 World Amateur title in Melbourne, albeit with a mediocre performance in the final against the Englishman Bob Close, whose mental resources appeared spent after his surprise semi-final win over Dagley. Ferreira's form was much more impressive in winning the unofficial 'World Open' in Christchurch which immediately followed, setting a new session average record of 189·8 in the final.

Ferreira reached new heights in the 1978 Indian Championship when he seized the world amateur break record with 1149 (superseding Dagley's 862 earlier that year). He compiled a 995 for good measure and raised the four hour and two hour average records to 158·0 and 243·6 respectively. His 1949 session aggregate in the latter was also a record.

With the rules changed from 'five pots' to 'three', Ferreira claimed a world record under the revised rules with a break of 566 in the Islam Gymkhana Open in 1979, superseding Dagley's 506 in the 1980 English Amateur final. His 3046 four hour aggregate in the 1980 Indian Championship was also claimed as a world record under revised rules.

Ferreira won the World Amateur Billiards Championship for the second time in New Delhi in 1981, beating Dagley by a mere 96 in an exciting final. Earlier in the event, he set new world amateur records under the three-pot rule of 191·8 (two-hour session average), 123·6 (four-hour session average) and 630 (break).

He retained the title in Malta two years later, scoring an amazing victory over Dagley by 64 points in the semi-finals after trailing by 735 going into the final session. He averaged 99 in this period.

In the final, he more comfortably disposed of his young compatriot, Subash Agrawal, whose quality and fluency had been shown the previous year when he deprived Ferreira of his two-hour aggregate record with 1596.

Agrawal later also deprived Ferreira of his break record under the two-pot rule with an effort of 716 against him in a tournament at BCA, Garware in which he also set new world amateur records of 1854 (two-hour aggregate), and 3485 (four-hour aggregate).

Agrawal's younger brother, Omprakash, gave India the world amateur snooker title for the first time in the 1984 Championship in Dublin in which he beat the defending champion, the Welshman Terry Parsons, 11–7 in the final.

India also held the world amateur break record through the 122 by Ratan Bader in the West Bengal State Championship in 1964. Bader's previous best had been 82 in practice and 50 in a match and he never again made a century, but his 122, a total clearance but for pink and black, remained the record until 1977.

Snooker, as it has in other countries, has overtaken billiards in popularity but India has continued to produce first class billiards player in greater numbers than can be found elsewhere. One important reason for this is that clubs employ markers to field out and, in effect, referee. The drudgery of fielding out, the bane of billiards, is thus removed.

MALTA

The games became popular on the island in the days when it was a key British base in the Mediterranean. National championships were instituted in 1947.

The outstanding early champions were Wilfred Asciak (six snooker titles and 18 billiards between 1950 and 1972) and Alfred Borg (13 snooker and one billiards between 1952 and 1974).

Far and away the most successful Maltese in inter-

Billiards Championship

1947	V. Micallef	1973	P. Mifsud	1961	A. Borg
1948	No contest	1974	P, Mifsud	1962	A. Borg
1949	E. Bartolo	1975	P. Mifsud	1963	M. Tonna
1950	W. Asciak	1976	P. Mifsud	1964	A. Borg
1951	W. Asciak	1977	P. Mifsud	1965	A. Borg
1952	W. Asciak	1978	J. Grech	1966	A. Borg
1953	W. Asciak	1979	P. Mifsud	1967	A. Borg
1954	W. Asciak	1980	J. Grech	1968	P. Mifsud
1955	W. Asciak	1981	No contest	1969	P. Mifsud
1956	W. Asciak	1982	V. Ellul	1970	P. Mifsud
1957	W. Asciak	1983	J. Grech	1971	P. Mifsud
1958	W. Asciak			1972	P. Mifsud
1959	W. Asciak	**Snooker Championship**		1973	A. Borg
1960	W. Asciak	1947	L. Galea	1974	A. Borg
1961	A. Borg	1948	T. B. Oliver	1975	P. Mifsud
1962	J. Bartolo	1949	L. Galea	1976	P. Mifsud
1963	J. Bartolo	1950	W. Asciak	1977	A. Borg
1964	W. Asciak	1951	W. Asciak	1978	P. Mifsud
1965	W. Asciak	1952	A. Borg	1979	P. Mifsud
1966	W. Asciak	1953	A. Borg	1980	J. Grech
1967	W. Asciak	1954	W. Asciak	1981	J. Grech
1968	W. Asciak	1955	A. Borg	1982	P. Mifsud
1969	P. Mifsud	1956	W. Asciak	1983	P. Mifsud
1970	W. Asciak	1957	W. Asciak	1984	T. Drago
1971	P. Mifsud	1958	W. Asciak	1985	P. Mifsud
1972	W. Asciak	1959	A. Borg		
		1960	A. Borg		

national competition has been Paul Mifsud, world amateur billiards champion in 1979 and runner-up in the world amateur snooker in 1976.

On home territory in 1978, in Malta's National Sports Pavilion, Mifsud found the burden of national expectation too heavy and was beaten by the Canadian Kirk Stevens in the quarter-finals but made unexpected amends by carrying off the world amateur billiards title in Colombo in 1979.

Mifsud, who had not competed in the world amateur billiards since 1973, when he had finished seventh of ten competitors, arrived only ten hours before his first match after being delayed 24 hours in Paris and 26 in Bombay. The physical reserves which had enabled him to withstand such an energy sapping journey also helped him cope better than the other players who were not from the continent of India with the sauna-like heat.

Qualifying in second place in his group, Mifsud overturned arrears of 618 halfway through his six hour semi-final against the Indian Michael Ferreira, the defending champion, to win by 633.

Having turned this match with a break of 338, Mifsud crucially played out time with 359 (completed next day to 361) to reach the halfway mark of his final against Dagley with a lead of 823 on which the Englishman never looked like making any impression.

Though he practised billiards much less than snooker, Mifsud had probably benefited from having to rise to the domestic threat posed by Joe Grech, who made breaks of 567 and 510 in winning the Malta Championship in 1978.

Grech, like Mifsud a quarter-finalist in the World Amateur Snooker in 1978, firmly established himself as Malta's no. 2 at both games while Mifsud came within striking distance of completing a unique world amateur billiards/snooker double.

Undefeated in his group of the 1980 World Amateur Snooker in Launceston, Mifsud beat the Australian John Campbell 5–3 in the quarter-final and led the eventual champion, Jimmy White, 3–0, 5–3, and 6–4 in the semi-final before losing 8–6.

Joe Grech holds the national championship break record with 567 (billiards) and 109 (snooker).

Tony Drago, who won Malta's snooker title in 1984, quickly made a name for himself by winning several amateur tournaments on the British circuit and turned professional in time for the 1985–6 season. Mifsud spent one year as a professional and reached 48th place in the world rankings before applying for reinstatement as an amateur.

NEW ZEALAND

Although the New Zealand Amateur Billiards Championship has taken place, except for 1909, annually since 1908, the New Zealand Billiards and Snooker Association was formed only in 1935 when competitors and delegates from four provinces, Auckland, Wellington, Canterbury and Otago, met at the Commercial Travellers Club, Auckland.

Far and away the outstanding cueist New Zealand has produced is Clark McConachy MBE, whose career is fully detailed on p. 107. Two other professionals, Norman Squire and Murt O'Donoghue, who spent most of their careers in Australia, were also New Zealand born.

Alan Twohill won five titles in succession from 1953 to 1957 and nine in all. His break of 204 in 1956 was the first double century in the New Zealand Championship. A year later, he made a break of 222 but it was not until 1966 that he improved the record to 238 unfinished, a timely effort as he was then trailing Herbie Robinson, who has himself won four titles, by 60 points with 20 minutes to play. His two hour session aggregate of 933 earlier in this competition remains a New Zealand record.

Twohill's break record was eclipsed by Robinson with 280 in 1979 but no New Zealander has yet made much headway in the World Amateur Championship even if Brian Kirkness, three times national champion, has at times threatened to do so.

With a good grasp of top of the table technique and an insatiable appetite for practice, Kirkness extended the national championship break record to 301 in 1978 and had a run of 326 in another competition.

New Zealand snooker standards, in international terms, generally remained modest although there was clear improvement in the seventies.

Dene O'Kane, who was only 17 when he was the New Zealand amateur title in 1980, became in 1984, the first New Zealander on the professional circuit. The break record in the national championship stands to Grant Hayward with 103 in 1978.

One curiosity of the 1976 New Zealand billiards final was that it is the only national final on record in which a father, Herbie Robinson, defeated his son, Russell Robinson.

Two administrators, Frank Holz and Brien Bennett, have made outstanding contributions not only to their domestic organisation but the international game.

Holz, who received the MBE for services to charity – to which virtually all his promotional enterprises were directed – in 1977, brought the 1964 World Amateur Billiards Championship to Pukekohe, a small South Auckland country town, and made it a resounding success.

He organised two unofficial World Open Billiards Championships in Pukekohe in 1972 and Christchurch in 1977 and his organisational abilities were so highly rated that he was brought in to organise the 1970 World Professional Snooker Championship in Australia. Other ventures included the match between McConachy and Rex Williams for the World Professional Billiards Championship in Auckland in 1968, the first time the event had been contested for 17 years.

Bennett, who won the New Zealand snooker title in 1971, maintained as president of the New Zealand Association the high standard of domestic adminis-

Billiards Championship

1908	J. Ryan
1909	No contest
1910	F. Lovelock
1911	F. Lovelock
1912	H. Valentine
1913	H. Valentine
1914	N. Lynch
1915	W. E. Warren
1916	H. Siedeberg
1917	H. Siedeberg
1918	W. E. Warren
1919	H. Siedeberg
1920	W. E. Warren
1921	H. Siedeberg
1922	E. V. Roberts
1923	E. V. Roberts
1924	R. Fredotovich
1925	C. Mason
1926	E. V. Roberts
1927	E. V. Roberts
1928	A. Bowie
1929	L. Stout
1930	W. E. Hackett
1931	A. Duncan
1932	C. Mason
1933	A. Albertson
1934	H. McLean
1935	L. Holdsworth
1936	S. Moses
1937	S. Moses
1938	L. Holdsworth
1939	R. Carrick
1940	S. Moses
1941	R. Carrick
1942	R. Carrick
1943	A. Albertson
1944	S. Moses
1945	J. Shepherd
1946	R. Carrick
1947	C. Peek
1948	R. Carrick
1949	R. Carrick
1950	R. Carrick
1951	R. Carrick
1952	L. Stout
1953	A. Twohill
1954	A. Twohill
1955	A. Twohill
1956	A. Twohill
1957	A. Twohill
1958	A. Albertson
1959	A. Twohill
1960	W. Harcourt
1961	A. Albertson
1962	W. Harcourt
1963	H. C. Robinson
1964	T. Yesberg
1965	L. Napper
1966	A. Twohill
1967	A. Twohill
1968	A. Twohill
1969	E. Simmons
1970	L. Napper
1971	W. Harcourt
1972	B. Kirkness
1973	H. C. Robinson
1974	H. C. Robinson
1975	T. Yesberg
1976	H. C. Robinson
1977	B. Kirkness
1978	B. Kirkness
1979	R. Adams
1980	D. Meredith
1981	D. Meredith
1982	D. Meredith
1983	D. Meredith
1984	D. Meredith

Snooker Championship

1945	S. Moses
1946	J. Munro
1947	W. Thompson
1948	L. Stout
1949	L. Stout
1950	L. Stout
1951	N. Lewis
1952	L. Stout
1953	L. Sout
1954	R. Franks
1955	L. Stout
1956	L. Stout
1957	W. Harcourt
1958	W. Harcourt
1959	W. Thomas
1960	T. Yesberg
1961	F. Franks
1962	K. Murphy
1963	W. Harcourt
1964	T. Yesberg
1965	L. Napper
1966	L. Napper
1967	R. Flutey
1968	L. Napper
1969	L. Glozier
1970	K. Tristram
1971	B. J. Bennett
1972	N. Stockman
1973	W. Hill
1974	K. Tristram
1975	K. Tristram
1976	D. Kwok
1977	D. Meredith
1978	D. Meredith
1979	D. Meredith
1980	D. O'Kane
1981	G. Kwok
1982	D. Kwok
1983	D. Kwok
1984	D. Kwok

tration he inherited from Holz and made a major contribution at international level in the difficult early years of the International Billiards and Snooker Federation, of which he was elected chairman in 1980.

SOUTH AFRICA

The South African Billiards and Snooker Association, founded in 1915, has organised a national amateur billiards championship since 1920 and a snooker championship since 1937.

In 1920, Arthur Walker, a millionaire South African, proposed an Empire championship which the BA & CC in London rejected as impracticable. However, it was approved in principle in 1922 and was held for the first time in 1926 at Thurston's with Walker's trophy, still in circulation for the World Amateur Championship, at stake.

Allan Prior, a 6ft 5in policeman won the 1927 event, also at Thurston's, to give South Africa the right, under the conditions then pertaining, to stage the event. They did so at the Carlton Hotel, Johannesburg in 1929 when Prior was beaten into second place by an Australian, Les Hayes.

Prior, who won seven South African titles at billiards and two at snooker, was third in London in 1933 and second to the great Australian Bob Marshall in Johannesburg in 1936. Prior, indeed, held Marshall until half an hour from time.

An expatriate Welshman, Glyn Rees won four billiards and three snooker titles between 1949 and 1953 and Gerry Povall, though he won only one billiards title, set a world amateur snooker break record of 106 in the 1956 South African Championship. Ken O'Kennedy made a break of 122 on a standard table in a non-championship match in 1955.

Mannie Francisco, who won twelve South African

illiards titles, and six snooker titles, set a new South African record of 518, albeit under the infamous 15-pot rule, in the 1964 World Amateur Billiards in Puke-kohe. In 1965, he set a South African championship record of 433 which still stands; and in 1967 in Colombo he led Leslie Driffield by 500 with an hour to play before the Englishman recovered to win by 162 and go on to take his second world amateur billiards title. Francisco, who also lost to Mohammed Lafir (Sri Lanka), was third.

In 1969, in London, Francisco was again well in the running. When he played the Englishman, Jack Karnehm, both players had one defeat. Francisco led by 152 with 17 minutes remaining but the fatal inhibitions which seemed to assail him throughout his career on the brink of important victories proved his undoing once more. He missed an in-off at the top of the table and Karnehm played out time to win by 9.

Though well beaten by England's Norman Dagley in the concluding four man round robin, Francisco followed his joint second place in London in 1969 with an outright second place in Malta in 1971.

He did not thereafter compete in a World Amateur Billiards Championship. As it gathered strength, the anti-apartheid movement increasingly limited South African involvement in international sport though the country was represented in the World Amateur Snooker Championships of 1972, their first partici-pation, and 1976 when they hosted the event lavishly in the President Hotel, Johannesburg.

In Cardiff, in 1972, Francisco demonstrated his determination when faced with defeat, when, after a series of nerve wracking group matches, he trailed the Indian Arvind Savur 0–4 in the semi-final before winning on the final black 8–7. He led Ray Edmonds (England) 6–0 and 7–2 in the final only to lose 11–10, a tribute to the Englishman's fighting qualities but also clinching evidence of Francisco's fatally flawed temperament.

Francisco won his group in the 1976 World Amateur but suffered his first competitive defeat to his younger brother Silvino in the quarter-finals. Silvino, with three South African snooker titles and three billiards, and Jimmy van Rensburg, a world amateur semi-finalist in 1976 who also won 11 South African snooker and one billiards title, were the other outstanding postwar South African amateurs.

South Africa's most successful professional has been Perrie Mans, only 20 when he won his national amateur title as his first and only attempt in 1960 and his coun-try's first ever world professional finalist in 1978.

His father, Peter Mans, South Africa's first

Billiards Championship

Year	Winner	Year	Winner	Year	Winner
1920	Sgt. Bruyns	1962	M. Francisco	1951	T. G. Rees
1921	A. Prior	1963	M. Francisco	1952	T. G. Rees
1922	A. Prior	1964	M. Francisco	1953	J. van Rensburg
1923	No contest	1965	M. Francisco	1954	J. van Rensburg
1924	A. Prior	1966	M. Francisco	1955	J. van Rensburg
1925	P. Rutledge	1967	J. van Rensburg	1956	F. Walker
1926	A. Prior	1968	M. Francisco	1957	J. van Rensburg
1927	A. Percival	1969	M. Francisco	1958	R. Walker
1928	P. Rutledge	1970	M. Francisco	1959	M. Francisco
1929–30	No contests	1971	M. Francisco	1960	P. Mans Jnr
1931	A. Prior	1972	S. Francisco	1961	J. van Rensburg
1932–36	No contests	1973	S. Francisco	1962	J. van Rensburg
1937	A. M. Burke	1974	M. Francisco	1963	J. van Rensburg
1938	A. Prior	1975	S. Francisco	1964	M. Francisco
1939	A. Prior	1976	No contest	1965	M. Francisco
1940–45	No contests	1977	M. Francisco	1966	M. Francisco
1946	P. G. Kempen	1978	C. van Dijk	1967	J. van Rensburg
1947	No contest	1979	C. van Dijk	1968	S. Francisco
1948	P. G. Kempen	1980	C. van Dijk	1969	S. Francisco
1949	T. G. Rees	1981	P. Spence	1970	J. van Rensburg
1950	T. G. Rees	1982		1971	M. Francisco
1951	I. Drapin	1983	P. Francisco	1972	J. van Rensburg
1952	T. G. Rees			1973	J. van Rensburg
1953	T. G. Rees	**Snooker Championship**		1974	S. Francisco
1954	F. Walker	1937	A. Prior	1975	M. Francisco
1955	F. Walker	1938	A. H. Ashby	1976	No contest
1956	G. Povall	1939	A. Prior	1977	S. Francisco
1957	F. Walker	1940–45	No contests	1978	J. van Niekerk
1958	F. Walker	1946	F. Walker	1979	F. Ellis
1959	M. Francisco	1947	No contest	1980	F. Ellis
1960	R. Walker	1948	F. Walker	1981	P. Francisco
1961	M. Francisco	1949	E. Kerr	1982	P. Francisco
		1950	T. G. Rees	1983	P. Francisco

Mannie Francisco

professional snooker champion, competed with fair success in the *News of the World* tournament in London in 1949–50, in which season he also reached the quarter-final of the World Professional Championship. Mans, who won his national professional title from Freddie van Rensburg, relinquished it in van Rensburg's favour in 1950. In turn, van Pensburg held the title until defeated 13–11 by Perrie Mans in 1965. Mans retained the title until sensationally defeated by Mienie in 1979 but regained it the following year.

Van Rensburg, who has also held the South African professional billiards title unchallenged since 1956, was a player of little cue-power but considerable touch. He gave Fred Davis his closest match, 5–4, in 'World' Open in Australia in 1960 but was past his best when, on the challenge system then in operation, he lost a

week's match 39–12 to John Pulman for the world professional title in 1965.

This match followed a 47 match series which Pulman and Rex Williams played for the world professional title throughout South Africa, the first time the event had been held abroad. It was during this series that Williams set a world championship record of 142, superseding his own 141 against Fred Davis at Birmingham in 1966. After the series Williams made a 147 maximum against Mannie Francisco which was recognised as a joint world record.

Professional tours to South Africa have been common since the days of John Roberts, Billy Matchell, H. W. Stevenson and Cecil Harverson, who settled in South Africa and whose son, Ronny, became a professional there. Frank Ferraro, who played with a 12 oz cue, was for some years in the inter-war period recognised as South African professional champion. Walter Lindrum, Joe Davis and Horace Lindrum each made several tours, as have Ray Reardon and Rex Williams in modern times.

It was Sid Gillett, a director of Thurston's, London, until he settled in South Africa as managing director of Thurston's (South Africa), who in 1952 asked the BA & CC to consider a world amateur snooker championship. The request was deferred but it at least started this particular ball rolling. Another trade personality, Ken Shaw of Union Billiards, has been South Africa's most persistent promoter.

When South Africa was barred from competing in the first two world amateur snooker championships in Calcutta in 1963 and Karachi in 1966 and anxious not to be left behind, the South African Association invited Ray Reardon and Jonathan Barron (representing England), for a Test Series against Mannie Francisco and Jimmy van Rensburg, representing South Africa.

In the course of the series, won 2–1 by England, Shaw offered to organise a South African tour for Reardon should he decide to turn professional. It was this tour which enabled Reardon's professional career to get under way in December 1967. In 1974, Reardon made a four month tour in which he made no less than 65 snooker centuries in public.

South Africa's unprecedented offer to pay air fares for one competitor and one delegate from each affiliated country to the 1976 World Amateur Snooker Championships in Johannesburg enabled some of the more impoverished national associations to be represented and others who would have been refused a grant by their government to be represented at no cost to themselves. The championship was conspicuously well staged but international governments were not impressed. South Africa has not since been allowed to participate in international amateur competition.

On the professional front, its players have been free to compete as individuals and a number of professional tournaments have been organised with an international flavour within South Africa.

Silvino Francisco, who is profiled on page 00, has

emerged as the outstanding South African on the professional circuit. Mannie Francisco has played only intermittently as a professional and never in Britain but his son Peter, the third member of the family to win South African amateur titles at both games, had an encouraging debut season as a professional in 1984–5.

SRI LANKA

The Billiards Association and Control Council of Ceylon, the precursor of the Sri Lanka Billiards and Snooker Association was founded only in 1948 though the games of billiards and snooker had been popular in the clubs of the island for many years. Its small population, isolated situation and for the most part poor playing conditions are all against producing large numbers of high quality players.

It was thus all the more remarkable that Mohammed Lafir, who learnt to play on an improvised table in which a sarong acted as the cloth and a bicycle tyre for the cushions, should become his country's first ever sporting world champion when he captured the World Amateur Billiards Championship in Bombay in 1973.

Having soon outclassed all his domestic rivals, both at billiards and snooker, Lafir developed his game by competing in the Indian and World Amateur Championships and learning from the players he encountered. In 1967, he was runner-up in the World Amateur Billiards Championship when it was staged before his own countrymen at the Samudra Hotel, Colombo; in 1973, after setting a new national championship break record of 500 unfinished, he won the title at the Cricket Club of India, Bombay in the course of which he set a new world amateur break record of 859.

His new status as an authentic national hero created a burden of expectation which he was nervous of being unable to fulfil. He did not compete either in 1975 or 1977 and, though he reached the semi-finals, looked only a shadow of his Bombay self in the World Amateur Billiards of 1979 in Colombo, when he was clearly unhappy with the factional splits in his own national association.

He rarely played to his full potential out of the tropics and his snooker was not quite of the standard of his billiards but he nevertheless reached the quarter-finals of the 1974 World Amateur Snooker in Dublin and also did well in Sydney in 1968, Edinburgh in 1970 and Malta in 1978. He died in 1981 at the age of 53.

OTHER COUNTRIES

In recent years, the number of countries involved in international amateur competition has risen dramatically. Whereas it used to be confined largely to Britain and its existing and former Commonwealth, the game is now spreading rapidly in all directions.

The most spectacular growth has been in the Far East, particularly in Thailand, Singapore and Hong Kong, and on the continent of Europe.

In Britain, television stimulated a high demand for tables, particularly in new snooker centres, but as this demand began to level out, the table companies sought the alternative markets necessary to maintain sales and therefore production.

Tours of the Far East by Steve Davis and other members of Barry Hearn's management stable produced many sales of the Riley tables with which the Hearn camp is commercially connected and domestic

Billiards Championship

1948	A. C. Cambal	1972	M. J. M. Lafir
1949	M. J. M. Lafir	1973	M. J. M. Lafir
1950	M. J. M. Lafir	1974	S. Shaharwardi
1951	M. J. M. Lafir	1975	M. S. U. Mohideen
1952	M. J. M. Lafir	1976	W. Weerasinghe
1953	M. J. M. Lafir	1977	W. A. J. Weerasinghe
1954	A. C. Cambal	1978	J. W. H. Boteju
1955	T. A. Selvaraj	1979	W. A. J. Weerasinghe
1956	T. A. Selvaraj	1980	
1957	M. J. M. Lafir	1981	J. W. H. Boteju
1958	n.r.		
1959	M. J. M. Lafir	**Snooker Championship**	
1960	M. J. M. Lafir	1948	M. J. M. Lafir
1961	M. J. M. Lafir	1949	M. M. Faiz
1962	M. J. M. Lafir	1950	M. J. M. Lafir
1963	M. H. M. Mujahid	1951	M. S. A. Hassan
1964	M. J. M. Lafir	1952	M. J. M. Lafir
1965	n.r.	1953	M. J. M. Lafir
1966	M. J. M. Lafir	1954	M. J. M. Lafir
1967	J. K. Bakshani	1955	M. J. M. Lafir
1968	n.r.	1956	M. J. M. Lafir
1969	M. J. M. Lafir	1957	M. J. M. Lafir
1970	M. J. M. Lafir	1958	M. J. M. Lafir
1971	n.r.	1959	M. J. M. Lafir
		1960	M. J. M. Lafir

1961	M. J. M. Lafir
1962	M. J. M. Lafir
1963	M. J. M. Izzath
1964	M. J. M. Lafir
1965	M. J. M. Lafir
1966	M. J. M. Lafir
1967	N. J. Rahim
1968	No contest
1969	M. J. M. Lafir
1970	N. J. Rahim
1971	No contest
1972	N. J. Rahim
1973	M. J. M. Lafir
1974	Abandoned
1975	N. A. Rahim
1976	M. S. U. Mohideen
1977	M. S. U. Mohideen
1978	N. A. Rahim
1979	
1980	
1981	J. W. H. Boteju
1982	J. A. Wahid
1983	
1984	K. Sirisoma
1985	J. W. H. Boteju

television stations also proved keen to televise tournaments of their own origination in addition to the footage which was bought in from Britain.

In Europe, where sales have also been stimulated by television, notably by BBC coverage picked up unofficially in coastal regions, tables have been sold in Spain, Sweden, France, Germany, Holland, Belgium and Iceland.

Belgium, Iceland and Sweden were all sufficiently advanced to send competitors to the 1984 World Amateur Championship in Dublin, an event which also attracted entries for the first time from the United States, where pool reigns and where still little snooker is played. Zimbabwe, Egypt, Mauritius, Fiji and Sudan have all sent competitors in recent years as snooker has maintained its progress to becoming a genuinely worldwide game.

ZIMBABWE

Snooker Championship
1981   A. Thomson
1982   A. Thomson
1983   J. Daly

Fred Davis

WORLD AMATEUR CHAMPIONSHIPS

In September 1922 the BA & CC approved in principle a British Empire championship though it was not until 1926 that the first event took place at Thurston's, London. Arthur Walker, a South African millionaire, whose conception the event had been, presented the trophy which is still in circulation although the title of the event was changed to World Amateur Billiards Championship in 1951.

Sid Gillett, a director of Thurston's until he settled in South Africa as managing director of Thurston's (South Africa), asked the BA & CC in 1952 to consider a World Amateur snooker championship and Australia made a similar request shortly afterwards only to have it 'deferred until some improvement in the BA & CC's finances takes place'. In 1958, the BA & CC announced its intention of inaugurating the event in London the following year but both India and Australia felt that London should not be the venue and persuaded two other countries likewise, so the event fell through until M. M. Begg, chairman of the BA & CC of India, donated a cup and concluded arrangements for the inaugural tournament in Calcutta in 1963 to which the BA & CC and other interested nations agreed.

The championships are held biennially with the billiards taking place in the odd years and snooker the even. A rota of venues is agreed several years in advance by the International Billiards & Snooker Federation. Each affiliated country is allowed to nominate two players for each event.

World Amateur Billiards Championships

	Won	Highest break	No. of centuries
1926 *London*			
J. Earlham (Eng)	4	282	18
G. Shailer (Aus)	3	203	13
M. Smith (Sco)	2	130	4
P. Rutledge (SA)	1	142	2
T. McCluney (NI)	0	144	4
1927 *London*			
A. Prior (SA)	3	184	9
H. F. Coles (Wal)	2	164	2
L. Steeples (Eng)	1	236	9
M. Smith (Sco)	0	158	1
1929 *Johannesburg*			
L. Hayes (Aus)	3	136	6
A. Prior (SA)	2	226	7
H. F. Coles (Eng)	1	170	7
P. Rutledge (SA)	0	164	1
1931 *Sydney*			
L. Steeples (Eng)	4	461	24
S. Lee (Eng)	3	433	18
L. Hayes (Aus)	2	167	6
H. Goldsmith (Aus)	1	179	4
W. Hackett (NZ)	0	97	0
1933 *London*			
S. Lee (Eng)	4	394	31
T. Jones (Wal)	3	144	8
A. Prior (SA)	2	235	13
M. Smith (Sco)	1	166	5
J. Blackburn (NI)	0	94	0
1935 *London*			
H. F. Coles (Eng)	4	267	33
J. McGhie (Sco)	3	207	11
I. Edwards (Wal)	2	196	11
S. Fenning (Irish Free State)	1	161	6
P. Deb (Ind)	0	123	5
1936 *Johannesburg*			
R. Marshall (Aus)	3	248	24
A. Prior (SA)	2	197	11
J. Thompson (Eng)	1	245	15
A. Bowlly (SA)	1	93	0
Three 2½ hour sessions			
1938 *Melbourne*			
R. Marshall (Aus)	6	427	59
K. Kennerley (Eng)	5	472	45
T. Cleary (Aus)	4	322	17
S. Moses (NZ)	2	129	4
M. M. Begg (Ind)	2	111	2
A. Burke (SA)	1	119	1
A. Albertson (NZ)	1	107	1
1951 *London*			
R. Marshall (Aus)	6	423	42
F. Edwards (Eng)	5	345	36
T. Cleary (Aus)	4	330	31

	Won	Highest break	No. of centuries
W. Ramage (Sco)	3	151	8
W. Pierce (Wal)	2	225	3
W. Jones (Ind)	1	138	10
E. Haslem (NI)	0	125	3
1952 *Calcutta*			
L. Driffield (Eng)	5	278	31
R Marshall (Aus)	3	351	27
C. Hirjee (Ind)	3	230	14
W. Ramage (Sco)	3	211	10
W. Jones (Ind)	1	253	6
A. Yunoos (Bur)	0	79	0
1954 *Sydney*			
T. Cleary (Aus)	4	682	35
R. Marshall (Aus)	3	407	35
F. Edwards (Eng)	2	328	26
W. Jones (Ind)	1	209	17
T. G. Rees (SA)	0	207	6
1958 *Calcutta*			
W. Jones (Ind)	5	501	56
L. Driffield (Eng)	4	499	48
T. Cleary (Aus)	3	431	52
C. Hirjee (Ind)	2	226	38
W. Asciak (Mta)	1	154	7
M. Hman (Bur)	0	215	8
1960 *Edinburgh*			
J. H. Beetham (Eng)	7	277	29
J. Long (Aus)	6	353	26
W. Jones (Ind)	5	589	30
M. Francisco (SA)	4	148	11
W. Ramage (Sco)	3	283	12
W. Asciak (Mta)	2	194	11
W. Dennison (NI)	1	155	4
A. Ramage (Sco)	0	101	2
1962 *Perth*			
R. Marshall (Aus)	5	348	57
W. Jones (Ind)	5	489	34
T. Cleary (Aus)	4	315	27
J. H. Beetham (Eng)	3	283	18
S. Benajee (Ind)	3	219	9
R. A. Karim (Pak)	1	130	3
W. Harcourt (NZ)	0	123	5
Play-off: Marshall beat Jones 3623–2891			
1964 *Pukekohe*			
W. Jones (Ind)	9	294	49
J. Karnehm (Eng)	8	390	28
M. Ferreira (Ind)	7	182	29
M. Francisco (SA)	6	518	38
A. Nolan (Eng)	5	259	26
T. Cleary (Aus)	4	241	19
H. Robinson (NZ)	3	85	0
T. Yesberg (NZ)	2	80	0
M. Mavalwala (Pak)	1	174	1
A. E. Redmond (SA)	0	107	1

	Won	Highest break	No. of centuries
1967 *Colombo*			
L. Driffield (Eng)	8	421	53
M. J. M. Lafir (Sri)	7	218	31
M. Francisco (SA)	6	301	32
M. Ferreira (Ind)	5	507	22
J. Long (Aus)	4	261	27
T. Cleary (Aus)	3	322	15
N. J. Rahim (Cey)	2	116	3
M. S. M. Marzuq (Cey)	1	88	0
F. Holz (NZ)	0	68	0
1969 *London*			
J. Karnehm (Eng)	9	232	27
M. Ferreira (Ind)	7	629	34
M. Francisco (SA)	7	335	35
M. J. M. Lafir (Cey)	7	296	28
R. Marshall (Aus)	6	216	33
M. Wildman (Eng)	6	274	22
R. Oriel (Wal)	5	297	30
S. Mohan (Ind)	5	219	24
P. Mifsud (Mta)	2	173	8
A. Twohill (NZ)	1	146	12
F. Holz (NZ)	0	65	0
1971 *Malta*			
Group A			
M. Francisco (SA)	4	321	15
M. J. M. Lafir (Sri)	3	233	4

	Won	Highest break	No. of centuries
P. Mifsud (Mta)	2	134	2
D. Sneddon (Sco)	1	121	2
L. Napper (NZ)	0	87	0
Group B			
S. Mohan (Ind)	4	188	11
N. Dagley (Eng)	3	330	11
M. Ferreira (Ind)	2	227	4
C. Everton (Wal)	1	205	5
W. Asciak (Mta)	0	188	7
Play-offs:			
Dagley	3	348	17
Francisco	2	353	11
Mohan	1	327	11
Lafir	0	211	5
1973 *Bombay*			
M. J. M. Lafir (Sri)	9	859	43
S. Mohan (Ind)	7	468	53
M. Ferreira (Ind)	7	421	41
P. Tarrant (Aus)	6	373	36
C. Everton (Wal)	5	240	17
A. Nolan (Eng)	4	265	31
P. Mifsud (Mta)	4	203	23
E. Simons (NZ)	2	94	0
B. Kirkness (NZ)	1	195	7
L. U. Demarco (Sco)	0	87	0

Bob Marshall

World Amateur Billiards Championships

	Won	Highest break	No. of centuries
1975 *Auckland*			
Group A			
N. Dagley (Eng)	5	477	24
D. Sneddon (Sco)	4	124	4
G. Parikh (Ind)	3	197	16
J. Reece (Aus)	2	125	4
H. Robinson (NZ)	1	123	2
M. Shaharwardi (Sri)	0	121	1
Group B			
M. Ferreira (Ind)	5	411	26
C. Everton (Wal)	4	272	13
R. Close (Eng)	3	164	10
T. Yesberg (NZ)	2	131	3
J. Long (Aus)	1	157	5
B. Bennett (NZ)	0	95	0

Play-offs
Semi-finals: Dagley beat Everton 1293–755; Ferreira beat Sneddon 2470–681
Final: Dagley beat Ferreira 3385–2268

	Won	Highest break	No. of centuries
1977 *Melbourne*			
Group A			
N. Dagley (Eng)	5	272	16
C. Everton (Wal)	4	170	7
S. Aleem (Ind)	3	263	11
G. Ganim Snr (Aus)	2	231	6
H. Robinson (NZ)	1	93	0
J. Nugent (Sco)	0	68	0
Group B			
M. Ferreira (Ind)	5	519	33
R. Close (Eng)	4	207	15
G. Ganim Jnr (Aus)	3	192	9
T. Yesberg (NZ)	2	109	1
W. Weerasinghe (Sri)	1	97	0
D. Pratt (Sco)	0	108	1

Play-offs
Semi-finals: Ferreira beat Everton 2155–1310; Close beat Dagley 1912 (234, 215)–1781 (236)
Final: Ferreira beat Close 2683–2564 (231)

	Won	Highest break	No. of centuries
1979 *Colombo*			
Group A			
M. Ferreira (Ind)	7	467	40
M. J. M. Lafir (Sri)	5	370	30
K. Shirley (Eng)	5	195	13
W. Barrie (Aus)	4	128	2
B. Kirkness (NZ)	4	214	8
H. Nimmo (Sco)	2	105	2
M. S. U. Mohideen (Sri)	1	76	0
R. Lim Sin Foo (Sin)	0	97	0
Group B			
N. Dagley (Eng)	6	466	39
P. Mifsud (Mta)	6	325	31
S. Agrawal (Ind)	6	355	30

	Won	Highest break	No. of centuries
G. Ganim Jnr (Aus)	3	267	15
C. Everton (Wal)	3	211	11
W. A. J. Weerasinghe (Sri)	3	202	7
B. Bennett (NZ)	1	101	1
E. Fisher (Can)	0	88	0

Play-offs
Semi-finals: Mifsud beat Ferreira 2489 (218, 338, 285)–1856; Dagley beat Lafir 2694 (266, 444, 289)–1692 (240)
Final: Mifsud beat Dagley 2943 (361)–2152

	Won	Highest break	No. of centuries
1981 *New Delhi*			
Group A			
N. Dagley (Eng)	6	416	42
S. Agrawal (Ind)	5	384	39
G. Ganim junior (Aus)	4	178	13
A. K. B. Giles (NZ)	3	162	5
D. Sneddon (Sco)	2	123	6
J. W. H. Boteju (Sri)	1	107	1
A. A. Essam (Egy)	0	59	—
Group B			
M. Ferreira (Ind)	6	630	58
L. A. Bux (Pak)	5	257	21
R. Close (Eng)	3	217	15
J. Grech (Mta)	3	402	9
D. Meredith (NZ)	3	154	7
H. Roberts-Thomson (Aus)	2	151	5
S. M. Shahawardi (Sri)	0	77	—

Semi-finals. Dagley beat Bux 2890 (359, 229, 217, 218)–1505 (257); Ferreira beat Agrawal 3272 (213, 532, 327, 527, 630)–1964 (233, 253)
Final: Ferreira beat Dagley 2725 (208, 349, 245, 244)–2631 (223, 296, 281)

	Won	Highest break	No. of centuries
1983 *Malta*			
Group A			
M. Ferreira (Ind)	6	463	31
R. Foldvari (Aus)	5	302	30
L. A. Bux (Pak)	4	177	9
H. Nimmo (Sco)	3	224	6
D. Meredith (NZ)	2	157	7
H. Griffiths (Wal)	1	112	1
A. Micallef (Mta)	0	122	6
Group B			
S. Agrawal (Ind)	5	635	42
N. Dagley (Eng)	5	368	30
J. Grech (Mta)	5	286	31
V. Ellul (Mta)	2	145	2
R. Lim (Sin)	2	96	—
W. Loughan (N)	2	198	5
H. Boteju (Sri)	0	120	2

Semi-finals: Agrawal beat Foldvari 2047 (240, 503)–1900 (302, 225, 231) Ferreira beat Dagley 1983 (463) — 1919 (258)
Final: Ferreira beat Agrawal 3933 (353, 398, 201, 254) — 2744 (242, 212)

World Amateur Snooker Championships

	Wins	For	Agnst	Highest break
1963 *Calcutta*				
G. Owen (Eng)	4	23	7	71
F. Harris (Aus)	3	21	17	52
M. J. M. Lafir (Cey)	2	19	18	67
T. Monteiro (Ind)	1	14	19	56
W. Jones (Ind)	0	7	24	36
1966 *Karachi*				
G. Owen (Eng)	5	30	7	118
J. Spencer (Eng)	4	26	14	101
W. Barrie (Aus)	3	23	22	73
M. J. M. Lafir (Cey)	2	22	20	45
L. U. Demarco (Sco)	1	14	28	36
H. Karim (Pak)	0	6	30	60
1968 *Sydney*				
Group A				
D. Taylor (Eng)	4	24	13	96
J. van Rensburg (SA)	3	22	14	
H. Andrews (Aus)	2	17	16	
T. Monteiro (Ind)	1	17	22	
L. Napper (NZ)	0	9	24	
Group B				
M. Williams (Aus)	3	22	14	
P. Morgan (Ire)	3	19	14	88
M. J. M. Lafir (Cey)	2	19	16	
S. Shroff (Ind)	2	20	19	
R. Flutey (NZ)	0	7	24	

Play-offs

Semi-finals: Williams beat van Rensburg 8–7; Taylor beat Morgan 8–3

Final: Taylor beat Williams 8–7

	Wins	For	Agnst	Highest break
1970 *Edinburgh*				
Group A				
S. Hood (Eng)	5	20	9	50
P. Mifsud (Mta)	4	22	11	61
M. J. M. Lafir (Sri)	4	20	16	50
J. Phillips (Sco)	4	19	18	62
D. Sneddon (Sco)	2	17	17	38
L. Glozier (NZ)	2	10	21	34
J. Clint (NI)	0	8	24	46
Group B				
J. Barron (Eng)	5	21	13	51
D. May (Wal)	4	22	18	64
S. Shroff (Ind)	3	18	14	47
E. Sinclair (Sco)	3	16	16	49
J. Rogers (Ire)	3	16	19	65
L. U. Demarco (Sco)	2	15	19	32
H. Andrews (Aus)	1	13	22	35

Final: Barron beat Hood 11–7

	Wins	For	Agnst	Highest break
1972 *Cardiff*				
Group A				
J. van Rensburg (SA)	3	12	6	45
K. Tristram (NZ)	1	8	8	50
G. Thomas (Wal)	1	6	8	32
L. U. Demarco (Sco)	1	6	10	41

	Wins	For	Agnst	Highest break
Group B				
M. Francisco (SA)	3	15	5	47
J. Barron (Eng)	3	15	10	50
A. Borg (Mta)	2	12	11	59
A. Lloyd (Wal)	2	11	14	41
T. Monteiro (Ind)	0	3	16	46
Group C				
P. Mifsud (Mta)	4	16	5	61
R. Edmonds (Eng)	3	14	7	101
J. Rogers (Ire)	2	8	8	36
M. Berni (Wal)	1	7	12	47
B. Bennett (NZ)	0	3	16	30
Group D				
A. Savur (Ind)	2	10	6	38
M. Williams (Aus)	2	9	7	48
D. Sneddon (Sco)	2	9	9	34
D. May (Wal)	0	6	12	42
Semi-final groups				
Group A				
Barron	3	12	4	35
Savur	2	10	8	68
Tristram	1	6	8	29
Mifsud	0	6	12	50
Group B				
Francisco	2	11	9	70
Edmonds	2	11	9	39
Van Rensburg	1	8	10	51
Williams	1	9	11	78

Semi-finals: Edmonds beat Barron 8–6; Francisco beat Savur 8–7

Final: Edmonds beat Francisco 11–10

	Wins	For	Agnst	Highest break
1974 *Dublin*				
Group A				
R. Edmonds (Eng)	7	31	11	66
M. J. M. Lafir (Sri)	6	30	19	77
E. Sinclair (Sco)	6	28	21	67
G. Thomas (Wal)	4	24	22	43
D. Sheehan (Ire)	4	25	24	43
P. Donnelly (NI)	3	21	28	42
S. Shroff (Ind)	3	16	26	44
N. Stockman (NZ)	2	18	29	51
J. Sklazeski (Can)	1	18	31	79
Group B				
A. Lloyd (Wal)	8	32	14	104
W. Hill (NZ)	5	26	21	58
P. Burke (Ire)	4	26	20	71
L. Condo (Aus)	4	26	21	53
A. Borg (Mta)	4	27	23	37
D. Sneddon (Sco)	4	23	21	54
A. Savur (Ind)	4	24	23	50
R. Cowley (Isle of Man)	3	16	27	50
N. J. Rahim (Sri)	0	2	32	25

Quarter-finals: Edmonds beat Condo 4–3; Sinclair beat Hill 4–2; Burke beat Lafir 4–3; Thomas beat Lloyd 4–2

Semi-finals: Edmonds beat Sinclair 8–4; Thomas beat Burke 8–2

Final: Edmonds beat Thomas 11–9

World Amateur Snooker Championships

	Won	Highest break	No. of centuries
1976 *Johannesburg*			
Group A			
D. Mountjoy (Wal)	7	28	9	107
J. van Rensburg (SA)	5	24	16	72
R. Edmonds (Eng)	4	20	18	77
N. Stockman (NZ)	4	21	19	45
E. Sinclair (Sco)	4	21	21	51
P. Burke (Ire)	2	17	25	48
J. van Niekerk (SA)	1	17	27	35
P. Reynolds (Isle of Man)	1	14	27	46
Group B			
P. Mifsud (Mta)	6	25	9	47
S. Francisco (SA)	6	27	12	68
T. Griffiths (Wal)	5	23	14	69
C. Ross (Eng)	4	19	17	58
R. Paquette (Can)	4	22	22	72
E. Swaffield (NI)	1	16	26	59
L. Heywood (Aus)	1	13	27	46
L. Watson (Ire)	1	9	27	45
Group C			
M. Francisco (SA)	6	27	12	62
R. Atkins (Aus)	6	25	12	45
R. Andrewartha (Eng)	5	25	14	100
J. Clint (NI)	4	17	18	33
L. U. Demarco (Sco)	3	21	21	75
B. Mikkelsen (Can)	3	19	22	60
K. Tristram (NZ)	1	9	27	46
R. Cowley (Isle of Man)	0	11	28	41

Elimination match: Griffiths beat Andrewartha 4–0
Quarter-finals: Mountjoy beat Atkins 5–1; van Rensburg beat Griffiths 5–3; S. Francisco beat M. Francisco 5–1; Mifsud beat Edmonds 5–1
Semi-finals: Mountjoy beat S. Francisco 8–2; Mifsud beat van Rensburg 8–4
Final: Mountjoy beat Mifsud 11–1

	Won	Highest break	No. of centuries
1978 *Malta*			
Group A			
K. Burles (Aus)	6	26	10	69
P. Mifsud (Mta)	6	26	10	62
J. Johnson (Eng)	5	23	9	101
J. Donnelly (Sco)	5	20	13	78
D. McVeigh (NI)	2	15	20	56
P. Reynolds (Isle of Man)	2	10	22	45
V. Cremona (Mta)	2	9	25	—
M. Mohideen (Sri)	0	8	28	—
Group B			
A. Lloyd (Wal)	6	26	12	65
K. Stevens (Can)	5	23	16	94
J. Grech (Mta)	4	23	16	63
E. Hughes (Ire)	4	23	21	56
M. J. M. Lafir (Sri)	3	19	20	50
D. Meredith (NZ)	3	18	20	81
S. Shroff (Ind)	2	14	23	39
L. McCann (NI)	1	10	27	40

	Won	Highest break	No. of centuries
Group C			
C. Wilson (Wal)	8	32	10	66
R. Paquette (Can)	5	24	14	81
D. Kwok (NZ)	5	23	20	49
A. Savur (Ind)	5	26	22	56
I. Willimson (Eng)	3	22	24	52
R. Atkins (Aus)	3	21	24	49
R. Miller (Sco)	3	18	24	48
A. Borg (Mta)	2	15	27	44
C. Cooper (Isle of Man)	2	13	29	33

Elimination match: Grech beat Kwok 4–0
Quarter-finals: Burles beat Paquette 5–4; Stevens beat Mifsud 5–0; Johnson beat Lloyd 5–0; Wilson beat Grech 5–4
Semi-finals: Johnson beat Burles 8–4; Wilson beat Stevens 8–2
Final: Wilson beat Johnson 11–5

	Won	Highest break	No. of centuries
1980 *Launceston*			
Group A			
J. White (Eng)	6	24	9	99
A. Savur (Ind)	4	20	11	67
E. Hughes (Ire)	4	21	13	127
J. Grech (Mta)	3	19	18	80
L. Adams (NZ)	3	15	18	54
Loo Yap Long (Sin)	1	6	23	57
R. Burke (NI)	0	11	24	50
Group B			
J. Giannaros (Aus)	6	24	11	54
S. Newbury (Wal)	4	20	14	100
R. Paquette (Can)	4	20	15	90
D. Meredith (NZ)	4	20	16	67
G. Parikh (Ind)	2	17	18	46
S. Clarke (NI)	1	10	22	44
Lau Weng Yew (Sin)	0	8	24	36
Group C			
P. Mifsud (Mta)	6	24	3	77
R. Atkins (Aus)	4	19	15	67
J. Bonner (Aus)	4	17	17	53
W. King (Aus)	3	19	15	57
E. McLaughlin (Sco)	3	16	16	67
J. O'Boye (Eng)	1	14	21	98
S. Padayachi (Fiji)	0	2	24	40
Group D			
A. Lloyd (Wal)	6	24	4	47
J. Campbell (Aus)	5	22	8	84
D. Sheehan (Ire)	4	17	14	69
M. Gibson (Sco)	3	16	20	80
H. Boteju (Sri)	2	16	20	45
P. Reynolds (Isle of Man)	1	11	23	35
W. Barrie (Aus)	0	7	24	39

Quarter-finals: Savur beat Lloyd 5–3; Atkins beat Giannaros 5–3; Mifsud beat Campbell 5–3; White beat Newbury 5–4
Semi-finals: Atkins beat Savur 8–6; White beat Mifsud 8–6
Final: White beat Atkins 11–2

	Won	Highest break		No. of centuries

1982 Calgary

Group A
Player	Won	Highest break		No. of centuries
J. Grech (Mta)	6	28	13	68
A. Kearney (Ire)	6	26	15	57
D. O'Kane (NZ)	6	28	18	68
B. McConnell (Can)	5	26	19	43
P. Kippie (Sco)	5	23	16	68
S. Habib (Ind)	4	22	21	52
V. Saengthong (Tha)	3	20	28	73
Lui Yew Keong (Sin)	1	13	30	60
J. A. Wahid (Sri)	0	6	32	26

Group B
Player	Won	Highest break		No. of centuries
T. Parsons (Wal)	7	31	7	63
P. Bronwe (Ire)	7	31	12	65
Kwok Kwan Shing (HK)	7	28	12	56
G. Parikh (Ind)	5	27	21	72
A. Thomson (Zimb)	4	17	23	36
G. Kwok (NZ)	3	17	26	62
H. Boteju (Sri)	2	15	28	31
W. Craig (Isle of Man)	1	14	29	35
T. Dada (Pak)	0	10	32	39

Group C
Player	Won	Highest break		No. of centuries
J. Bear (Can)	7	30	12	71
M. Bradley (Eng)	7	30	12	68
J. Jorgensen (Can)	6	25	17	46
W. Mills (NI)	5	26	17	89
J. Giannaros (Aus)	5	25	21	68
P. Reynolds (Isle of Man)	3	23	23	36
Cheung Che-Ming (HK)	2	17	25	40
E. Amro (Egy)	1	11	31	40
V. Yassa (Sudan)	0	3	32	22

Group D
Player	Won	Highest break		No. of centuries
W. Jones (Wal)	6	27	13	70
P. Mifsud (Mta)	6	29	15	80
W. King (Aus)	6	29	17	83
R. Chaperon (Can)	5	24	18	56
D. Chalmers (Eng)	5	25	24	57
R. Lane (Sco)	3	23	23	44
S. Pavis (NI)	3	19	27	82
Lau Weng Yew (Sin)	2	15	29	53
S. Sherif (Egy)	0	7	32	27

Quarter-finals: W. Jones beat A. Kearney 5–1; T. Parsons beat M. Bradley 5–0; J. Grech beat P. Browne 5–3; J. Bear beat P. Mifsud 5–2.

Semi-finals: Parsons beat Jones 8–5; Bear beat Grech 8–7.

Final: Parsons beat Bear 11–8.

1984 Dublin

Group A
Player	Won	Highest break		No. of centuries
A. Micallef (Mta)	9	38	16	75
T. Parsons (Wal)	8	37	11	102
P. Ennis (Ire)	8	34	28	110
V. Saengthong (Tha)	7	34	19	86
J. Sigurossonn (Ice)	6	29	29	70
T. Finstad (Can)	4	28	28	85
B. Bjorkman (Swe)	4	26	27	52
A. Thomson (Zim)	3	24	34	36
D. Feeney (USA)	3	21	35	42
K. Sirisoma (Sri)	3	16	33	40
L. Talman (Bel)	0	11	40	37

Group B
Player	Won	Highest break		No. of centuries
D. John (Wal)	9	37	10	72
T. Drago (Mta)	8	35	15	132
A. Robidoux (Can)	8	36	20	107
S. Sim-Ngarm (Tha)	7	33	20	70
J. Long (Ire)	6	30	24	62
M. G. Jayaram (Ind)	5	30	23	84
A. Campbell (Aus)	4	25	29	96
J. McIntyre (NI)	4	21	30	91
R. Cowley (Isle of Man)	3	20	30	52
M. Sedupathi (Sri)	1	6	36	37
C. D'Avoine (Mau)	0	3	40	38

Group C
Player	Won	Highest break		No. of centuries
G. Wilkinson (Aus)	8	30	13	68
J. Wright (Eng)	7	27	14	68
H. Haenga (NZ)	7	26	14	66
H. Bakahati (Egy)	6	26	21	73
M. Colquitt (Isle of Man)	5	24	20	57
S. Hendry (Sco)	5	23	22	118
T. Kollins (USA)	3	16	27	92
K. Friopjofssonn (Ice)	3	15	28	28
H. Thwaites (Bel)	1	3	32	21
L. Yew Keong (Sin)	scr.			

Group D
Player	Won	Highest break		No. of centuries
C. Archer (Eng)	9	32	15	80
O. B. Agrawal (Ind)	7	33	16	68
D. Kwok (NZ)	5	27	21	64
G. Kwok Kwan-Shing (HK)	5	26	23	129
H. Morgan (NI)	5	27	27	78
J. Selby (Wal)	4	24	23	72
L. Yew (Sin)	3	25	28	55
G. Carnegie (Sco)	3	22	32	69
M. Hallgren (Swe)	2	17	32	43
M. Sadek (Egy)	2	15	31	59

Quarter-finals: O. B. Agrawal beat D. John 5–4; J. Wright beat A. Micallef 5–1; C. Archer beat T. Drago 5–4; T. Parsons beat G. Wilkinson 5–2.

Semi-finals: Agrawal beat Wright 8–5; Parsons beat Archer 8–3

Final: Agrawal beat Parsons 11–7

WORLD AMATEUR CHAMPIONSHIP RECORDS

Billiards
1954	T. Cleary (Aus)	682 (2 post)
1973	M. J. M. Lafir (Sri)	859 (5 pots)
1979	M. Ferreira (Ind)	467 (3 pots)

Snooker
1984	T. Drago (Mta) 132

World Records

BILLIARDS
There have been so many changes in the rules of billiards that any list of records requires a note stating the precise variant of the rules under which each break, aggregate or average was made. In broad terms, the stricter the limitation incorporated in the rules, the more control and skill is required to make a large break.

Briefly, the changes in the rules may be codified thus:

	Pots	Hazards	Cannons	Code
1898	2	–	–	A
1926	2	25(p)	–	B
1927	2	25(a)	–	C
1931	2	15	–	D
1932/3	2	15	100 baulk line	E
	2	15	200 baulk line	
	2	15	180–200 every 200	
1960	2	25	35 direct	F
1964	15	15	35 direct	G
1968	5	15	35 direct	H
1970	5	15	75	I
1979	2(p)	15	75	J
	3(a)	15	75	K
1983	2	15	75	L

(a)–amateur (p)–professional

World

PROFESSIONAL		AMATEUR	
Walter Lindrum (Aus) 4 137 E*		M. Ferreira (Ind) 1 149	I
*35 direct cannons		M. Ferreira (Ind) 630	K
		S. Agrawal (Ind) 716	L

National Amateur Championships

England	N. Dagley 862	I
	N. Dagley 506	K
Northern Ireland	R. Taylor 278	E
Repbulic of Ireland	J. Bates 370	F
Scotland	J. Bates 323	F
Wales	R. W. Oriel 345	I
Australia	R. Marshall 702	E
India	M. Ferreira 1 149	I
	A. Savus 556	K
Malta	J. Grech 567	I
New Zealand	B. Kirkness 326	I
South Africa	M. Francisco 433	G
Sri Lanka	M. J. M. Lafir 500	I

SNOOKER
World

PROFESSIONAL	AMATEUR
Joe Davis (Eng) 147	J. Johnson 140
Rex Williams (Eng) 147	
Steve Davis (Eng) 147	
Cliff Thorburn (Can) 147	
Kirk Stevens (Can) 147	

National Amateur Championships

England	T. Chappel 138
Northern Ireland	M. Gill 87
Republic of Ireland	P. Morgan 89
Scotland	E. Sinclair 91
Wales	T. Chappel 123
Australia	M. Williams 101
	J. Campbell 101
India	S. Shroff 98
Malta	J. Grech 109
New Zealand	G. Hayward 103
South Africa	G. Povall 106

Note: Joe Johnson's world amateur record of 140 was made in the Tyne Tees Television tournament in 1978. There have been many breaks in excess of national championship records recorded in non-championship events.

To be accepted as a world record, a break must have been made (a) on a standard table on which the pocket openings conform to the approved templates; (b) in a match to which members of the public are admitted; and (c) with a qualified referee officiating.

Right: Stacey Hillyard, winner of the Women's World Amateur Championship 1984.

THE WOMEN'S GAME

The Women's Billiards Association (later Billiards and Snooker Association) founded in 1931, took responsibility for the Women's Amateur Billiards Championship since 1931 and Snooker Championship since 1933.

The association fell on hard times in the late sixties and early seventies but was spectacularly revived by Wally West, a well known London amateur, who became secretary in 1978. Given a free hand, he employed his entrepreneurial talents to secure a variety of sponsors for the tournament circuit he built up, culminating in the Women's World Open, first sponsored by Guinness in 1980.

Women's standards have been and to some extent still are affected by restricted opportunities. In the game's early days, it was socially unthinkable for a woman to play in a public saloon and most clubs were likewise implacably male bastions though in the kind of socially privileged homes spacious enough to accommodate a billiard room, a degree of cuemanship was regarded as an acceptable feminine social grace.

A few women nevertheless did play in public. Ruby Roberts, a niece of the Australian Charles Memmott, could make century breaks and John Roberts Jnr toured at one time with Madam Strebor, a less curiously named lady if one discerns that, backwards, it spells 'Roberts'. Eva Collins, daughter of the 19th-century professional George Collins and sister of Frank, who refereed at Burroughes and Watts, Soho Square until well into his eighties, was a well known coach.

The Women's Professional Billiards Championship, instituted in 1930, was won seven times by Joyce Gardner, once by Ruth Harrison and on the four occasions it was last staged by Thelma Carpenter. It

Women's Professional Billiards Championship

1931	Joyce Gardner
1932	Joyce Gardner
1933	Joyce Gardner
1934	Ruth Harrison
1935	Joyce Gardner
1936	Joyce Gardner
1937	Joyce Gardner
1938	Joyce Gardner
1939	Ruth Harrison
1940	Thelma Carpenter
1941–48	No contests
1949	Thelma Carpenter
1950	Thelma Carpenter

Women's Professional Snooker Championship

1934	Ruth Harrison
1935	Ruth Harrison
1936	Ruth Harrison
1937	Ruth Harrison
1938	Ruth Harrison
1939	Ruth Harrison
1940	Ruth Harrison
1948	Ruth Harrison
1949	Agnes Morris
1950	Thelma Carpenter

Women's Amateur Billiards Championship

1931	R. Harrison
1932	T. Carpenter
1933	T. Carpenter
1934	T. Carpenter
1935	V. Seals
1936	V. Seals
1937	G. Phillips
1938	V. McDougall
1939	V. McDougall
1940–46	No contests
1947	S. Isaacs
1948	E. Morland Smith
1949	M. Keeton
1950	H. Futo
1951	No contest
1952	E. Morland Smith
1953	E. Morland Smith
1954	H. Futo
1955	M. Barrett
1956	M. Barrett
1957	No contest
1958	No contest
1959	M. Hazeldine
1960	M. Barrett
1961	No contest
1962	T. Hindmarch
1963	S. Isaacs
1964	M. Baynton (née Barrett)
1965	V. Youle
1966	M. Baynton
1967	T. Hindmarch
1968	M. Baynton
1969	T. Hindmarch
1970	V. Selby
1971	V. Selby
1972	V. Selby
1973	V. Selby
1974	V. Selby
1975	No contest
1976	V. Selby
1977	V. Selby
1978	V. Selby
1979	M. Baynton
1980	No contest

Women's Amateur Snooker Championship

1933	M. Quinn
1934	E. Morris
1935	M. Hill
1936	V. Seals
1937	E. Morland Smith
1938	E. Morris
1939	A. Morris
1940–46	No contests
1947	M. Knight
1948	J. Adcock
1949	R. Davies
1950	P. Holden
1951	R. Davies
1952	R. Davies
1953	R. Holmes
1954	M. Barrett
1955	M. Barrett
1956	M. Barrett
1957	R. Holmes
1958	R. Holmes
1959	D. Thompson
1960	M. Hazeldine
1961	M. Barrett
1962	M. Baynton (née Barrett)
1963	R. Holmes
1964	M. Baynton
1965	S. Jeffries
1966	M. Baynton
1967	H. Futo
1968	M. Baynton
1969	R. Craven
1970	M. Hazeldine
1971	M. Hazeldine
1972	V. Selby
1973	V. Selby
1974	V. Selby
1975	V. Selby
1976	A. Johnson
1977	A. Johnson
1978	A. Davies (née Morris)
1979	V. Selby
1980	S. Foster

Women's World Open Snooker Championship

1976	V. Selby
1977–79	No contests
1980	L. McIlrath
1981	V. Selby
1983	S. Foster

has not been contested since 1950.

Miss Gardner, born in Gloucester but a Londoner by adoption, made a break of 96 in the 1930 championship which was the first certificated women's record. It was superseded by Margaret Lennan, a Scot, with 176 in 1931 and Miss Harrison, a Tynesider, with 197 in the 1937 women's championship, still the women's world record.

Miss Gardner, a gifted auctioneer and commere, fulfilled exhibition engagements in her youth with Tom Reece and Tom Newman and toured extensively for charity until the late seventies, playing at one time or another with all the leading male professionals. Her lifetime best breaks in public were 318 at billiards and 82 at snooker.

Miss Carpenter, whose father kept the Solent Cliffs Hotel, Bournemouth, a favourite haunt of professionals, retired after her marriage, having also won the Women's Professional Snooker Championship in 1950, the last time it was held, though Miss Harrison, with eight title successes, was by the far the most successful exponent of the 22 ball game in her day.

The 1949 winner, Agnes Morris, learnt to play in the one table billiard hall started by her father in Amman-ford with his miner's disability pension. She retired from the game for almost 30 years but returned as Mrs Davies to win the women's title (amateur/professional distinctions having been abolished in the interim) in 1978. She scored other notable successes on the expanding women's circuit of the late seventies and was losing finalist in the Guinness Women's World Open in May 1980.

Among the outstanding women's champions, Maureen Baynton (née Barrett) won eight snooker titles between 1954 and 1968 and seven billiards titles between 1955 and 1980. She would have assuredly won more if she had not retired from competitive play for several years.

Vera Selby, who captains a men's team in the Gates-head League, won eight billiards and five snooker titles

and also the Embassy Women's World Open Snooker Championship at Middlesbrough in 1976 which was run in conjunction with the men's World Professional Championship. Though that sponsorship, which included a £500 first prize, was not repeated, it broke new ground in bringing together an international field in the women's game for the first time with Australian, Canadian and Irish as well as British competitors. The event also broached the need to differentiate between British women's champions and world champions who had hitherto, in default of any other arrangements, been regarded as synonymous. Mrs Selby regained the Women's World Open Championship in 1981.

Two recent British champions, Ann Johnson and Susan Foster, came through fields growing both in quality and numbers while standards also improved strikingly in both Australia, where a national cham-pionship involving all state champions was inaugurated in 1976, and Canada, where women were encouraged to play in public halls.

The Australian Championship was dominated by Fran Lovis, champion from 1976 to 1980 and Lesley McIlrath and the Canadian scene by Natalie Stelmach, who won the women's section of the Canadian Open from 1977 to 1979.

In an entry of 46 for the inaugural Guinness World Open at Warners Sinah Warren Holiday Camp, Hayling Island, in May 1980 there were three English, one Welsh, two Australian and two Canadian quarter-finalists.

The latter stages of the event resulted thus: *Quarter-finals*: Ann Johnson (Eng) beat Vera Selby (Eng) 3–2; Lesley McIlrath (Aust) beat Mary Ann McConnell (Can) 3–1; Agnes Davies (Wal) beat Fran Lovis (Aust) 3–2; Natalie Stelmach (Can) beat Susan Foster (Eng) 3–2; *Semi-finals*: McIlrath beath Johnson 3–1; Davies beat Stelmach 3–0; *Final*: McIlrath beat Davies 4–2.

Miss McIlrath's £700 first prize was a record for the

Mandy Fisher, winner of the National Express Women Grand Prix 1984.

women's game. Mrs Davies took £350 as runner-up.

The 1981 Guinness Women's World Open at Thorness Bay, Isle of Wight saw Mrs Selby's cool temperament, sure grasp of tactics and safety play overcome technically more gifted players as she went through the championship without losing a frame.

Miss Stelmach, who again lost in the quarter-finals, had a few weeks previously made a break of 56, the first ever half century by a woman in competition, in winning her sixth Canadian Women's title.

Quarter-finals: Sue Foster (Eng) beat Lesley McIlrath (Aust) 3–2; Mandy Fisher (Eng) beat Ann Johnson (Eng) 3–1; Fran Lovis (Aust) beat Natalie Stelmach (Can) 3–1; Vera Selby (Eng) beat Mary Ann McConnell (Can) 3–0; *Semi-finals*: Fisher beat Lovis 3–1; Selby beat Foster 3–0; *Final*: Selby beat Fisher 3–0.

Mrs Selby took £2000, a new record prize for the women's game, and Miss Fisher £1000.

The women's game then fell into disarray with the Women's Billiards and Snooker Association losing control to the newly formed World Ladies Billiards and Snooker Association. There was some overlap in personnel between the latter and Ladies Snooker International, a management and promotions company, who signed most of the leading women players either just before, during or just after the Pontins Women's World Open at Brean Sands in May 1983.

Sue Foster won the £2000 first prize with Maureen Baynton taking £1000 as runner-up. Miss McIlrath and a Canadian, Sue LeMaich who had made a break of 85 in competition in Canada took £500 as losing semi-finalist.

At this point, the game separated, without any obvious benefit to the players, into amateur and professional categories with LSI announcing ambitious plans for the professional game. LSI secured sponsorship from National Express, the bus company, of £60 000 for a five week grand prix circuit, a sum more appropriate for an event with considerable television coverage than the three and a half hours in Welsh and three and a half hours in English it actually received within the HTV region for the first leg only.

Various dissatisfactions with LSI surfaced as the circuit proceeded and attention tended to focus on these rather than the modest but real improvement in playing standards which the better women players demonstrated.

Mandy Fisher won two of the five tournaments and reached two other finals in earning £14 000 from the circuit. Two Canadians, Mary Ann McConnell and Sue LeMaich finished second and third in the overall standings with two Englishwomen Sue Foster and Georgina Aplin fourth and fifth and another Canadian, Grace Nakamura, sixth. Each leg carried a first prize of £2500 with £1500 for the runner-up, £750 for the losing semi-finalists, £500 for the losing quarter-finalists, £250 for the first round losers in the invited field of 16 and £500 for the highest break. There were six snowball prizes of £5000, £2500, £1000, £750, £500 and £250. Miss Fisher's break of 62 was the highest by a woman in competition in Britain.

Not surprisingly, LSI found it impossible to secure sponsorship of this magnitude again and the focus of interest reverted to the more broadly based 'amateur' game. Since there was no restriction on amateurs accepting prize money, professional status proved to be a liability for those players were simply excluded from competition except for events in which they were permitted to enter on condition that they conceded 14 start.

LSI, which had been virtually synonymous with the WLBSA, lost much of its influence and a modest but at least regular circuit of amateur events started to be established by WLBSA's new administration.

The first Women's World Amateur Championship sponsored by First Leisure, at the Hertford Sporting Club, Coventry in October 1984, was won by Stacey Hillyard, 15, a Christchurch, Dorset schoolgirl, who beat Natalie Stelmach 4–1 in the final.

Allison Fisher, her senior by a year, also established a reputation by winning several events including an open women's tournament at Pontins, Prestatyn in September 1984 in which she made a break of 67. A couple of months earlier, another teenager, Angela Jones from Poole, had made a break of 63 in a women's tournament at Windsor. Miss Fisher made a break of 71 against male opposition in a men's amateur tournament at Witham in December 1984 but instead of the highest break by a woman pushing up by degrees to the century mark, Miss Hillyard shattered the century barrier with an effort of 114 in the premier division of the Bournemouth League in January 1985.

INDEX